Will Love For Crumbs

A memoir

Jonna Ivin

This book is a work of non-fiction. I have changed some names, and at times combined characters, conversations and events to allow for better narrative flow. All events of this book are told to the best of my memory in how I saw the truth.

Copyright © 2012 by Jonna Ivin

For Krystal Engel

Who always asked for more pages

even when I didn't want to write them.

Acknowledgements

There are not enough variations of the words "thank you" that I can express to my family. Jodi, Jenn, Cami, and Hannah, you have supported me in so many ways over the years and my heart is filled with love for you.

To my Arkansas family, our bond may be new but it runs deep. Jake, Erica, Brett, Cleatus, thank you all for the support and understanding during difficult times. And a special thank you to my sister Judy for bringing my father back into my life. I love you all.

Numerous people along the way have given their feedback, help or advice. Special thanks must go out to Raquel Valdivia, Sherrill and Gary Giusti, Tommy Kabat, Hillary Smotherman, Janet Minton, Marty Beaudet, and Kerry Logan.

Kerry Cohen, thank you for your invaluable guidance on the beautiful and sometime torturous process of memoir writing.

To Erika Worth, Baby, Monkey and Woody, I cannot express how indebted I am that you accepted a rag-a-muffin like me into your home when I had nowhere else to go. I will be eternally grateful for your love and friendship.

Jill Piwowar, I can't imagine my life without you in it. I love you like a sister.

To Adam Chase, simply put, you are one of the best people I have ever known. You have always supported me through the toughest times, and I am forever grateful that I have you in my life.

And most of all, to my mother, Sandra Kay Paulus-Quinn, I hope I was able to make you proud.

Prairie Creek, Arkansas

My eyes opened before the alarm went off. I was immediately wide-awake as I lay in bed listening for the sound of footsteps. The footsteps would tell me when it was safe to get up. The footsteps would tell me if my plan was going to happen or if I would have to call it off for another day. But all I heard breaking the silence was the thumping of my own heart. Everything I'd been planning for the past two weeks, every nitty-gritty detail depended on those footsteps. The silence told me nothing.

And then I heard them. Moving throughout the house, each clunk, clunk, clunk, caused my heart to race faster. This was it. This was the day. I lay perfectly still, until I heard the final confirmation I needed. The front door opened then closed; the footsteps were gone.

I jumped out of bed, found my cell phone, and used it to call my younger sister Judy. "Okay, it's safe to come over."

"I'll be right there." She sounded as nervous as I felt.

I scrambled to get dressed, then paused for a moment, looking down at the disheveled bed. Making a spur of the moment decision, I yanked up the sheets, flung the comforter over the top, and then tossed the pillows into place. Never having run for my life before, I didn't know the rules, but it seemed to me that making the bed would be the polite thing to do.

With that out of the way, I immediately went to the closet and pulled out the boxes and plastic tubs I'd been secretly packing for over a week. The few things not already packed were thrown into containers I'd hidden throughout the house.

By the time Judy arrived, everything I'd be taking was stacked in a neat pile in the center of the room.

"Is this it?" she asked as I ushered her in the back door and showed her what was left of my life.

"Yep," I answered. With reality sinking in, I muttered to myself, "Wow, Is that really everything I own?"

It was quite a pitiful little stack, now that I'd put it into perspective. I couldn't shake the feeling that this might be the perfect time to sit down and reflect on the mistakes of my past. Having a short window of time, I would unfortunately have to wait to do any reflecting; instead I made a mental note: "Don't forget this moment. Surely there is meaning here."

Judy and I each picked up the end of a heavy plastic tub. We maneuvered our way out the back door, around the side of the house, up and over a low brick wall, and across the front lawn to my truck parked out front. "Are you wearing flip flops?" I asked as she slipped on a few loose rocks in the driveway.

"I always wear flip-flops," she answered. Her hillbilly twang contrasted with my valley girl inflection.

As I said, I was no expert on secretly skipping out of town, but flip-flops felt a little casual for the occasion. Yet, even with my sister's impractical choice of footwear, it didn't take long for us to load my truck. I'd bought a tarp the day before; we threw it over the back and tied everything down.

It was time to say goodbye. It didn't seem fair really. We'd only just reconnected two years earlier after being separated as kids. She'd grown up with our father and her mother, and I'd been raised by my mother. Now we had to say goodbye again.

We hugged each other tightly. "Call me when you get to wherever you're going," she said.

I could hear the lump in her throat as certainly as I could feel my own. "I will," I said.

Although I'd been preparing for this day for weeks, I'd told no one of my plans. A few days earlier, I finally let my sister know I was leaving. We both agreed it was best if she didn't know where I was going - at least not right away. Prairie Creek, Arkansas, where we lived, was an itty-bitty place tucked away in the Ozark Mountains. The people might move slowly there, but a good, juicy secret could shoot through the town like a bolt of lightning.

"I'm going to miss you," she said. "It's not right."

I sighed with a heavy heart. "I'm going to miss you too, but I don't see any other way."

I noticed the neighbor watching us from his deck. He was a nice, older man I had visited with on a number of occasions. But I couldn't say goodbye to him; I knew my secret wasn't going to stay secret for long, and I needed to buy as much time as possible.

I pretended I didn't see him. It was time to go.

Judy and I hugged once more. We quickly turned away from each other, since neither of us wanted to cry. We walked to our own vehicles not knowing when we would see each other again.

I had two stops to make before leaving town: my first at the bar where I'd worked for the past eight months. It was payday. I needed to pick up my check, although my employer had no idea it would be my last one. Judy had agreed to call my boss the next day to let her know I wouldn't be back. I'm sure I wasn't the first person to leave this job without notice, but still, I felt like a rat.

I walked into the bar and allowed my eyes to adjust to the light for a moment. The regulars were all in their places like any other day. There was Smiley, A/C Joe (he was in the heating and cooling business), and Long-Haired Larry (as opposed to Scooter Larry, who had short hair and rode a red scooter. They were a rough-and-ready group and they'd become my friends. It had been hard over the last few weeks to not let anyone know I was leaving. Now it was going to be even harder not being able to say goodbye.

I walked behind the bar and found my check where the owner always left them. I ripped open the envelope, threw it in the trash, and shoved the check into the back pocket of my jeans.

"Hey, Little Shit, what are you up to?" It was A/C Joe who spoke. He'd started calling me "Little Shit" one day when I cut off his rum and Cokes. It was a name that stuck.

"Just came into get my check, Joe. And stop calling me Little Shit."

"You know I love you. I wouldn't tease you if I didn't love you," he said, batting his eyes in a playful way.

"I know. I love you too."

Long-Haired Larry leaned in a little closer over the bar, "You workin' tomorrow?" he asked.

"I always work on Thursday. You know that."

He glanced at the bartender on shift. She stood off in a corner looking into a little mirror, piling on more makeup than needed. "You make better drinks," Larry whispered."

I laughed. What he meant was I made *stronger* drinks. I'd never bartended in my life when I got this job, so I just made the drinks as strong as they wanted them. This usually meant that most my customers were totally shit faced by the end of my shift.

I'm gonna be smokin' a pork roast tomorrow," Smiley added. "I'll bring ya some when it's done."

Smiley was a master at smoking meats. Although he rarely tipped, he made up for it by bringing me food on a regular basis. His pork was amazing I was bummed I wouldn't be getting any.

"Cool. Thanks, Smiley. I gotta go guys," I said as I headed toward the door.

"See ya tomorrow," Smiley called out.

"Yeah, see ya." I opened the door just as Scooter Larry was entering. "Hey, Scooter."

"Hey, Jonna."

We ducked past each other in the doorway. "See ya, Scooter."

"See ya, Jonna."

I turned back, giving a final wave, not knowing when or if I would see my friends again. As much as I cared for them, I could not share my plans. The next journey of my life, I would have to take alone.

The next stop was the bank, which conveniently, was next door. I hurried to cash my check and close my account. As I walked back and climbed into my truck, I took one last look at the bar. I was going to miss this place. I turned the key and the engine turned over. So did my stomach.

This was it. There was no going back now.

I'd been on the road for barely three hours when I received the first of what would be a barrage of text messages and voice mails.

WTF is going on? People r telling me they saw u driving with truck full of your stuff and tarp on back. Call me!

That was faster than I expected. I shut off my phone, tossed it onto the passenger seat, pressed down on the gas and headed west.

Los Angeles, California

I was living in Los Angeles, managing a spiritual gift store called Aum and Garden, and I loved it. It was the kind of place you could get away with calling in sick if you felt your chakras were out of alignment. Having a bad day? Take some "me time" and relax in the meditation room. We may not have received health insurance, but all employees were offered integrated energy treatments and a fifty-percent discount on all the Marianne Williamson and Wayne Dyer books you could ingest. Who needed a 401K? I had universal energy supporting me.

The movie "The Secret" had just come out and all of Los Angeles was buzzing with a newfound connection to using our thoughts to manifest the heart's desire. Everyone who came into the store was super nice and on their best behavior, as they were all in the process of creating positive vibes in their lives. It would be bad karma to be rude to a shop girl while Mary, Jesus, Buddha, Lakshmi, Saint Anthony, and the Dalai Lama stared at you from every corner of the store. I loved my job.

When the writers' strike hit Los Angeles, the housing market collapsed. All those extremely nice, tuber-rich, super-skinny, slightly orange women with their tightly stretched skin and big, puffy lips stopped needing expensive Buddha statues and healing crystals. I quickly discovered that when the economy is in the crapper, people let go of God real fast and cling to their cash. In no time I found myself unemployed.

I looked every day for a job, any job. I was so desperate I even worked one afternoon as a maid on a "trial basis." After one family interviewed me, the housewife couldn't decide between me and another applicant. She wanted us to each work one day so she could "get a feel" for us. I figured I had two advantages. One, I spoke English. Two, I could legally work in the United States. My disadvantage? The other applicant had been a maid before.

Early one morning I drove my clunky little Mitsubishi into the Hollywood hills, among the mansions and celebrities. I was prepared to kick some major Mr. Clean ass and send that little Hispanic woman packing. I scrubbed the inside of the refrigerator until it sparkled and did piles of laundry. And when the phone rang I jumped to answer it, taking a detailed written message with my best penmanship. This was a competition. I needed the wife to know that my ability to speak English was a vital job requirement. By the end of the day, speaking with such clear enunciation, I was beginning to sound a lot like Mary Poppins. "Why of course, milady. I cherish the opportunity to clean the wee nuggets from said litter box. I shall begin this delightful task immediately."

Two days later she chose the other woman, saying, "I feel more comfortable with her on a day–to-day basis, but I'd love to keep your number for special occasions.

I politely declined. It was fine being a maid, but I certainly wasn't about to be the back-up white maid to be paraded out at dinner parties so her rich friends could ooh and ah."

Around this time I picked up work with a landscaper. My boss was a socialite who made it crystal clear to me on my first day that we were landscapers, *not* gardeners. "What we do," she said, flipping blond hair over her shoulder, "takes precision and an artistic eye. Anyone can push a lawnmower. We create beauty." I didn't know much about all that, but I did know it was really fucking hot creating beauty during a Southern California heat wave.

One of her clients had their front yard landscaped in all white. Roses, gardenias—a bunch of other stuff I couldn't name—were all white with one exception: the Dusty Miller lining her long, curving driveway. Although it had silver-whitish leaves it also (gasp!) sprouted teeny tiny yellow flowers; hundreds and hundreds of teeny tiny yellow flowers. Yellow is not white. This travesty needed to be righted. And so, once a week I drove to the client's house to snip hundreds upon hundreds of teeny tiny yellow flowers.

I wouldn't have minded being a maid or a gardener—sorry, "landscaper"—if I'd been happy in my personal life. But I wasn't. I was missing something. I was missing a purpose. I was missing the joy, the love, the gratitude I was told by those around me that I should feel simply for being alive.

I didn't feel any of that. I felt abandoned by God, discarded by the Universe, forgotten by Love. Each night before I went to bed I would meditate and I would pray. "Please God, show me what I'm supposed to do. This can't possibly be the life I was meant to live. I don't know what you want. I'll do whatever it takes if you just show me the path to creativity, joy, and love."

On September 13, 2008, Hurricane Ike made landfall, devastating the coast of Texas. I joined up with the Red Cross to help with the relief effort. The truth was I was broke with no employment prospects, so it was an easy decision to volunteer. I was running away from a mundane existence, a pile of unpaid bills, and a feeling of being los

Driving US-412

Somewhere in Oklahoma

Leaning against my truck, pumping gas, I wait for the tank to fill. I hear my cell phone beeping through the driver's window; yet another text I will ignore. The sun is hot on my skin. The air is dry. I feel like a fugitive, like I have a secret that makes me different from the people around me. My eyes wander around the steaming parking lot as I play the guessing game "coming or going." People excited and energized are going somewhere; the stressed out, exhausted ones are coming back.

Nearby is a family clearly coming back. Mom is tired, the kids are fussy, and Dad is waiting with arms crossed for the gas to pump. A little girl, around five or six, is licking an ice cream cone that is rapidly losing its fight against the heat. I watch with knowing amusement as her tongue delicately gives the final lick that sends the scoop tumbling off the cone. It lands on the blacktop with a splat. This is followed by an ear-piercing scream.

Her father looks over, rolls his eyes in frustration, and turns back to pumping the gas. His face and body language tell me this is but one of many meltdowns he's witnessed lately. The mother takes a gentler approach. She removes the messy, sticky, now-empty cone from the little girl's hand and throws it away. Picking up the child, she pats her daughter on the head and soothes her with quiet whispers as they head back into the convenience store.

I haven't felt the comfort of my mother's touch in nearly nine years. It seems unreal that she's been gone this long, but when I quiet my mind I can bring her back, if only for a moment. I look up at the big, puffy clouds and allow the memories to drift in.

It was December 1, 2001, the day my boyfriend Adam and I picked up the last of my mom's belongings to move into our new house. I was anxious to get back quickly. Although Mom had been staying on her own for short periods of time, I didn't feel good leaving her alone.

She had become so ill that Adam suggested we rent a house together and move Mom in with us so he could help me with her care. Adam and I had only been dating for about a year; I couldn't believe anyone would be so loving and kind as to take all this on so early in a relationship.

It had been an exhausting week of moving Adam, myself, and my Mom into the new house. Finally, finally, we were nearly done. Just a few more boxes and it would be over. We were driving Adam's little pickup from my Mom's apartment in West Hollywood, and were nearly to the new house in Pasadena when my cell phone rang.

I answered.

"Can't... breathe..." Mom gasped.

"Mom? What's happening? Are you okay?" I turned to Adam, "Drive faster!"

Adam pressed hard on the gas, maneuvering quickly through the freeway traffic. He told me once that all men, when driving fast, pretend they are racecar drivers. If this is true, he was doing an excellent job. I grabbed hold of the door with my free hand to stay balanced.

"My... my... the trach... come home," Mom said before the phone went dead.

"Mom? Mom?" I shouted in the phone. I immediately tried to call her back, telling Adam, "All I got was she can't breathe and something about her trach. I should never have left her. I'm such an asshole." Mom's phone went straight to voicemail.

Adam tried in vain to reassure me. "We're only a couple of minutes away. It's going to be okay."

I thought about calling 911, but I knew all the doors were locked. We would already be home by the time any rescue workers showed up and figured out they'd have to break down the front door. When we arrived, Adam had barely shut off the motor before we were both out of the truck, running for the door.

By the time I entered my mother's room, I was out of breath. But she appeared to be okay—I was so relieved. She was in her hospital bed looking as calm as could be. "Are you okay?" I panted, trying to catch my breath and settle my nerves. Mom always amazed me with her ability to remain calm when all common sense indicated someone should be freaking out. That someone was usually me.

I was immediately reminded of the previous year, when she called me at work to tell me that they'd discovered a tumor in her brain stem. She mentioned this as casually as if we were making lunch plans: "So it seems I have a brain tumor."

"What? When did you find that out?" I asked, shocked by the news.

"I just came from the doctor."

I bolted out of my chair and began gathering my belongings from my desk. "Okay, I'm leaving now. I'll be home in a minute."

"Why are you going home?" Mom asked.

"So I can be with you," I nearly shouted.

"But I'm not at home," she replied calmly.

"Well, where *are* you?"

"I'm at work."

"You went back to the office?" I was completely confused. If ever there were a doctor's note to get out of work, "brain tumor" had to be at the top of the list.

"Where else would I go?" Mom sounded confused by my confusion.

"Um… home!" I said. "I'll leave now and meet you there."

Mom sighed, "And what are you going to do? Stand there and stare at me?"

I thought about this as I slowly sank back into my chair. What *would* I do once I got home? I knew for certain that I wouldn't just stand there staring at her. That seemed not only rude, but also a little creepy. I could listen. Well, I could listen under the condition that my

14

mother would ever be willing to share even a smidge of information about her feelings.

The truth was I didn't know what I would do, so I answered her with the only thing that made sense to me. "It seems to me if someone is told they have a brain tumor then they should go home. *Normal people* go home when bad stuff happens. I don't know *exactly* what they do, but I'm pretty sure they do it *at home*."

My coworker's head popped up at the words "brain tumor." She mouthed, "Are you okay?"

I shrugged, throwing one hand in the air.

"Don't worry," Mom reassured me. "I'm not going to die today, so there's nothing for us to do. The tumor didn't appear overnight. It's been there for a while and it will still be there when I get home. But, Jonna, if you want to go home you should. Don't let me stop you."

I leaned back in my chair, tossed my keys on the desk and tried to explain. "I can't go home if *you* don't go home. *You* have the tumor. If I'm all dramatic and go running home while you stay at work, then I just look like an asshole. It only makes sense if we both go home."

"Oh, okay. I see what you're saying," Mom said, and then added, "I'm sorry if I ruined your day."

"You didn't ruin my day," I said, laughing sadly. "Well actually," I added, "you *did* ruin my day, but only because I love you and it sucks you have a tumor."

"I love you too," she answered. "And I don't think you're an asshole."
"Thanks."

My mother had been right, she didn't die that day. But a year later, as I stood in her bedroom door still trying to calm my nerves, I could see the tumor was taking a serious toll on her.

"What happened?" I asked. "All I heard was, 'can't breathe' and then nothing. You scared the shit out of me."

"She's okay," I told Adam as he entered the room behind me. "I think she just got scared."

She raised a shaky hand and placed a finger over the hole where the tracheotomy tube had been inserted into her neck a few months before. She struggled to form words, trying to cover the hole so I could hear her. "It's... It was..." She began to fiddle with the trach tube moving it around.

Seeing all was okay, Adam went outside to get the remaining boxes from the truck.

I came to her bedside and tried to move her hand from the tube so I could get a better look. "Don't touch it. Let me see."

Mom didn't listen. She kept her finger where it was, forcing her breath to make the words. "Crooked. Feels crooked."

"Your trach is crooked?" I asked.

She rested her head back on the pillow and nodded having used up what little energy she had.

I took a closer look. "It doesn't look crooked."

Mom glared at me and covered the hole once again. "Crooked."

"Okay. Okay." I said. "It feels crooked on the inside, like in your throat?"

She nodded, her eyes indicating with frustration, *how many times do I have to repeat myself?*

"Do you think I should take it out?" I asked, really hoping she would shake her head no.

Instead, Mom shrugged, as if to say, "Beats the hell out of me."

The hospital had sent us home with every supply imaginable; I had boxes of new, sterile tracheostomy tubes. The problem was that so far I had only removed and replaced the inner disposable tube. I had never actually switched out the entire mechanism. A nurse had quickly spent five minutes talking me through it before they released my mom into my care, but other than that I was going to have to wing it. I took a deep breath and told myself, *I can do this. What can be so hard—just take one out and put another back in, right?*

I pulled on a pair of hospital gloves and carefully undid the ties that kept the trach securely in place at her neck. I wiggled it a little; it seemed loose enough. Just give it a soft tug, it would slip right out; pop a new one in, tie it off, and I'd be done. Simple.

"Okay, I'm going to take out the old one," I told her.

Mom shrugged. *Go for it.*

I pulled gently on the tracheotomy tube; just as I'd hoped, it slid out easily.

"Oh. Okay. Cool. That was easy," I said, smiling at Mom. I felt quite proud of myself. I tossed the old trach into the trashcan. Mom seemed relieved as she inhaled deeply.

And then I watched in horror as flaps of skin growing around the edges of the incision were quickly sucked into the hole blocking her airway. Mom's eyes grew huge as she realized no air was entering her lungs. I froze, staring at her and thinking, *Oh Dear Lord, I've just killed my mother.* Mom stared back, no doubt thinking, *my stupid kid is trying to kill me.*

In a moment of complete panic I did the only thing that came to mind: I stuck my index finger into the hole. In all my life I never imagined that my finger would be in my mother's throat. There had been numerous fantasies throughout the years involving my foot up her ass, but never once did I imagine finger in throat.

I slowly removed my finger and the skin flaps followed, clearing her airway. As long as I held the skin pulled back and open she could breathe easily.

I looked down at her as she took in a deep breath, "It's okay. It's cool. We're cool," I said, trying to convince myself as much as her.

She nodded.

"It's okay. It's okay." I repeated, visually scanning the room. I couldn't let go, so I stretched out my free hand, blindly searching for anything that might help. On a low table near the head of the bed, the tips of my fingers were just barely able to reach a small, clear, plastic tube that was meant to go inside the larger tracheostomy tube. I inserted it into the hole; as I did, the skin flaps disappeared back into her neck. Fortunately, she was still able to get air through the tube. Unfortunately, the tube was too small; it was the diameter of a drinking straw. The hole in my mother's neck was the diameter of a dime. If I let go the smaller tube would slide inside her throat.

"Ah crap!"

Mom looked at me.

"Everything is going to be okay," I said again.

She nodded calmly.

I was afraid of making anything worse. All I wanted was to sit down and cry. My mother had taken care of me my entire life; now she needed me to step up and return the favor and I was failing miserably. It took everything I had to keep from crying. I wanted her to have faith in me. A bawling, sniveling caretaker does not fill one with confidence. If she could remain calm then, dammit, I needed to pull myself together and do the same.

The only thing I knew for sure was that I didn't trust myself to go back to the original plan of inserting the new tracheotomy. So, as calmly as I could, I called out for help. "Adam? Hey, Adam."

He poked his head in the door a moment later. "Hey."

"Could you do me a favor," I said, "and call 911?"

He looked worried. Ten minutes earlier everything was fine. "What's going on?"

I explained the recent events and he left the room to make the call. After a few minutes I could hear him banging around in the living room. "What are you doing out there?" I shouted.

"Trying to clear a path through all the moving boxes, so they can get in," he yelled back.

Mom and I looked at each other. *Made sense.* "Thank you," I called out.

It wasn't long before we heard the sirens approaching. The lights through the window splashed the walls with red. A moment later, eight huge firefighters crowded into my mother's small bedroom and gathered around her bed looking at the two of us.

One of the firemen stepped forward. I assumed he was the captain because he was older and had a clipboard. He may have been an EMT, who knows. All I knew was, he was the only one saying anything. "What seems to be the trouble?" he asked.

"I took out her tracheotomy and then she couldn't breathe."

He scrunched his brow and cocked his head, suspicious—probably questioning if it was, in fact, me who should be examined. "Why would you do that?" he asked in a very deliberate tone.

I took a deep breath and raced through the explanation. "It was crooked, so I was trying to change it, but when I took it out," I said, pointing, "See these two flaps of skin? They were sucked into the hole, so I grabbed this tube because it was the only thing I could reach and I stuck that in the hole. But now if I let go, it will slide down her throat. When she takes a breath I feel it pulling, so I can't let go." I exhaled hard.

The firemen exchanged glances, then looked at me. Mom and I looked at each other then back at them. I guess they were expecting me to elaborate, but that's all I had.

Finally the captain broke the awkward silence. He bypassed me and spoke directly to my mother, "Ma'am are you okay?"

She smiled and nodded. I was starting to get the feeling she was enjoying the attention.

"Without her trach, she can't speak," I sighed, feeling incredibly stupid and very small.

The captain looked back at me. "Well, she seems to be doing okay otherwise. Do you have the other trach?"

"Yes," I said pointing to a large box on the other side of the room. "There's a bunch in there."

A young, fresh-faced fireman, who couldn't have been more than twenty, reached into the box and pulled out a package containing a tracheostomy. He handed it to the captain.

He turned the package over in his hands, and then looked back at me. "So what do you need me to do?"

"Um... put it in?" I replied, not understanding why he would ask such a ridiculous question.

He shoved the package at me, "Oh, I can't do that."

I pushed it back, "Of course you can."

"No. I can't."

Mom's eyes followed the pushing of the box like a tennis match.

"Why not? You're the fireman." I reminded him.

"Yeah, but I don't know anything about this. Are you her fulltime caregiver?"

"Yeah."

"Then you know more about it than we do."

"No. I don't. Clearly," I said, indicating the situation, "I'm not qualified."

"Well, the only other choice is take her to the emergency room like this. You can ride in the ambulance and hold the tube. Then they can put a new one in at the hospital."

I shook my head with disbelief. I was petrified of making the situation worse, but felt backed into a corner. I was the one who screwed it up so I would have to fix it. "Okay fine." I said, "I'll do it." I looked at Mom and asked, "Are you okay with that?"

She shrugged and nodded.

The captain put on gloves while I opened the package. I made a mental note: *perhaps I should have done this first.*

"Okay, what do you need me to do?" he asked.

"When I pull this tube out, I need you to poke your finger in the hole and kind of wiggle those flaps of skin—"

"How about if I just hold the tube?" He said, cutting me off with a smile.

The absurdity of the situation made me smile as well. I nervously joked, "Fine, ya big chicken, I'll do the hard part."

I shifted to the other side so he could hold the tube.

"I guess, just take it out slowly," I said as the other firemen crowded around, leaning in to get a better look. My hands shook as he started to remove the tube, but I was able to work the sides of the hole and ease the skin out along with it.

"Okay… um… hold these pieces of skin back so the hole stays open."

The captain did as I asked. I took the tracheotomy out of the package, mentally said a quick prayer: *Please dear God, don't let me fuck this up;* then asked Mom, "You ready?"

She nodded, encouraging me with her eyes. If she was scared she didn't show it. I tried to be as brave as she was, but my trembling hands gave me away. I took a deep breath and held it while slowly sliding the curved end of the trach into the hole and down her throat. The captain released the flaps of skin. When I felt it was all the way in, I slowly held up my hands, stepped back, and asked Mom, "Does that feel okay?"

She reached up to cover the hole and answered, "You did good."

It felt as if the entire room exhaled with relief. I wasted no time in excusing myself to the bathroom down the hall. Once there I shut the door behind me, and using a towel to cover my mouth, sobbed as quietly as I could. My entire body shook with fear at what I had done. I was completely overwhelmed and couldn't catch my breath. My mother was the one who was always strong and calm in a crisis. Not me. This was supposed to be her job. I was just the kid. A thirty-four year old kid, but still a kid, her kid.

I heard a light knock on the door. Adam asked, "Jonna, are you okay?"

I exhaled slowly; pulling myself together the best I could before answering, "Yeah, I'm fine. I'll be right out."

After everyone had gone and the excitement died down, the house was still and quiet. I pulled a chair next to my mother's bed. I could see she was tired. We both were. She looked into my eyes and I couldn't hold back the tears as I whispered, "I am so sorry."

I covered my face with my hands and pressed my forehead to the edge of her bed. Then I felt her hand gently rubbing the top of my head, telling me everything was okay. It was a lie, of course. Nothing was okay. She was dying and we both knew it. But no matter how sick she was, or what little time she had left, she was still the mother and I was the daughter that needed comforting.

I am jarred back to the gas station by the sound of the father's voice. "Are you happy now?" he asks as the little girl returns with her mother. She nods, carrying a new cup of ice cream, which she eats with a plastic spoon.

"Well, get in the car," he says. "We have a lot of miles to cover."

I absentmindedly nod my head in agreement.

Beaumont, Texas

I arrived at the Red Cross Headquarters in Dallas and checked in. After looking around at the hundreds of volunteers gathered in the sprawling warehouse, I was struck by a single thought, "A lot of people who do volunteer work are really old." My fantasies of being surrounded by super-hot firemen and sexy search-and-rescue workers were quickly dashed. I realized that Red Cross work has to do with food and shelter and nothing to do with running out of a collapsing building with an orphan under one arm and puppy in the other.

I was assigned to a small group of six volunteers and sent to Beaumont to work on an ERV (Emergency Relief Vehicle). We would be staying in a small Baptist church until the Red Cross could set up a shelter for us. All of us piled into a van to begin the six hour drive south. The closer we got to Beaumont the less traffic we saw. The highways were empty except for the occasional convoy of rescue vehicles and utility trucks. We knew we were getting closer when we began to see twisted, mangled billboards; massive trees ripped out of the ground; and miles of downed power lines. Every now and again the volunteer driving the van would slow down to maneuver around some object that was far from where it belonged, such as a refrigerator lying in the middle of the road.

I'd never been a part of something so big. It was sad, and I felt bad for the people who had to go through it, but at the same time it was exciting. I felt a little rush every time we passed an overturned car or a building with its roof ripped off. They were signs that something with unimaginable power had been here.

I saw him the moment I entered the little church. He was sitting in a chair in the entryway looking really sexy. The way one leg bent and the other was thrown casually out front, I could tell he would swagger when he walked. I caught his eye as I passed by. It was one of those rare movie moments when one holds a stranger's look long after it would normally be appropriate. I had no idea who he was or what he was doing there, but my intuition told me that this wasn't the last time I would see him.

It had been a long day and we were all exhausted. Well, most of us were exhausted. The exception was LuAnne, whose energy I can only describe as a cat in heat. Not that she was looking to get laid, it was that she was wound so tightly with such a nervous crazed look in her eye, that I got the feeling that if she were stuck indoors she would snap and begin hissing and spitting and howling. While the rest of us settled into our cots to relax or read or call family, LuAnne went on the prowl looking for someone, anyone, to talk to.

A couple hours later LuAnne returned and excitedly began telling us about her night. "Oh my God, ya'll, you won't believe this guy I met downstairs! His name is Chris and we started talkin' and I don't know why, poor thing must have needed someone to talk to, but he started tellin' me his whole life story and it was all just so tragic I didn't know what to say."

Instinctively, I knew exactly whom she was talking about. "The hot guy in the chair, right?"

LuAnne nodded her confirmation with such enthusiasm I thought she might explode if she didn't get the story out soon.

"So, what was so tragic about him?" I asked.

Her super-fast speech touched with a strong southern twang began to pick up speed. It felt as if we should have been sitting at the plantation, sipping lemonade and fanning ourselves as she retold the juicy gossip. "Well, for one, he was married when he was, like, seventeen, and he joined the Army because his wife was pregnant. Then one day he came home on leave to surprise her and she got hit by a train right in front of him."

There was an audible gasp from the other volunteers. As LuAnne's story continued her eyes grew wider than I thought humanly possible, "He lost his wife and his baby! After that it's like he wanted to die, so he joined the Special Forces and would volunteer to go to the worst places. He's been to Iraq like four times, Afghanistan a whole bunch and he's watched almost all of his friends die. Then, he tells me that he eventually remarried and his sister-in-law had this boyfriend that beat her. Chris went to her house one night, like a few years ago, and got into a fight with the boyfriend, who apparently was this big huge guy. In the middle of the fight he dropped Chris over his knee breaking Chris's back. Then the boyfriend pulls out a knife and is about to stab him, but Chris was able to pull his gun out of the back of his pants and shoot the guy first. The guy died and fell on top of him. Right there in the front yard.

"Did he go to jail?" I asked.

"No the cops pulled up and seen that it was self-defense. Plus they all knew him, and knew he was Special Forces, so no charges were filed. But he was in the hospital for ages recovering from his broken back. Oh and get this: his wife, well his ex-wife now—her sister never forgave Chris for killin' the deadbeat boyfriend. How's that for gratitude?"

"So why is he here?"

"Well here's the thing, ya'll. He's pretty messed up in the head. I just didn't know what to say to the poor guy. I guess about a month ago, he was driving a big truck, transporting a tank for the military. He was in New Mexico on the highway and a car full of teenagers crossed the line hitting him head on. All the kids were killed, and as horrible as that is, the worst part was that, driving in the car behind them were their parents. They saw the whole thing. He said he has just flipped out because it brought back all the memories of losing his first wife and their baby. The Army forced him take a leave because he's too messed up and unpredictable. I guess he's suicidal or he was. The minister in his hometown said he needed to do somethin' for others to get his thoughts off himself, so he came down here with the Texas Baptist Men. He's on the chainsaw crew."

The room fell silent with each of us lost in our own thoughts. Eventually I could not stomach it a moment longer. "What a load of bullshit," I blurted out. "No one's life is that dramatic."

They looked at me as if I'd dropkicked a kitten across the room. Wide eyes and closed mouths spoke volumes about my perceived character. I knew I was skating on thin ice. Here I was, a volunteer for the *American* Red Cross, sitting smack in the middle of Bush's home state, having the gall to doubt an American soldier's—hell, an American hero's—word.

I saw myself, in that moment through their eyes; an artist, a writer from The Devil's Playground of Los Angeles, a hippie who had dared to protest the war. They saw me as a cynic, one of those Hollywood types that wouldn't be happy until I had stripped away the very last fibers of good American values. I wasn't being looked at like I was clever or witty. I was being looked at like I was mean; a mean, bitter girl with a cold heart.

I glanced down at my hands, mumbling, "Look, I don't know this guy, but I can tell you, no one ever goes through that much drama and tragedy." I glanced up and continued, "Sure one or two things may happen, but regular life isn't like movie life. Mostly it's just boring."

I'd officially sucked all the fun out of the conversation. Everyone quietly returned to whatever they were doing before LuAnne came in with the Story of the Century. As I lay down on my cot I had no idea that very soon I would be moving to the swamps of Louisiana with this larger-than-life man I had yet to meet.

****

Over the next few days, I continued to see Chris around. The small Baptist Church where we were temporarily housed made it impossible not to see everyone every day. With two organizations under one roof it was tight quarters. The Texas Baptist Men and The Red Cross have been serving together during disaster relief efforts for ages, and although they are distinctly different organizations, they work as one. The Texas Baptists cook the food. The Red Cross serves the food. It's the Yellow Hats and the Red Vests working side by side.

I've never seen people work as hard as those Yellow Hats. They woke up early, worked and sweated all day in the heat, prayed, and went to bed.   Although Chris was a yellow hat, it didn't fit. He didn't strike me as a "get on your knees and pray" kind of guy. Every time I saw him, he was outside smoking, in the kitchen playing cards, or flirting with various women.   In a short time he'd become the most popular man around.

I found myself watching him with more and more interest. He would be leaning back in his chair, casually smoking and talking, while others leaned toward him, particularly the women, but the men too. I never heard what he was saying, but I thought whatever it was, he certainly had their attention. More important than seeing him, I *heard* about him. Each day bits of information would filter down the pipeline adding to the already grand tale that LuAnne told the first night.

"Did you hear he tried to kill himself? A minister sent him here to get his head straight."

"Apparently, he hung himself from a tree. At the last second the limb snapped; he was knocked out for twelve hours until someone found him in the morning."

"No, that's not it. His brother stopped by and when he walked in he saw him with a gun in his mouth. If the brother had gotten there ten seconds later, he'd be dead. I'll tell you what, ladies, that there is the power of God."

"Amen."

"Did you see the pictures in his phone?"

"What pictures?"

"Of his dead wife. She's so pretty, barely a teenager. Can you imagine? Loving the same woman for twenty years? So sad."

"He said that's why he joined the Special Forces. When she died he had a death wish."

These hushed conversations took place early in the mornings while we waited for the ERVs to be loaded up with food. They took place while we crowded around small tables in the dining room eating dinner. They took place in the bathrooms while we brushed our teeth before bed. Who was this guy? After the first night, I learned to keep my comments to myself. When you're the weird, artsy girl sitting in the back of the class, you don't call out the star quarterback in front of the whole school. Besides, who was I to judge anyone, to question another's life story? What had I ever done that was exciting or interesting? Just because my life had become as dry and boring as Melba toast it didn't mean other people weren't out there living full, rich, passionate, exciting lives.

From what I could tell, this man didn't sit around, weeping and praying, hoping a reluctant God would someday show up and make everything better. My skepticism for his story was quickly turning to a fascination. The more I heard the more I realized this would make an amazing book.

And there it was. *Could this be why I came here? Could it be that "The Secret" actually worked?* All those years of wish lists, the meditations with Healing Angels, the God Boxes, the prayer circles, the visualizations, and the positive affirmations had brought me here. I'd spent the past two years immersing myself in spiritual practices that would bring love and creativity into my life. The Universal Energy Flow had brought me here to this little church in Beaumont Texas to meet this broken soldier and write his life's story.

God had finally shown up in my life and I'd nearly blown it with my cynicism and mistrust. How many times did I need to be told, "Jonna, you must believe it to receive it? The Universe can only give us what we already know we have." I'd always been the problem child in any of my countless spiritual classes, because I could never believe. Countless instructors, teachers and ministers told me the same thing over and over, "Know it to be true and it is." But I could never do that one simple thing.

A spiritual teacher would take my hands, look in my eyes and say, "I know that right here, right now, Jonna is living in prosperity. She is surrounded by Universal Abundance."

And I would think, "No I'm not. I'm broke. If I'm living in so much prosperity, why is my rent late?"

Hearing Chris's story and realizing how a quickly I'd snapped to judgment helped me see how my negative thought patterns had once again nearly blocked my energy from attracting to me my life's purpose.

One morning Chris held the door open for me. I looked back as I passed him and caught him checking out my ass. He glanced up, catching my eye. Knowing he was busted he gave a little shrug and a smile as if to say, "I can't help it. I'm a guy." I smiled back. He was cute.

We introduced ourselves and started chatting. I mentioned I had not been able to sleep and was up all night wandering the halls.

"Well, Darlin', you can wander these halls with me anytime," he said with a grin, in his slow southern drawl. Since I had never heard him speak before, I was taken aback at how... well... how *country* he was.

"Oh no," I said, "You've got trouble written all over you. I can smell it a mile away!" And with that I left him standing in the doorway looking confused.

I meant it too. He really did have an air of trouble. There was something about him that said he wasn't your run of the mill nice guy. He had an air of baggage, or turmoil.

But that's not why I said it. I said it because I had spent the last three or four days becoming totally intrigued with this man and now I wanted him to become intrigued with me. I figured he had women around him all the time. I had seen "An Officer and a Gentleman." I knew the drill. He was the rebel, the bad ass.

If wanted his attention I had to be the girl who didn't give a shit, the tough girl, the girl with a chip on her shoulder. *Hey Buddy, you may be broken, but I'm broken too. You're not the only one who's walked a tough road and come out the other end.* Of course my road wasn't littered with so many dead people, and no one ever got shot. Still, I knew pain.

It worked. The following morning as I was preparing to go out on our first run of the day, Chris sidled up next to me, leaning in close.

He nudged my arm and cocked his head, "Hey, if I'm trouble, then you, little gal, are gonna be in trouble."

The writer in me thought it was pathetic that it took him over 24 hours to come up with that ridiculous comeback. But the woman in me thought it was adorable. Then the writer was disgusted that the woman was being such a sap. The woman quickly told the writer to get over it and stop being a pessimist or else we would end up alone for the rest of our lives. The writer got the message and shut up.

I smiled at Chris, as he laughed hard at his own joke. He nudged a guy standing next to him and repeated, "Did you hear that? If I'm trouble then you're in trouble."

I knew in that moment I was than smarter he was, but I glanced at his arms—which were absolutely perfect, strong, and muscular—and thought, "What's so great about being smart?"

LuAnne dashed over at that moment. She was always dashing somewhere. *Zip. Zip. Dash. Dash.* It was as if her body was constantly trying to keep up with her energy. She rushed up to the kitchen manager who stood on the other side of Chris.

"Lieutenant Dan," she said with urgency, "do you think we could get a vehicle tonight? I heard there was a bar near here that was still open, and some of us want to go. If I don't get out of here and have me some fun, I'm just gonna go crazy." The faster she talked, the more she sounded like Scarlett O'Hara. At any moment, I expected her to swoon.

"Well, let me see what I can do." Lt. Dan dragged out his words, underscoring the importance of this decision.

We called him Lt. Dan after the character in *Forrest Gump* because he was missing a leg. Actually, he called himself that and we just followed his lead. Lt. Dan took his volunteer position as kitchen manager very seriously. So seriously, I felt sorry for him. Maybe this was all he had. At first we thought he must have lost his leg in the war, but it turned out that it was a tractor accident when he was a teenager. Lt. Dan said he'd joined the Army and was waiting to go to basic training when the accident happened. He never realized his dream of being a soldier.

I imagined his life was pretty sad back home in Michigan, living on disability, managing an apartment complex, and thinking about what could have been. But here, here in this little Baptist church in Beaumont, Texas with a fleet of Red Cross vehicles outside, he was somebody. He was Lt. Dan, our boss who made all the big decisions.

Chris turned to me, "So what about you? Ya'll goin' out tonight?"

"I don't know." I scrunched up my face and eyed him with mock suspicion. "Maybe."

"Well, maybe I'm jus' fixin' to join you," he said, rubbing the stubble on his chin.

"Well maybe you should," I smiled.

I wanted to lick his face. I've never had any desire in my life to lick another person's face, but I wanted to lick his. I imagined he would taste salty, not gross salty, but hot, sexy salty. The guys in L.A. didn't seem like they would be salty. They're too over-processed and groomed for that sort of thing. They wax their eyebrows, have spray tans and get chemical peels. Who wants to lick that?

"All right, all right," Lt. Dan broke in. "Stop flirting and go back to work. Don't you have somewhere you need to be?" "I   am   so   *not* flirting!" (I so totally was.) As I walked away, I turned back to Chris. "I hope I see you later.

"Darlin', you will most definitely see me later," he said with a wink.

Funny how a wink from a city guy can come across as cheesy or condescending, but a wink from a southern boy will send shivers up a girl's spine.

After a hard day of work, our ERV crew returned later that evening to find out two things: One, that the Red Cross volunteers were being moved. The little Baptist church was overwhelmed by our presence. Turns out we were never supposed to be there in the first place. The kitchen was supposed to be staged there, but it was never established that we would be sleeping at the facility. The first night we piled in the pastor and his wife didn't know what was going on, so they simply did what came naturally: they took care of us. Over the following four or five days, more and more Red Cross volunteers kept arriving, until we had taken over. Now it was time to go. The Red Cross contacted a local high school a few blocks away, and we were told to pack it up and move it out.

The second thing we learned was that Lt. Dan had come through and LuAnne got her wish to have a vehicle available to take us out. Once all the volunteers were moved over to the high school, we could take one of the vans and go out to blow off some steam. I looked around for Chris, but didn't see him anywhere, so I quickly went upstairs, threw together my belongings, and caught the first van over to the high school.

I had learned from LuAnne the importance of being first in the Red Cross. This was not her first disaster. She had spent months in New

Orleans after Katrina. Being first for everything was huge. First to the shelter to pick the best area, first in line for food, to eat and get out. Above all things, LuAnne taught me to always, always, *always,* be first in line for showers.

The last thing anyone wanted was to be stuck in line waiting to shower behind a couple of elderly volunteers who were at that moment casually sucking away every last drop of hot water while nonchalantly discussing the entire history of their lives.

"You know, I think I forgot my cream rinse."

Does cream rinse even exist anymore? I would wonder as I rolled my head against the wall and silently begged them to hurry.

"Here honey, you can borrow mine."

Apparently it does.

"Now, you were saying you live in Peoria?"

"Yes, my husband Norman and I owned a print shop for thirty-five years. Now my daughter and son-in-law run things. We're retired. Did I tell you that my granddaughter Jenny just lost her first tooth?"

"Oh isn't that the sweetest thing."

Rinse. Lather. Repeat. Then get out!

"Is your water getting cooler?"

"It sure is. Now where exactly is Peoria?"

Aaaahh, fuck!

Before climbing into the van I quickly scanned the church to look for Chris, but didn't see him. I knew to sit in the first seat by the door, so I could be the first out of the van, first to get my stuff, throw it on the best cot at the new shelter, and be the first to hit the showers. I flung open the side door, and there sat LuAnne in the first seat. I was okay with that. She was the master and I was happy to be her second.

My butt barely landed on the second seat when LuAnne quickly started laying out the plan. "Now listen up, we're not wastin' no time tellin' everyone we got the van for the night. I'm not waitin' on no pokey pants. I told the others that ya'll better light a fire under your ass, 'cause I want to go out. If I don't have some fun, I'm jus' gonna die!"

I knew LuAnne was bat-shit crazy and I couldn't help but love her. But I decided that this wasn't the best time to let her know I had every intention of commandeering the van later. My plan was to swing back by the church and try one more time to locate Chris to invite him along.

Within an hour we had relocated shelters, unpacked, and showered, and were ready for a night out. There were three vans that were meant to be shuttling volunteers from the church to the high school until everyone was relocated. *Technically* our van should have kept making the trip back and forth until *all* the volunteers were transferred, but that could have taken *hours,* so LuAnne hid the keys and we all played dumb. The best part of disaster relief is the confusion. No one ever really knows what's going on, so as long as you act like you're just as confused as everyone else you can get away with a lot.

"There's a van parked outside. Shouldn't it go back to the church and pick up some of the others?"

"Oh I don't know. I just caught a ride here. I don't know who has the keys."

"We should ask someone."

"Yeah. Totally. Maybe that guy over there knows. You should ask him."

The six of us that were in the know quickly piled into the van, making sure no one was watching, and took off. Once out of the driveway, I leaned forward to the guy who was driving.

"Swing back by the church," I whispered quietly.

Apparently it wasn't quiet enough because the ever-vigilant LuAnne shot forward, "We can't go back to the church. If anyone sees us we'll get stuck shuttling people all night and never get out. I just got to get out and—"

"I know, I know, LuAnne. Don't worry." I turned back to the driver, "Park around the corner and I'll hop out. I'll be two seconds. It's fine. I just forgot something."

When we pulled up to the church I quickly got out while the others waited in the van. "Why are we here?" I heard LuAnne sigh as I closed the van door.

I entered through a side door and hurried through the halls not seeing him anywhere. There was one last place to check before I would have to give up: out in back where everyone went to hang out and smoke. It was also where the other volunteers, the slowpokes, were lined up still waiting for the vans. I felt kinda bad when I came outside and saw them sitting there with all their belongings, waiting for a van that I knew was sitting around the corner. But then I saw Chris and thought, *it's not like we took the only van. There are still two others. And if they stopped being so dang slow, maybe they wouldn't be so selfish and make the rest of us, who have things to do, wait for them.*

(Whenever I know I'm wrong, I can't keep my brain from trying to over justify being right.)

I caught Chris's eye. He smiled wide, "Hey, gal!"

I motioned for him to be quiet and follow me inside. As the door closed behind him, I asked, "Did you still want to go out?"

"Heck yeah. I got back here and ya'll were gone. Then I heard they moved ya'll and I thought, oh well, guess I'd see ya tomorrow."

I couldn't help but smile when he said. "Heck yeah." *Who talks like that?*

"We have one of the vans outside. If you want to come, we have to go now cause LuAnne's about ready to have a fit." I was already headed down the hall toward the side door.

"Shoot yeah, let's go."

Seriously, who talks like that?

When we reached the van, I turned to Chris and asked, "Are the Baptists going to be mad if they know you went out?"

He looked at me sideways and grinned, cocking one eyebrow. "No one tells me what to do." And I believed him. He reached out and slid the van door open. As I stepped up to get in, he placed his hand on the small of my back. God I love it when a man places his hand on the small of my back. It's a small gesture with a huge impact. It says *I've got you. You're safe. I'm here.*

I sat down and scooted over to make room for Chris. As soon as the others saw his head poke in, I got the razzing I deserved.

"Ohhh, so this is what you forgot!"

"Now we see how it is."

We pulled a U-turn and headed out with everyone in good spirits.

It was a short drive to the local bar. Most of the streets had been cleared of debris by this time, but every now and again we would still have to maneuver around a fallen tree or telephone pole. There was a curfew for most of the town, and with a lot of the electricity still knocked out the city was dark and eerily quiet.

The curfew didn't apply to relief workers, so a few businesses were able to stay open on a limited basis. We walked into the near empty bar and picked a table. I was happy when it seemed that Chris made an extra maneuver to make sure he sat next to me. After we ordered drinks the conversation quickly turned to the relief effort.

"We ran out of peaches half way through the dinner services."

"That happened to us yesterday. I just gave everyone an extra granola bar."

"The neighborhood we were in today has had their electricity on for three days. People are just coming out for free food. They don't *need* it."

"I *know*! We were stationed in a Walmart parking lot and people were coming out of the store with a cart of groceries and *still* coming by to get a free lunch."

"When are they sending us to Galveston?"

This question had been on everyone's mind. Galveston was where the real damage was. Everyone was itching to get there and see it for themselves. I was too, but more importantly, at this moment I was just itching to get away from this conversation.

I leaned over to Chris and asked, "You wanna play a game of pool?"

Judging from how quickly he jumped up out of his chair I guessed that he didn't care much for peaches and granola bars either. "Lead the way, gal."

We found a pool table on a quiet side of the bar and started to play. I set up the balls so that he could break. When he leaned over the table to take that first shot I noticed a tattoo on his upper arm. It was a blue arrowhead with yellow lightning bolts crossing through it. It wasn't a particularly nice tattoo, looking like it was done in someone's garage or perhaps in prison, if colored ink is available in the slammer.

"What's the tattoo?" I asked.

He came around the table and lifted the sleeve of his T-shirt so I could take a better look. "Special Forces Airborne. It's for the guys in my unit I've lost." He went back around the table to take another shot, having sunk one of the balls on the break.

"How many did you lose?" I had to ask as he squatted down to peer at the table from a lower angle.

He raised his eyes to meet mine and held them there for a long moment. "All of them." Then he stood up and cracked the cue ball so hard the colored balls flew around the table in uncontrolled chaos.

What do I say to respond to this? Sorry? I'm sorry I flippantly told everyone you were full of shit? I'm sorry I diminished your suffering to a Lifetime movie of the week? I'm sorry that you are going through

42

such tragedy and all I can think about is how hot it would be to make out with you?

I decided it best to say nothing letting the moment pass. It was my turn. When the balls settled into play I halfheartedly took a whack at one. I didn't even know if I was stripes or solids, and really didn't care.

"You're not much of a pool player," he laughed.

I turned around leaning on the cue stick. "Why are you here?"

What was wrong with me? Why couldn't I just let this guy have some fun? Why was I so hell bent on bringing up his past? I already knew all his tragic stories. I'd been hearing them for over a week. Did I really want to break him into a post-traumatic-shock meltdown?

"I had an accident about a month back and since then…" He trailed off, lost in thought. When he came back he continued with, "Let's just say I've been on medical leave."

It was obvious he didn't want to talk about it. "So what happened?" I asked.

It was as if I had no control over what was coming out of my mouth. My brain was screaming, "Let it go," but my mouth kept pushing forward.

He stood up from the barstool and took the stick out of my hands. We stood face to face for a long moment and I thought for a second he might kiss me. Instead he grinned and said, "You ask a lot of questions, don't you?"

I grinned and shrugged my shoulders.

"I tell ya what. You give me a little kiss on the cheek and I'll tell ya all about it."

I knew all about this little game. You lean in to kiss a man on the cheek and at the last second he turns his head so you kiss his mouth. Of course I was absolutely thrilled he was planning this, but I didn't want him to know that. I was still playing the role of tough, unattainable, distant girl.

"No way. I know that old trick," I said.

"What trick?" he protested.

"I go to kiss your check and you turn your head. Do you think I'm new?"

He dropped his head back laughing. "Little girl, you need to trust people more. That thought never crossed my mind."

Ouch. I hid my disappointment by squinting my eyes as though I were deciding if he was trustworthy.

"Right here," he tapped his check.

I paused long enough to give the appearance of reluctance, and then I leaned in.

Damn. He didn't turn his face. My lips landed on his cheek just as he had promised.

"See," he smiled, "I wouldn't lie to you."

His face was inches from mine. The butterflies in my stomach fluttered around as if they had taken a huge hit of crack. I swallowed hard. "It's your turn," I murmured, pushing the cue stick in his direction.

He looked into my eyes and I recognized in his that he already knew he had me. So much for being the cool chick, he held all the cards and now we both knew it.

He took the beer out of my hand and lifted the bottle to see that it was empty, "You want another?"

"Sure."

He left me and headed toward the bar. Returning a short time later, with a fresh beer, he sat down on a bar stool next to me. It was a few moments before he spoke.

"A couple months back I was driving a big rig haulin' a tank for the Army across New Mexico. Out of nowhere this car going the opposite way crossed into my lane. There was nothin' I could do. I blasted the horn, but it was too late. They hit me head on. All traffic stopped. People were screaming and running, but there was nothin' anyone could do. The car was a mangled hunk of shredded metal. I walked away without a scratch, but four teenagers were dead."

"Wow," was all I could say.

"Their parents were driving a few cars behind them when it happened. They saw the whole thing. I couldn't look at them. I just couldn't. I mean what am I supposed to say? One of their mamas just couldn't stop screaming and I... I just couldn't... Everyone says it wasn't my fault but..."

He stared off for a long while lost in thought, then sadly shrugged. "The Army decided it was best if I didn't come back for a while, so they put me on what you could call medical leave."

"I don't even know what to say," I mumbled, more to myself.

"No one ever does."

I looked at his face seeing such a deep sadness, the kind I'd never seen before. Although he was sitting only inches away, in his eyes he was somewhere else.

"Anyway," he continued, "I went through a depression and, well, things got bad."

I knew what he was dismissing was the attempted suicide I'd heard about. Even thought there'd been conflicting stories about what happened there was no way I was going to ask him about it.

"So Randy, who is the pastor of the Baptist church in my town, came to see me and basically said, 'You're gonna go to Beaumont to help with the hurricane relief effort.' I guess he figured if I was helpin' others it would do me good." He laughed, adding, "I don't think I had much choice. Between him and my mama they'd made up their minds. I may try and act tough, but my mama still makes the rules."

"So is it helping? I mean, do you feel any better?"

"Well yeah," he smiled, grabbing my knee. "I'm sittin' here with you aren't I?"

There was something that still didn't make sense to me. I debated about whether to let it slide or just ask. It was such a touchy subject, but he had come back from the bar and answered my question like he promised. So I asked, "Why were you transporting a tank? I thought you were more of a like, I don't know, like a fighting war guy."

He must have found my lack of military knowledge entertaining because he threw his head back and laughed. "A fightin' war guy? Damn girl, you are cute."

"Well, I don't know about this stuff," I smiled.

"I *am* a fightin' war guy, but I'd been on light duty for the past year cause I was shot in Afghanistan."

"You got shot? I want to see it."

He stood up asking, "You really want to see this?"

"Um, yeah!" I'd never in my life known anyone who had been shot. Of course I wanted to see it.

He sighed while pulling off his boot, then pulled down his sock and lifted his ankle up for me to see. It looked like a big chunk had been blown away. There was a gnarly scar and my first thought was, *that shit had to hurt.* On impulse I reached out a finger to touch it. He jumped back. "Don't touch it."

Pulling his boot back on, he grimaced as it went over his ankle. "I saw the guy in a window right before he fired off the shot. I thought I was a goner, but the asshole was such a lousy shot he hit my ankle. Can you believe that? He had me right in his sights and he fuckin' hit my ankle. I couldn't move, so I just start laughin' and flippin' the guy off."

"You were laughing?"

"Yeah," he laughed, reliving what I guess was a comical memory. "I started yellin' all kinds of stuff like, come on you fuckin' pussy, do it! I'm thinkin' maybe I was in shock."

"You think?"

"Then I hear a crack right behind me and that guy dropped like a ragdoll. That's the difference between us and them. Our guys don't miss."

"So once you get shot, doesn't that kind of get you a get-out-of-Army-free card?"

He looked at me like I was crazy. "Darlin', I've been Special Forces for eighteen years. I don't know anything else. I don't want to get out. But if this ankle doesn't heal right, then I put my guys at risk and I become a liability."

"You seem to get around okay."

At this point, he'd looked at me with so many variations of confusion that I was beginning to think he wondered if I'd lived under a rock. When it came to the military, I guess I had.

"If I parachute out of a plane behind enemy lines and my ankle snaps, then my guys have to drag me along. That puts all of us in danger. I can't do that, and they would never leave me behind. I go to the VA next month, so they can test it again."

"What happens if you don't pass?"

"I don't know," he answered, and then changing the subject he asked, "You want to go outside and smoke?"

I'd quit smoking six months earlier, but after two beers and his stories, I picked up right where I had left off. We moved to the patio area meeting up with the other volunteers. The intensity of our time spent together instantly vanished as we joined in the casual conversations that were going on.

Eventually it was time to go. Our group started walking toward the front door. On the way, I stopped to use the restroom, telling the others to go on and I'd meet them outside.

When I came out of the restroom, I headed to the front door. Someone grabbed my hand from behind and pulled me back. When I turned, there he stood. He stepped forward and took my face in his hands while moving me up against the wall. It was a kiss that nearly buckled my knees. He ran a hand through my hair and held onto the back of my neck. His other hand slid down my body and grabbed hold of my hip. My skin was on fire as his body pressed against my own, and I thought, *I might just die right here.* After a moment he pulled back, "I've been wantin' to do that all night."

"Uh huh," was all I managed to get out.

"Let's go," he said, taking my hand.

****

The next morning I got the first van over to the little church with the rest of my crew. The Yellow Hats had been up early and already had all of the food for the day prepared for us. As we loaded up the ERV with supplies to take out into the neighborhood, I stole moments here and there to look around and try to spot Chris. No luck. I figured the chainsaw crew had probably already left for the day.

Those guys had a tough job. Beaumont had sustained a lot of wind damage from Ike and there were mangled, twisted trees lying all throughout the city. The difficult part wasn't the trees that had fallen. Those were hauled away. It was the trees that hadn't completely fallen but where hanging on by a few roots. This isn't such a big deal to someone with a good income and extra money. You just call a tree service and have it taken care of. But if you're an elderly person living on a fixed income, having a giant oak tree dangling precariously over your home can be scary. That's where the chainsaw crew came in. They removed dangerous trees for people, and they did it for free. Sure, Chris was a yellow hat, but he was part of the badass Yellow Hats, and that made him even sexier.

We were loaded up ready to go when we got called back into the church for a meeting. As we piled into the gymnasium and took our seats in the bleachers, Lt. Dan limped back and forth in front of us.

"Last night we were told to move shelters, but some of the volunteers were left behind because the keys to one of the vans couldn't be located," he said, looking straight at our crew.

I did what came naturally: I looked to the other volunteers with an expression that read, *who would do such a thing?*

"Now," Lt. Dan continued, barking his orders as though we were troops being sent into battle, "I don't mind if you want to take a van to go out in the evenings, but we don't leave others behind. We all go together. We're a team!"

LuAnne, who was sitting behind me, leaned forward and whispered in my ear, "We ain't never gonna have no fun waitin' for these dilly-dallies. They're slow as molasses."

My loud burst of laughter caught everyone's attention and I quickly slapped my hand over my mouth. I liked LuAnne. She was crazy, but she was my kind of crazy.

As the meeting broke up and the crowd filed out, someone grabbed my arm from behind and pulled me to the side. I turned to see Chris smiling at me; I was beginning to wonder if this guy ever approached anyone head on. I figured it must be a Special Forces thing to always sneak up from behind.

"Hey, gal." He moved in closer as though he were giving me top-secret information. "I'm gonna take you out on a date tonight, just the two of us."

"There's no way they'll let us take a vehicle out on our own. Plus, you're not even in the Red Cross, so—"

"Don't worry, I got this. You just be ready." He quickly kissed me on the cheek and was out the door.

I was left standing there thinking, *this guy has some balls.* Of course it would never happen, but I appreciated the thought.

Later that evening I was mopping out the ERV, nasty and dirty, covered in whatever happened to be on the lunch menu that day, when Chris approached. He put one foot up on the bumper and leaned in shaking a set of keys.

"I'll meet you back here in an hour and a half," he said with a wink, and then he was gone.

When I was finished cleaning, I ran to catch the first van back to the shelter, then ran to get to the showers before anyone else. I was dressed and ready in lightening speed. I caught another van back to the church before some of the other volunteers were even finished unloading their ERVs. I was a woman on a mission.

I did, however, slow down long enough to give the appearance that I was casually sauntering back to the church. Having spotted Chris standing inside, I made it a point to stop and chat with others who were hanging around. I told myself I was "easy-breezy girl," who didn't rush for no man. The truth was, with my back turned to the doors, it was taking every ounce of willpower I had to not turn and peek to see if he had noticed me yet.

A short time later I felt him behind me. "You ready?" he asked.

I looked back, smiling casually, hoping the sound of my pounding heart wouldn't give me away, "Uh huh, just one second." I turned back to the woman in front of me, giving her my most undivided fake attention, "A print shop in Peoria huh? That sounds sooooo interesting."

My plan backfired. After the most boring minute and half of my life, hearing about the print shop in Peoria I turned to discover Chris had found a group of guys nearby and was talking up a storm. I approached him, "I'm ready."

"Just a second," he dismissed me with a nod, turning back to his captive audience.

Twenty minutes and two cigarettes later I was still standing around waiting like a pathetic lost puppy. I was beginning to think he had completely forgotten about our date. I had to take a risk or we were never getting out of here. Easy-breezy girl wasn't working, but tough girl had shown positive results in the past, so I took a chance.

I approached the circle of men and snapped at Chris, "Seriously? Are we gonna eat? I'm fucking starving."

Chris threw up his hands in mock surrender and laughed, saying to the others. "Gotta go, the lady is hungry." He turned back to me, "All right, gal, let's get you fed."

Note to self: Quietly trying to manifest what you want doesn't work, being a bitch does.

I followed Chris to an SUV in the parking lot. I found out later that it was issued through the Red Cross to Lt. Dan. Of course Chris's "best buddy" would let him borrow it. Since the town continued to be under curfew, there were few restaurant choices, but there were still some places serving from a limited menu. It all depended on what supplies they could get.

We found a country-western–themed chain steak house that had peanuts on the floor and served baked potatoes the size of your head. Chris opened the door for me, and continued to hold it for an elderly couple that was exiting.

"Thank you," the woman said as she passed.

"Yes, ma'am" Chris replied.

Chris addressed everyone he met with either "yes, ma'am" or "yes, sir." I didn't know if that was a southern thing or a military thing, but I liked it. I was used to L.A. guys who could barely look up from their cell phones long enough to even acknowledge another person, let alone politely open a door for them.

We found a booth and Chris slid in beside me. He sat *beside* me, not across the booth at some distance, but right next to me on the same seat. And to top it off, he threw his arm over the back of the booth so it was almost like his arm was around me. Almost.

The waitress brought our menus, and then proceeded to list all the things that weren't available. "We don't have any seafood. It went bad when the power went out. You can get a burger, but we don't have any buns; the bread truck never arrived this morning. There isn't any salad, and the only vegetable we have left is broccoli. We have brownies if you want dessert, but all the ice cream melted." She smiled and left us to decide.

While he scanned the menu, Chris asked, "So what looks good to you?"

"Um, I don't know. Maybe I'll get chicken," I shrugged.

He whipped his head in my direction with an eyebrow raised in disapproval. "What" He shook his head? "No," he said definitively. "Get a steak. You need a steak." With that, he turned his attention back to the menu, ending any further discussion.

Did this cowboy just tell me what I was going to eat? My head was spinning. I'd been preparing my own bowl of cereal or peanut butter sandwich for dinner since I was seven. If that wasn't available, I would always find some chips or candy. I knew how to survive. I knew how to take care of myself. No man had ever come into my life and told me what I should or should not eat. *Ever.*

I could feel my face grow hot. All the blood in my body rushed to the surface as my nerves jumped to attention. If it hadn't been frowned upon in public, I would have ripped his clothes off and fucked him right there under the wagon-wheel clock. This was a man—a *real* man—who had just told me what I was going to eat, a man who took charge, a man who knew what was best for me, a man who could take care of me.

"No. Get a steak. You need a steak." It was the single hottest moment of my life.

I looked at him and replied, "Okay." It was so simple. He made the decision. All I had to do was let him. Where had he been all my life?

When the waitress came back, Chris ordered our steaks. She asked me how I wanted mine cooked and instinctively I looked to Chris.

"Medium rare for her, extra rare for me," he answered.

After dinner we intended to get a drink at the bar where we'd played pool, but we never made it. We did get as far as the parking lot. A storm had rolled in and it was pouring rain. Huge, fat, Texas-sized raindrops like I had never seen before. Chris and I began making out in the back of the SUV. As things became more heated the windows fogged up giving us our privacy. Unfortunately, I couldn't shut my mind off and simply enjoy the moment. I went back and forth: we should stop, I don't want to stop, we should stop, I don't want to stop.

Finally, after the third time I'd mumbled, "We shouldn't do this," but then continued doing it anyway, Chris stopped kissing me. He looked in my eyes and panted with a heavy breath, "Do you need me to take over?"

If the steak thing didn't kill me, this just might. Did I want him to take over? Of course I wanted him to take over! I slowly nodded my head. That's all the encouragement he needed. He yanked me down lower on the seat and within five seconds had both of us stripped. When he pulled his shirt over his head I nearly passed out. He was perfect.

Every muscle in his shoulders, chest, and abs, was tight and clearly defined. Not like a beefy, pumped-up body builder, but like a statue carved in stone.

"Oh my God, are you serious?" I blurted, while eyeing his body from head to toe.

"What?" Chris asked. He looked down at his own chest causing his stomach muscles to tighten which only outlined his six-pack.

I quickly said a silent prayer thanking Baby Jesus I was on my back. My squishy imperfections had safely sunk into the seat cushion.

"Look at you! You're perfect," I said, waving my hand toward his body. "I don't know what to do with all that."

A sly grin came over his face. "I do."

And he wasn't lying. He absolutely knew exactly what he was doing. I couldn't believe this was actually my life. The intensity of the summer storm, in a hurricane ravaged town, in the back of a Red Cross vehicle with a sexy Special Forces soldier was bigger than any fantasy I could dream up.

An hour later, we finally came up for air and started pulling our clothes back on. There was a lot of fumbling around in the dark trying to figure out whose jeans were whose and squinting to see if our shirts were on backwards or inside out. I fished around on the floor to find my cell phone and check the time.

"Oh shit," I said. "I missed the curfew. They lock the shelter at midnight. Damn it, I'm locked out."

"Come on, let's get you back," he said. "Someone will still be up."

On the drive to the shelter, neither of us said anything. The longer the silence lingered the more uncomfortable it became. I've never been a big fan of one-night stands. I'd had them of course, but usually not by choice; when I slept with a man who never called again, by default it became a one-night stand. But my intention was usually to see them again. I've never been the chick that walked away after sex like it was nothing.

Obviously I wasn't expecting Chris to immediately become my boyfriend just because we'd done it. I wasn't completely out of touch with reality. We were basically strangers and, in all likelihood, this was a one-time thing. But still, I wished he would at least *say something*. I hated the feeling that once the sex was over, the guy had nothing left to say. Chris was a talker, telling one story after another. Now, suddenly he'd gone mute.

Once we were at the shelter, I pointed to the window where I thought my team was staying. Chris parked the SUV and I got out in the pouring rain to go tap on the window. I was hoping someone would wake up, while simultaneously hoping not everyone would wake up. By the time a familiar face pulled back the curtains and peered outside, I was completely soaked. I motioned toward the front door to let me in.

I gave Chris a wave to let him know it was okay to leave. Before I turned to run inside, Chris rolled down the window and whispered, "Hey, gal, what are you doin? Get over here."

I walked over to the driver's side.

"You were just going to run inside without saying bye?" he asked.

I shrugged, "You didn't say anything the whole way here. I figured—I don't know—whatever."

"Darlin', I'm a guy. I can't talk after sex." Then he added with a grin, "I barely remember my own name."

"Oh."

Chris took my face in his hands giving me a long, slow kiss. No one had ever kissed me in the rain before. It was like a movie kiss. Of course, I was the only one actually in the rain. He was comfortably dry in the car, but who cared? I was having a genuine chick-flick moment.

He slowly pulled away and said, "Go on now, get yourself inside before you drown."

"Okay. See ya."

****

The next morning, as our crew was loading up the ERV to go on the morning run, I glanced around, but didn't see Chris anywhere. I was half disappointed and half relieved. Disappointed because I was dying to see him. Relieved because I was scared to see him. I knew from experience that although the night had been amazing, in the light of day, things often changed. I dreaded the horrible feeling of being excited to see a guy I'd slept with, only to have him pull that bullshit attitude that said, "Since my penis has been in your vagina, I will act like you have cooties." I fucking hate that. There is absolutely no reason to be a dick, just because you have one.

When this happened in my twenties (Who am I kidding? Well, well, into my thirties), I would quietly go away. I pretended it was cool so the guy didn't see I was hurt. But that was no longer the case. If Chris wanted to act like an immature jerk, then he would hear a few choice words from me. I wasn't about to let some guy, Special Forces or not, treat me—

"Hey there," his voice whispered in my ear. I jumped about five feet and spun around to see to see him laughing at my fright. "Damn, girl, you were a million miles away."

"You scared me." I laughed while slapping him on the chest. Mmmmmm, his chest.

"What were you thinkin' 'bout?" he asked. "You looked like you were fixin' to kill someone."

I laughed nervously, "No, not at all. I was just... nothing... just doing my thing."

"Well, I gotta go, but I was thinkin' we need to get you back over here so we can hang out at night. I plan on seein' a lot more of you."

"I don't think that's possible. They don't just randomly let us go wherever we want. I have to stay where they tell me."

Chris rejected this with a shake of his head. "Nah."

Nah? He said this as if he actually had a say in the matter. I thought it was endearing—arrogant sure, but endearing all the same.

Chris saw his crew was ready to leave. "I gotta go. You just get packed and ready to move back." He gave me a quick kiss and left.

Having spent the last ten minutes fantasizing on the tongue-lashing I'd give him after he blew me off, I was completely unprepared for this turn of events. This guy kept surprising me, and hardly anyone ever surprised me. It was fun and exciting, if only I could relax and trust. I decided in that moment that no matter what the future held, I was going to have some fun and be grateful for this time I got to spend with Chris.

Later that afternoon, while walking out of the church, I passed Lt. Dan, who called out to stop me, "Hey, I want to talk to you."

My heart sank; he'd heard I'd come back late the night before. I knew I wasn't in any serious trouble, but I didn't feel like hearing a lecture about following rules.

I turned back smiling. "What's up?"

"You're on the cleanup crew."

"We have a cleanup crew?" I asked, having never heard of this before.

"We do now," he answered flatly.

So he *had* heard and now I was being punished. Great. I didn't want to be part of a cleanup crew. I wanted to stay on the ERV with my team. Now I was going to miss out. I guess that's what I got for acting like a horny teenager.

"What do you need me to do?" I asked.

Lt. Dan waved his hand casually, "Oh, you know, if you see a paper on the ground, throw it away—that kind of stuff. Maybe empty the ashtrays outside. Pick up around here."

It hardly sounded like enough to keep me busy all day. "That's it?" I asked, confused. "What about the ERV? We get those raviolis and strained peas out to the people like a well-oiled machine. You can't break up our team now," I said trying to joke with him.

Without a flicker of a smile he responded, "You'll stay with your ERV. The cleanup crew takes place after you get back."

"Who else is on the cleanup crew?" I felt this was a little unfair. Sure I had been late, but we were all adults here. I was a volunteer, not a student at boarding school.

"Just you."

I looked at Lt. Dan, trying to decide if I should put up a fight or just suck it up, when he said. "You need to go get your stuff and bring it back here." He winked and added, "The cleanup crew sleeps at the church, so they can be around to, you know, clean up."

I smiled widely, having finally been let in on the joke. "Where is he?"

He shrugged, "I don't know. He was here earlier but he disappeared."

While I packed my bags, my friends at the shelter lovingly glared at me. At the church I wouldn't have to wait in line to brush my teeth or take a shower. I could sleep an extra half–hour, since I no longer had to wait outside for a van to pick me up. But the best part: every morning the Yellow Hats made a huge breakfast, biscuits and gravy, eggs, sausage, French toast, donuts, and bagels. Unfortunately it was mostly gone by the time the Red Cross showed up, but not for me. Not anymore.

When I walked back into the church, I saw Chris pushing a large television on a wheeled stand. "Well, hello there, Sweetheart," he beamed as he saw me.

I laughed, "What is that?"

He patted the top of the television. "It's a television. And look there's a DVD player too."

"I can see that, but what are you doing with it?"

He looked very proud as he said, "Taking it to our room. Here, give me your bag."

"I got it," I said with a wave of my hand.

Chris fixed me with a look and I handed over the backpack. He threw it over his shoulder and pushed the TV stand down another long hallway. He stopped at one of the many doors and held it open, letting me go in first. I looked around in awe, not believing how lucky I was. It was a tiny room where the church taught Sunday school. There were kids' drawings on the wall and tiny chairs stacked in the corner, but to me it might as well been a palace. There was a double sized blow up mattress on the floor and a working sink. I no longer had to crowd around with ten other people trying to brush my teeth.

I turned to Chris, who was busy plugging in the television, "How did you do all this?"

Chris told me when he got back to the church that afternoon he saw Lt. Dan and told him to figure out a way to get me back to the church. It was Lt. Dan who came up with the idea for the cleanup crew.

"Do people usually do what you want?" I asked.

"Well, shoot yeah," he answered, as though this were common knowledge.

Chris then found the secretary for the church and explained to her that he was suffering from post-traumatic stress disorder. It was difficult for him to sleep, so he needed to watch a movie in bed to quiet his mind. She arranged for the room and the television.

"What about the blow up mattress?" I asked.

"Borrowed it from my crew leader."

"Well, okay then." I smiled as Chris came over hugging me tightly.

That night, lying on a blow up mattress in the little classroom with Chris's arms wrapped around me, I slept better than I had in years. If God had planned that I lose my job so that I would meet this man and have this amazing experience, then all I could say was, "Thank you."

****

Unfortunately, even the best of times eventually come to an end. After nearly three weeks, the city of Beaumont was back on its feet and the Red Cross was moving its available people to Galveston. That's where the real damage was. I was dying to get down there and see it for myself. We were given the choice, extend our volunteer commitment and go south, or fly home.

Either way, it was time to say goodbye to Chris. As much as I thought we couldn't be more different, I still had an amazing time with him. The surprise of a mini-romance just added to the volunteer experience. His crew was staying in the Beaumont area and wouldn't be going down to Galveston. There were no homes left after the destruction of Ike, so there wasn't a need to cut down fallen trees.

We said our goodbyes one morning and told each other we would keep in touch. I tried to fight back the tears as he held me tightly and said, "Girl, I am gonna miss the heck out of you. My little tree hugger."

"I'm going to miss you too," I said, wiping my eyes. I laughed and looked away. "I don't know why I'm crying. It's stupid."

He wiped a tear off my cheek. "No it's not. I think it's sweet."

I climbed into the van with the other volunteers. As I waved goodbye I hoped maybe one day I'd see him again.

A couple of hours later we arrived in Galveston. Like everyone else, I was shocked at the devastation. Miles and miles of homes were gone. All I could see as I gazed out the van window were massive piles of debris strewn in every direction. And this was after weeks of clean up. One of the volunteers, an older man, tapped my shoulder and pointed out the window. "Now that's something you don't see every day." I turned my head to see a house completely flipped upside down, sitting at a precarious angle, resting on one side of the pitched roof.

The Red Cross Volunteer base was much different too. I was used to our little Baptist church kitchen and our crew with ten ERVs going out a day. This was an enormous FEMA site stationed on the runway of the local airport, which also housed an aviation museum. All around the perimeter of our camp were the tattered remains of old vintage planes that had been twisted around and spat out by Ike. It was now an aviation cemetery.

The National Guard, The Salvation Army, AmeriCorps, The Red Cross, The Texas Baptist Men, and countless other relief agencies had set up camp. There were so many uniforms from so many different places I couldn't tell who was who. I guessed that there were well over a thousand people, a hundred big-rig trucks and emergency relief vehicles, and so many giant white tents that it resembled a small city.

Because this operation was run by FEMA, it meant no one was let in or out without a FEMA badge. We stood in line to enter a trailer and give our information to one of the many military personnel sitting behind long tables. They would type all of our information into a computer, check our Red Cross ID, then take our pictures. Within minutes a new FEMA badge would pop out of a machine and we would be allowed to enter the premises.

Our little team was finally processed through the system and shown to the tent where we would be sleeping. We carved out our own space, wanting to stick together in a tent that housed nearly 400 Red Cross volunteers. I looked down at the hard cot and stiff blanket with a longing for the blow up mattress I'd shared with Chris.

Later in the evening while wandering around taking it all in, I received a call from him. "Hey, gal, how are you?"

"I'm good. How are you?"

"Well, it sure is a lot quieter since ya'll left," he said sounding kind of sad.

"It's crazy here. It looks like—I don't know—like there's a war going on or something. There are military people everywhere and we're staying in this massive tent city. You should see it."

"I have a pretty good idea what it's like."

"Oh yeah, right," I said, then added, "Well, I never saw anything like it in my life. It's super cool!"

Chris laughed. "I miss you, girl."

"I miss you too. I wish you were here."

"Yeah, me too," he said. "Listen, John is waving at me to hurry up. We're going to the bar to get a drink, but I'll call you later, okay?"

John was Lt. Dan's real name. Chris refused to call him Lt. Dan like the rest of us. I think since Lt. Dan had never actually served in the military, Chris found it somehow insulting. Also, he'd told me his rank in the Army was sergeant, and although I was no military expert, I knew a lieutenant was higher than a sergeant. So Chris called "Lt. Dan" John.

After we hung up I stood in line to take a shower. When I finished my shower, I stood in line to use the restroom, then stood in line to brush my teeth. On my way back to the Red Cross tent my phone rang again.

"Guess what? Chris sounded excited. "I'm coming to Galveston."

"What? How did that happen?" I said thrilled at the news.

John and I were sittin' at the bar and I was bein' all mopey cause I was missin' you, then this lady comes over and sits down. We all get to talkin' and turns out she's the head of the Beaumont Chapter of the Red Cross. I tell her I want to go to Galveston. John is drivin' down tomorrow so I could get a ride with him if I were in the Red Cross. Get this, she tells me to come by the chapter in the morning. She'll sign me up as a volunteer and put the paperwork through to send me down there." Chris laughed. "I'm comin' to get ya, gal."

"What about the Texas Baptist Men? Are they going to be mad that you left?" I asked.

"Baby, who cares? No one can tell me what to do. I do what I want."

He'd never called me Baby before. My stomach did little flip-flops.

Chris continued, "Besides, they were all givin' me a hard time today 'cause they could tell how much I was missin' my little hippie. They'll understand."

I could barely contain my excitement that night as I tried to sleep. This kind of stuff didn't happen to me. I'd never had a guy follow me across the street—let alone across Texas—because he missed me. Once again, I found myself amazed that this was actually my life. For the first time, I allowed myself to consider that maybe Chris was the one.

The next day, I spoke with him numerous times. Things in Beaumont weren't going well. He'd gone to the Red Cross chapter, but they were having computer problems and unable to process his paperwork. Chris spent the entire day sitting at the chapter waiting. Each time we spoke I could hear the frustration in his voice growing. Then I stopped hearing from him. When I tried to call, it went straight to voicemail. I told myself it had been stupid to get my hopes up in the first place.

That night, after everyone had eaten and were getting ready for bed, I got another call.

"Hey, gal, we're here!" Chris said. "How do you get in?"

"You're *here* here?"

I could hear Lt. Dan laughing and talking in the background as Chris laughed too. "We're drivin' around, but can't find the way in. Where's the entrance?"

"I don't know where you are, so I don't know how to tell—"

"Whoa, man, stop!" Chris shouted at Lt. Dan. "Is that a fucking plane? Where the hell are we?" The two of them burst into fits of laughter again. "Watch the road, Dumb-ass!"

Chris composed himself, lowering his voice to say to me, "He's gonna get us killed."

"I'm walking to the front gate now. I'll meet you there. Do you see all the ERVs?"

"What ERVs?"

"There's like fifty of them. You don't see them?"

"It's pitch black out here. Where the fuck you going, John? We just came from there. Turn around."

"Well, what do you see?" If I could figure out where they were, then maybe I could figure out how to get them in the right direction.

"I see planes."

"Are you on the *runway*?"

It took about twenty minutes but eventually Lt. Dan and Chris pulled up to where I was standing at the front gate. Chris jumped out of the SUV and gave me a big hug. He whispered in my ear, "I've had easier drives through Baghdad; this guy can't drive for shit."

I stepped back, bobbing up and down on my toes. "I can't believe you're actually here! When I didn't hear from you, I figured you weren't coming."

"Well, shoot, gal, I told ya I was."

"Yeah, I know. But people say stuff all the time; doesn't mean it will really happen."

"Damn, girl, you really need to have more faith. My phone went dead. I didn't have the charger with me." Chris turned his attention to Lt. Dan. "Hey, how long did we sit in that office?"

"Six hours, maybe seven." Lt. Dan was busy pulling a bag out of the SUV.

"So you got in? Let me see your badge. I want to see your picture."

Chris opened the back door pulling out his duffle bag, "Nah, we got tired of waiting and left."

I stood there stunned while Chris and Lt. Dan closed the car doors.

"Is it this way?" Chris asked me as they took steps toward the front gate.

"Wait. They're not going to let you in."

Chris turned and looked at me like I was crazy, while Lt. Dan continued toward the gate. I guess he figured he got Chris here, now Chris was on his own. "Of course they'll let me in. I'll show them this."

He reached in the back pocket of his Levi's pulling out a rolled up, squashed, wrinkled packet of papers which he handed to me. I unrolled the papers and tried to straighten them by rubbing them against my leg. I flipped through the pages then looked at Chris with disbelief.

"Is this all you have? It's nothing. This is just an application to apply for the Red Cross. It doesn't say anything. You can't get a FEMA badge unless you are actually *in* the Red Cross."

I could tell he was getting annoyed at these technicalities that were ruining the fun. "All right then, where are these Red Cross people? Go get one and tell them I'm here. They can sign me up."

"Chris, they've all gone to bed. It's late."

A look of surprise crossed his face. "They still have food, right? I'm starvin'."

"Yes, but it's on the other side of the fence which you can't get to without a FEMA ID."

Chris took a deep breath, exhaling loudly as he looked around. "Alright where are the FEMA people that give out badges."

I pointed to a nearby trailer that Lt. Dan had already entered. "In there."

"Well let's go." Chris took my hand as we walked across the blacktop toward the trailer. Lt. Dan was already getting his picture taken when we walked in. Chris looked around and saw three young Military guys sitting at the long table. He muttered under his breath, "Damn girl, why didn't you-? Trust me. I got this."

Chris walked up to the table sliding into a chair with the same swagger I'd noticed the first night I saw him. He handed the young soldier his paperwork—his ridiculously stupid paperwork that meant nothing. I realized I was holding my breath and slowly forced myself to exhale.

The soldier noticed the Special Forces pin that Chris always wore in his baseball cap. "You Special Forces?" the kid asked.

Chris nodded. "Nearly twenty years."

"I met some of you Special Forces guys. You're some crazy motherfuckers."

Chris grinned and nodded. "We can be."

And just like that, I watched as the young soldier placed Chris application for the Red Cross into a shallow wire basket without even glancing at it. As the two of them continued to talk about a bunch of military stuff I didn't understand, troop numbers and names of bases where they had both been, the young soldier simultaneously entered Chris's information into the computer, took his picture, and handed him a FEMA badge.

We headed over to the giant sleeping tent where I'd already saved him a cot next to mine. He set his bag on his new bed while scanning the giant tent with its sea of sleeping volunteers. Glancing at me he muttered, "We're not staying here."

I shook my head and chuckled, "This isn't like Beaumont. It's all organized. You can't just do what you want."

Chris flipped up the FEMA badge hanging around his neck. "You can't?"

"Okay *that,*" I said, pointing to his chest, "was just plain lucky."

"Luck ain't got nothin' to do with it, Babe."

That night we slept with our cots pushed together, holding hands. In the morning we were told to pack up our belongings. As we later heard through the rumor mill, there had been complaints about the sleeping quarters, so the Red Cross arranged for all its volunteers to be relocated to a four-star hotel across the street. Since no one could get into Galveston, the rooms sat empty and the hotel agreed to let us stay there.

Chris had nothing to do with the move, but I was beginning to wonder if he didn't have a direct line to God. I'd never seen anything like it. It seemed any desire he spoke magically appeared. That morning while we were carrying our bags into the new room, I asked him, "Have you ever seen the movie *The Secret*?"

"No, what's it about?"

"It's all about how our thoughts create the world around us. Like, what we believe to be true is true, and how if you want to manifest something into your life, you need to speak of it as though it already exists, and then it will."

Chris raised his eyebrow, "Sound like a bunch of hippie bullshit to me."

"It's not hippie bullshit!" I protested. "It's how the energy of the Universe works. What you put out is reflected back to you. You do it all the time."

"What do I do?"

"Manifest."

"What the fuck are you talkin' about?"

"It's true," I said. "You wanted a car to take me out, and you got it, you wanted us to have a room with a television, you wanted to come here, you didn't want to stay in the tent and look, we're in this amazing hotel room."

Chris didn't look like he was buying into any of this. "I just know I always get what I want. I'm not doing anything."

"That's manifesting, knowing that you already have it."

Chris walked over placing a hand on my shoulder. I felt pressure as he pressed down on me, while starting to unzip his jeans. "What am I manifesting now?" he asked.

"You're an ass!" I said with mock anger while slapping his arm.

Chris laughed and wrapped his arms around me holding me tightly. "Okay little tree hugger, don't get all mad. I'm sorry I made fun of all your hippie bullshit."

I tried with all my might to twist around and give him a shove, but he had my arms pinned to my chest. I finally resigned that it was useless and gave up with a sigh. "Please let me go. *Some* of us have to work around here."

Chris loosened his grip and I turned around. He gave me a kiss and said, "Have a nice day." Then he leapt onto the bed, landing in a reclining position with his legs crossed. He picked up the remote and flicked on the television. "Don't work too hard."

"You suck, you know that?" I said with a smile.

"Hey, if they have those little packets of Oreos on the ERV will you bring some back? Mammy hmmmm, I love me some Oreos!"

I had to laugh as I turned to go. "Yes, I will bring you back some Oreos."

Since Chris didn't technically belong to any organization, he was basically on a free vacation. He would come to the FEMA site in the morning and eat breakfast with us, then while we were out slopping raviolis, he would hang around the hotel making new friends. In the evening he would join up with us again for dinner.

One afternoon after finishing a long shift, I walked over to the hotel and saw Chris sitting out front.

He stood up. "I've been waiting for you. I want to show you something," he said as he took my hand and led me across the hotel parking lot toward a very large building. As we got closer I realized it was the Galveston Aquarium. Chris grabbed the door and held it open for me. The building was empty.

"I don't think we're supposed to be in here," I whispered.

"It's fine," Chris answered, continuing further into the building.

I saw a man ahead of us. He was looking at one of the enormous fish tanks that reached all the way from the floor to the extended ceiling. It was incredible. Everywhere I looked we were surrounded by glass walls. I felt like I was in an airtight bubble in the middle of the ocean. The man must have sensed someone else in the room, because he turned in our direction.

"Ah you made it!" he said, reaching out to shake Chris's hand.

"You've been here before?" I asked Chris.

"Yeah, I was lookin' around today and met Richard. We got to talkin' and I told him I wanted to bring my fiancée by. He said that was okay."

Fiancée? Where did that come from?

I shook Richard's hand. "I'm Jonna."

"Yes, I've heard a lot about you. I'm Richard. I'm the curator here at the aquarium. If you like, I'd love to show you around."

For the next two hours, Richard gave us a private tour of the aquarium. Everywhere I looked massive tanks filled with every kind of imaginable fish surrounded us. He told us about staying with some of the staff in the aquarium to ride out the hurricane, how a couple of the tanks were damaged, and how they had to scramble to save the fish inside. It was incredibly interesting, and I was missing most of it because all I could think was… *fiancée?*

Although I'd only known Chris for three and half weeks, I couldn't help but hope, whether he thought it was hippie bullshit or not, that this was something we could manifest. Fiancée. Fiancée. I said the word over and over in my mind, as Richard walked us to the front door.

We thanked Richard and said our goodbyes. As we were walking away, he called out to us, "Hey, if you want to come back in the morning around seven, I'll take you into the back and you can watch us feed the sharks. It's pretty exciting stuff."

Chris and I looked at each other, bummed at the missed opportunity. We wouldn't be able to feed the sharks, because the adventure was over. In the morning we would be saying goodbye and heading home.

Driving US-54 W

Somewhere in New Mexico

I am exhausted from a long day of driving as I lug my Mac desktop computer up the steps and into the hotel room. It is the only possession that I bother taking out of the truck to keep with me in the room. If the thieves want any of the other stuff, there isn't much I can do about it. But I need my computer. Meanwhile, everything I own is under that blue tarp; all I can do is hope that it will still be there when I wake up in the morning.

I think about going out to try to find something to eat, but dismiss the idea as soon as I see the bed. I set the computer box down, pull off my jeans, and climb under the stiff sheets. I am asleep before my head hits the pillow, dreaming of New Year's Eve, 2001 and the news I wish I'd never awakened to hear.

Adam and I had just arrived home from the hospital. We had been there all day. When it seemed Mom would make it through the night, we'd decided to leave. We wanted to get home before the streets filled up with New Year's Eve crowds. As soon as I walked through the front door I felt such a heaviness consume me that I immediately had to lie down.

I don't know how long I had been sleeping when the phone began to ring. It felt somewhere far off in the distance. Finally it went quiet. Then, just as I was drifting back to sleep, I felt Adam's hand gently shaking my shoulder. I forced my eyes open to look at him. I knew who was on the other end of the line. I could feel it in the deepest part of me; I dreaded hearing what they had to say.

"It's the hospital," Adam said with deep sadness filling his dark brown eyes.

I reluctantly took the phone. "Hello."

"Is this Miss Ivin?" the female voice on the other end asked.

I sighed. As soon as I identified myself she was going to use that professional but compassionate healthcare voice to break the news to me gently. There was no way to put it off. "Yes, this is she."

"I'm really sorry, Miss Ivin, but unfortunately I have to inform you that your mother passed away a short time ago. We estimate around seven o'clock this evening."

I looked over at the alarm clock. It read 7:15. Had I really only been asleep for forty-five minutes? It seemed so much longer than that.

"We'll be right there. Thank you." I hung up the phone and handed it back to Adam. "She's gone," I said as I pulled myself to a sitting position. Adam sat down on the bed next to me and put his arm over my shoulder. There was nothing to say. We were cried out and emotionally drained.

Our big plan to move the three of us into this house, so Adam and I could take care of her, was for nothing. The first night, I removed her trach and nearly killed her. A week later, I poured a can of Ensure into her feeding tube and she immediately began to vomit. I was still emptying the can into her stomach as it was coming out of her mouth.

We immediately called 911 and the exact same firefighters that had been there the week before piled back into her room. As they were wheeling Mom out to the ambulance, one of the firemen commented to Adam that we were doing a great job on the house and had gotten a lot of unpacking done. It was nice of him to notice.

Mom never came back from that trip to the hospital. It was becoming clearer every day that her body was shutting down and she needed a level of care that I was not equipped to give her. So nearly every day for the past three weeks Adam and I had gone to the hospital to stay with Mom. In the last week she had slipped into unconsciousness. We would sit for hours watching her sleep, gasping for each breath. And each time we would think, *was that that the last one?*

It didn't surprise me at all that my mother waited until we were gone to leave this earth. I guess she had been right all along. When it came down to it, all I could do was stand there and stare at her. No, it made perfect sense that my mother would leave her body just as she had lived: on her own.

Now, as Adam and I sat quietly in our bedroom, I could hear noisemakers and horns in the distance; people had begun to celebrate the coming of a new year. Our house was less than a block away from the parade route for the Tournament of Roses. All week people had been arriving from all over the country to stake out a spot. The parties had already started.

I called Jodi and we met her at the hospital. The moment I walked into the room where my mother lay, my numbness flew out the window; her death became very real. The hospital staff had pulled a curtain in front of Mom's bed and all I could see were her feet under the blankets. That was enough for me. Just knowing she was on the other side of the curtain, dead, I came unglued.

One of the nurses came into the room and asked me if there was someone that we could call, such as a funeral home or priest or something. I had no idea. I suddenly turned on her and snapped, "I don't know what to do!" She quickly realized that I wasn't going to be of any help and immediately left.

There were decisions and arrangements that needed to be made and all I could do was cry while standing in the middle of the room saying, "I don't know what to do!

Jodi stepped forward and took my arm, looking me in the eyes, "Do you need me to handle this?" she asked.

Since our Mom had become ill, I had been her primary caregiver. I'd made all the decisions regarding her health. I'd been in charge of all her medications, her doctor's appointments, delivery of all her medical equipment, her physical therapy, even her finances. And now it was Jodi's time. She was stepping up and being the big sister. I may have taken care of our mother, but now she was taking care of me.

I nodded. "I'm done," I said quietly.

Jodi motioned for me to sit on an empty bed on the other side of the curtain from Mom. I did. And that is where I stayed. I stared at the curtain, knowing my mother lay dead on the other side, while Adam and my sister cleared out Mom's belongings and made arrangements with the hospital to take care of her body.

When everything was done, Jodi came back into the room. It was her time to say goodbye. She stepped behind the curtain, and after a moment came back. I stood up and took a step toward Mom's bed but Jodi reached out and stopped me.

"I don't think you should see her," she said, pulling me in the opposite direction.

Jodi was right and I would forever be grateful that she knew better than I did in that moment what was good for me. I have no visual of my mother in death. I can only remember her being alive.

Adam and I said goodbye to Jodi in front of the hospital. She was having a New Year's Eve party at her house and needed to get back. I never understood her ability to plan a party while our mother lay in the hospital dying. But the relationship that I had with Mom was different than the one Jodi had with her. Their relationship was their own, and it was none of my business. Besides, Mom loved nothing more than a good party, so I'm sure she understood. Maybe now that she was free from the body that had failed her she might even stop by.

When we arrived back at the house, Adam and I sat down on the couch. I could still hear the early celebrations going on outside in the streets, but the house felt quiet, as if it were encased in its own silent bubble. The world outside continued to spin freely, but everything within the walls of our home had stopped.

I decided that I should probably call a couple family members and friends to let them know that Mom had passed on. What I didn't count on was that each person I called would be in the middle of a New Year's Eve party and wouldn't be able to hear me.

"Mom passed away this evening."

"What?"

"Earlier tonight Mom passed away."

"Hold on. I can't hear you. *What?*"

"Mom died tonight."

"Is she okay?"

"No! She's dead! Dead!"

I hung up the phone, dropping it to the floor. Looking at Adam, I stated "Fuck that. I'm not calling anyone else. People will just have to find out tomorrow. I'm not going to keep shouting 'Mom's dead' over dance music and noisemakers."

Although, I could almost imagine that Mom planned it exactly this way: sneak quietly out the back door while everyone continued to party.

After a while the stillness started to become unbearable. We were just sitting there doing nothing, because there was nothing left to do; yet doing anything seemed inappropriate. I wanted a beer, but was that okay? Can you have a beer after your mother dies? *My mom died and I drank a beer* seems mean or disrespectful. What if I ate a sandwich? Was that dismissing the significance of her life having ended? *My Mom died and I ate a sandwich.* I couldn't stop thinking about how everything sounded. *My Mom died and I checked my email. My Mom died and I went to bed.* Nothing felt okay. It all felt flippant and cold. So I did nothing. *My Mom died and I did nothing.*

"I don't know how I'm supposed to be right now. It feels like I should be doing something, but everything I think to do feels wrong," I said to Adam.

He nodded in agreement, "I know what you mean. I really want to smoke some weed, but I feel selfish, like, 'sorry your mom died, but I'm gonna get high.'"

I laughed, "This is so weird. I want a beer, but I can't have a beer because Mom died. I don't know. I just feel like I should be doing something."

"Maybe," Adam said, "we could build, like, a little shrine to Sandi."

"What do you mean?"

"We'll go around the house and find things that meant something to her or that remind us of her, and we'll just build a little shrine and light some candles."

"It sounds like the perfect thing to do," I said.

Los Angeles, California

Returning to Los Angeles after the adventure of being with Chris completely deflated my spirit. Slogging my way through traffic and smog to find a low-paying job in order to scrape by month-to-month was disheartening at best. I felt like a prisoner who'd been allowed to run free for an afternoon, only to be locked back in a dingy cell. Maybe it would have been better if I'd never met him. At least then I wouldn't know what I was missing.

Chris and I spoke to each other every day on the phone, multiple times a day. I had to admit, it did make me feel better that he was as lonely and sad as I was. Yes, I know, real love meant wanting nothing but joy and happiness for the person I desired. But in my experience, aching for someone who seemed perfectly happy without me sucked ass. Call me selfish—or at least call me honest—but I slept better at night knowing I wasn't pining alone.

On one particular day Chris called from his neighbor's house, an old military guy that he often checked in on. The old man's health wasn't good and Chris didn't think he would be around too much longer. He had told me that the two of them would pass the time exchanging war stories and telling dirty jokes. Apparently, the old man loved a good dirty story, and Chris had plenty to tell. I didn't even want to imagine what Chris told him about me. Some things are better left unknown.

Although Chris had told me about the man in earlier conversations, I never expected to hear, "He wants to talk to you."

"Me? Why?"

"I don't know," Chris laughed. "He just wants to talk to you."

"Okay, I guess."

"Hold on." I could hear the phone being passed and Chris laughing, "Now don't you say anything dirty, old man."

"Hello," the voice on the other end of the line was deep, rough, and very, very old sounding.

"Hello," I said. "How are you today?"

"Well, every day that I'm still here is a good day."

I heard Chris in the background say, "Don't let him fool you. He's gonna outlive us all, the ornery old bastard."

The old man ignored Chris. "I won't keep you long," he told me, "I just wanted to say hello and tell you how glad I am that Chris met you. He seems like a new man since he's been back."

"Ahhh, thank you. That's very sweet. I'm really glad I met him too. Chris tells me you were in the military."

"Yeah, served twenty-five years in the Marine Corps," he said.

"Well, you must be very proud of Chris for serving his country for so long."

"Chris is a good man. I'll tell you, we were all worried about him. He's been through an awful lot in his life. A lot more than most men could handle."

"I know."

"I'm just glad he met a nice girl. Maybe things will turn around for him now. You know he talks about you all the time. The boy is smitten."

"Okay that's enough. Give me the phone back," Chris said in the background.

"It was nice talking you," I said.

"You too."

I never did catch his name. Chris got back on the phone and we continued our conversation. He told me he had an upcoming appointment with the VA and would find out if they were going to give him the okay to go back on active duty. If so, he would most likely be sent back to Afghanistan.

It was about a week later that I got the call from Chris. He sounded really depressed. I knew he must have found out about his future with the Army.

"What did they say?" I asked.

"It's no good. I'm out."

"Just like that?" I asked.

"Yep," he sighed. "They offered me a desk job if I wanted to stick it out and wait for my retirement."

"How long would that be?"

"About two years."

"Are you going to take it?"

I could hear the sad smile in his voice as he answered, "Can you see me sittin' behind a desk?"

"No, not really."

There was a long silence as words failed me. I didn't know how to comfort him. He wanted to return to a war that I'd stood in the streets protesting against. What was I supposed to say?

When Chris spoke again, I could hear the strain in his voice as he fought back tears. "This is all I've ever known. I don't know what I'm supposed to do with my life."

"I'm sorry." It was all I could think to say.

"I've been doin' this since I was eighteen years old, and now it's…" His voice cracked. "It's just over."

"You should come to Los Angeles." I blurted out. It was breaking my heart to hear the pain in his voice and I just wanted to fix it for him. I wanted to make that pain go away. "I don't have much going on, but you could stay at my place if you want to check it out. Maybe it will give you some time to figure out what you want to do. Who knows," I added, trying to lighten the mood a little, "maybe you'll get discovered and become a famous actor."

I was relieved when I heard that familiar laugh. "Well, I don't know about that," he joked, "but it'd be cool to be the guy who blows stuff up. That seems like fun."

I laughed, "I could see you blowing stuff up."

Then Chris surprised me when he became serious again. "Do you love me?"

"What do you—?"

"Do you love me?" he said again, cutting me off. "If we're really gonna do this I need to know that you love me, because I am crazy in love with you, Jonna. But if it don't mean nothin' to you. I've had too much in my life to—"

"Yes, I do. It's crazy and it's fast, but I love you too."

Chris laughed with happiness. "My Baby loves me! And I love my Baby."

****

We talked a few more times over the next couple of days making plans for Chris come out for a visit. The idea was that he would stay for a couple of weeks; then if we both wanted to move forward, we would decide what to do at that time. Maybe we would stay in Los Angeles or, who knew, maybe I would even consider moving to Texas. Anything was possible. Neither of us was tied down. We could go anywhere, do whatever we wanted. It felt good to be calling the shots in my own life. Being with Chris made me feel safe to do so.

The day Chris arrived I was a nervous wreck — excited, but nervous. I couldn't wait to see him. At the same time I was paranoid he would take one look at me and realize what a huge mistake he'd made. My insecurities nagged at me. They told me he was in an emotionally vulnerable place, that he'd convinced himself he loved me, but was really just confused and depressed from being released from duty.

I was glad my sister Jodi offered to drive me to pick him up. As jumpy as I was, I didn't think I could maneuver my car safely though the L.A. freeway system. Waiting outside the gate for his arrival, I had to remind myself to breath.

And then he was there. Seeing him again wasn't at all like I had pictured it was going to be. We awkwardly hugged and he kissed me on the cheek. I couldn't think of anything to say and he wasn't being much help. We were like two pimply-faced teenagers on a first date. As we went to get his bags, we held hands and stole little nervous glances at each other.

Thankfully it didn't take much time for us to become reacquainted with each other. Over the next day or two we fell back into the easy comfortableness we shared in Texas. I was thrilled that Jodi and Chris immediately hit it off. Jodi had been in the Air Force in her early twenties, so they had that in common. Also, I got the impression that she really liked having another "guy" around—someone who appreciated the immaculate condition of her BBQ, who took an interest in taking apart the dishwasher, and who understood the importance of owning a handgun. She never got this with her partner Jenn or me.

Jenn was more reserved in how she felt about Chris. She was more like me—an artist and all around hippie at heart. I think she was waiting to see if Chris—being a Republican, military, Southern boy—was going to turn out to be homophobic or racist. Jenn was from Louisiana, and having grown up a lesbian in the South, she knew very well what some opinions were. As a Southern woman she felt an even greater need to fight the stereotype. I admit: before I got to know Chris I assumed he would be all of these things too. But just as he had won me over, he eventually won Jenn over too.

Everything was going great with everyone getting along, but I still had not found work. It was also becoming obvious Los Angeles wasn't the place for Chris. He didn't seem to have any interest in even going out to explore the city. The few times we had to drive on the freeway I thought his head was going to explode. Chris was a guy that needed to be on the move all the time; sitting for forty-five minutes on a congested freeway to go five miles was not good. I could feel his energy building like a pressure cooker.

Something had to change and it became clear one morning when I woke up to find Chris already out of bed. I looked around the house but didn't see him. My car was still there, so I knew he hadn't gone anywhere. Figuring he went for a walk—although Chris wasn't a "go for a walk" kind of guy—I went to the backyard to smoke a cigarette and wait for him to come back.

After quite a bit of time had passed I was starting to wonder where Chris could be; then I heard a whistle. Looking around the yard I didn't see anything. Then I heard it again, louder this time. It seemed to be coming from near the back fence. I walked further into the yard, looking around before I heard, "Up here."

"Oh Jesus!" I said jumping back. Chris was sitting in the branches of a tree above my head. Placing a hand on my beating chest, I nervously laughed. "What are you doing up there?""You're just in your own little world, aren't you, Babe?"

"No, I'm not."

"I've been sittin' in this tree for about twenty minutes, just watchin' you, and you had no idea."

"Well yeah, that's because you're being all sneaky and Special Forces like. I'm not typically on the lookout for a sniper in the backyard."

Chris looked over the row of fences, "Did you know a few doors down they have an orange tree? Tonight when it's dark, I'll sneak over and get some."

I looked up at him shading my eyes from the rising sun. He looked really cute sitting in his lookout post. He also looked like a bored child. "Babe, it's California. You don't need to pull off a top-secret mission to get oranges. They pretty much sell them on every corner."

"Yeah, but it will be fun."

"Please don't sneak into the neighbor's yard in the middle of the night." I said.

Chris shrugged. I didn't know him well enough yet to read this as *Okay I won't* or *I'm not gonna listen to you.*

"Are you coming down from there anytime soon?" I asked.

"Yeah, in a bit."

"Okay, well I guess I'll see you inside."

"See ya, Babe."

Los Angeles wasn't working for us. I couldn't remain unemployed while my boyfriend stayed up in a tree. It was Jenn who came up with the perfect solution. One night while we were eating dinner, she asked us, "What would you guys think about moving to Louisiana?"

She and Jodi had bought a second home in Abbeville, Louisiana a few years earlier. But with the sea surge caused by Hurricane Ike the house had flooded. While Chris and I had been in Texas Jenn had gone down to see the damage to the house. With the help of her family, they'd removed all the drywall, doing what they could to keep out the mold. Now Jenn needed someone to repair the damage so she could rent it out. While sitting empty, it had already been broken into once, so having someone living there while doing the remodeling would help.

It took Chris and me about twenty seconds to decide that yes, we would love to do this. I was tired of living in Los Angeles. I needed breathing room and space. More than anything, I was ready to make a big change in my life. I wasn't exactly sure what path my life was on, but I sure was in a hurry to get on it and see.

We very quickly put plans together. There was no point in wasting a lot of time. We we're both more than ready to go. I had a big garage sale, getting rid of nearly everything I owned, except the absolute essentials. Once that was done we began the task of selling my car. It never would have made the trip and we were going to need a truck to make the move.

One afternoon Jenn and I were out doing errands when she got a call from Jodi. She and Chris were at a car lot and wanted us to come by. When we arrived, we found the two of them standing near a very large white truck.

I barely got out of Jenn's car when Chris approached, all smiles, "What cha' think, Babe?" He was like a kid at Christmas.

"It's a really pretty truck," Jodi added in agreement. Clearly their minds were already made up.

"It's um… well… it's big." I said.

Chris's eyes glazed over as he gazed lovingly at the truck, "Wait until I lift it."

"Absolutely not." I stated, giving a verbal smack down on that dream. I was all about embracing this new Southern lifestyle we were embarking on, but some things are simply too redneck for me, and a lifted truck was one of them.

"Alright," Chris said, coming up behind me and hugging me close. "I won't lift it." After a moment I heard him mutter, "Yet."

"What kind is it?" I asked. In that moment, I think both Jodi and Chris were embarrassed to know me.

"Baby, that's an F150."

"How much is it?" Jenn asked. She was already on her iPhone looking up prices on Bluebook to see its worth. Out of the four of us, Jenn was the most business savvy. Actually, truth be told, she was the only one with *any* business savvy.

Two hours later, Jodi had signed for the truck and we were driving it off the lot. We had agreed that Jodi would sign for the truck, since my credit was shot from being out of work for so long. It had taken years for me to build up good credit, but just few short months to rip it all apart. When the truck was paid off, she would sign it over to me.

Chris and Jenn worked out a budget of what they thought it would cost to fix up the house including, materials and Chris's labor. With everything worked out we were ready to go. The only thing left to do was throw a huge party, introducing Chris to all my friends while saying goodbye to them at the same time.

On the night of the party my heart swelled with joy at having been so lucky to meet this amazing man. I said a silent prayer thanking God for bringing him into my life. Even though everything about him was completely different from most of my friends, Chris was charming and funny, and I was proud to be with him.

Plus, I'll admit, there is something really sexy about having "Rambo" as your boyfriend. Toward the end of the party, when the logs in the fire pit needed arranging, Chris reached into the fire picking them up with bear hands. It totally turned me on that my man was a badass. I felt protected and safe: the two things I'd longed for my entire life.

I loved the balance of male and female energy between us. While his strength and confidence made me feel physically safe, it was my gentleness and compassion that allowed him to open up and feel emotionally safe. One night I was lying in bed, waiting for Chris to pick out a movie. He still needed to watch one every night and I was finally getting used to falling asleep with the TV on. Chris got into bed and sat looking at a DVD in his hand for a long time.

"What did you pick out?" I asked.

He answered by giving me the box. "I've carried this with me for a long time, but I've never watched it."

It was the movie *Blackhawk Down*. I flipped the box over and read the description; it was a true story about an American military battle in

Somalia. I wasn't surprised, since Chris almost always chose to watch war movies. "Why don't you want to see it?" I asked, looking up.

He had the same distant look in his eyes that I'd seen in the bar playing pool. "Chris, are you okay?"

"Yeah, Babe. I'm okay," he said, coming back to me. "I was there. It was a long time ago, but it was one of the worst days of my life. We lost a lot of good guys that day."

"Oh, wow. I'm so sorry." I reached out placing my hand on his. I knew there was nothing I could say to make it better. There was no way to "fix" this kind of pain. All I could do was listen if he wanted to talk. And if he didn't, that was okay too.

Chris reached out and touched my face. "But I think I'm ready. I want to watch this movie with you."

"Okay."

Chris put the movie in and climbed into bed. I propped myself up with pillows so he could rest his head in my lap. As we watched the movie I let him talk without interrupting or asking too many questions, just letting him talk. He gave me a running commentary of events, talking about the real guys being portrayed by the actors, telling me funny stories about them or the little bits of personal information he knew. "That man right there was one of the most honest and loyal guys I've ever known."

But not everyone was Chris's best friend and he let that be known too. "He was a dick," Chris said, pointing to the screen while shaking his head. "I near 'bout punched him in the head one night. Fucker."

During one of the more painful scenes, when one of the soldiers was killed, Chris broke down and cried. Neither of us said anything. We didn't need to. He needed to release some of the pain from his past and I was glad that I was able to be there for him when he was ready.

I thought there had to be a reason that the two of us were brought together. The liberal war protester from Los Angeles, and the Republican soldier from Texas; it didn't make any sense and yet it worked. I thought if the two of us could see past our differences and fall in love, then maybe there was hope for the world yet.

I saw this move across country as a new beginning for both of us— a fresh start—and I was more than ready to get on the road and start building our life together.

Driving I-40 W

Somewhere in Arizona

I pull off the highway and stop at a red light, trying to find a convenience store where I can buy more cigarettes and a Diet Pepsi. Standing on the corner near the driver's side is a homeless man holding a cardboard sign that reads: *Why lie? I want beer.*

I roll down the window and hand him a few dollars. *Why not? At least he's honest.*

"God bless you," he says.

I have no response. The light changes. As I make my turn, I glance back once more at the man and wonder if he has children. Is he as honest with them as he is about his need for beer?

I am reminded of the first time I can recall knowing my mother was lying to me. It was Christmas Eve. My sister Jodi and I were at home alone. I was around eight. She was four years older, which I guess, made her in charge. But I don't recall her ever doing anything that indicated she was drunk with power. Mostly we just did our own thing.

We'd been raised by a single mom in the 70s, so this wasn't unusual. Our mother had taught us enough survival skills to call for help if the house caught on fire, and if a bad man approached to "kick 'em where it counts and run like hell."

On that night, it was getting late and had long since grown dark out when we saw the headlights of our mother's car pull up in the driveway. I immediately knew she was drunk. I didn't need to see her wobble or hear her slur; I just knew. Thousands of dollars in therapy and years of Al-Anon would later tell me that this was called "being hyper alert"; I just called it "Mom's smashed *again.*"

Quite a bit of time passed without our mother appearing, but neither Jodi nor I made any move to see what was going on. We had learned the number-one rule early in life: ignore, ignore, ignore. Over the years many a concerned neighbor would come to the front door to inform us that our mother was passed out on the front lawn. Our response was always the same: "Yeah, we know. She does that."

Eventually the neighbor would learn, like all the others that came before them, that it was best to leave these people to their own business. Each time we moved away, I always imagined there was a collective sigh of relief from the surrounding homes. On the positive side: we never stayed anywhere long enough to become a real nuisance. Yes, we were *those* people.

After what seemed like ages, I heard my mother stumble to the door and fumble with the lock. The sound of dropping keys followed by a muttered "God damn it" or "shit," confirmed that Mom was definitely on the far end of drunk. Sure, Jodi or I could have gotten up and opened the door for her—it was Christmas Eve after all—but that would have broken rule number one. And we never broke rule number one unless absolutely forced to.

Eventually Mom got the lock and key to cooperate and the door swung open. She began dragging huge plastic bags filled with Christmas presents into the living room. Our eyes lit up at the sight of all that loot, but we still didn't help her.

"You'll never guess wha' happened on my waaaaay home," Mom slurred as she began pulling the gifts out of the plastic bags and placing them under the tree. She was still in her business suit from work and teetered precariously on her high heels.

This piqued my interest enough—or perhaps it was the abundance of presents that had. I asked, "What?"

Mom finished unloading the presents and plopped into a chair, lighting a cigarette. "First go get me a beer, then I'll tell you."

"Great," I muttered, then flung myself off the couch with a huge sigh and skulked into the kitchen.

This behavior on my part would continue for nearly thirty more years. Any time my mother would ask me to bring her a beer, I would sigh, roll my eyes, groan—any number of passive tactics that said, "I don't approve." Never once did any of these tactics work. Never once did my mother say, "You know, Jonna, your deep sigh has convinced me that I need help and will immediately check myself into Betty Ford."

Normally I would draw out the process of getting her a beer by taking as long as humanly possible to drag my feet into the kitchen, hanging on the refrigerator door swinging back and forth for some time, pretending I couldn't see the six-pack of tall Budweiser. Then I'd

98

drag myself back. But this time all those brightly wrapped presents called to me to move quickly. Of course, as I handed her the beer I threw in a disappointed sigh. But we were both used to this and it was ignored.

"Okay, so you waaana hear wha' happened?" she asked. "Jodi leave the presents 'lone and come listen."

Jodi was under the tree and had started to separate the presents into piles by nametag. She turned slightly so she was somewhat facing our mother, enough to pretend that she would listen to the story. At twelve, Jodi was already reserved and guarded. Listening to a drunken tale from Mom held no interest for her. I was still young enough to have curiosity, and finding out where those presents came from was a must-know.

"So, I was jus' gettin' off work an walkin' to the car when I ran into Saaana Claaaus! He asked me if I knew two girls, Jodi and Jonna." She took a long swig of her beer while removing her high heels.

"He did?" I asked.

"Yeah. He told me that he was runnin' late and would I mind bringing these presents to you." She waved her cigarette in the general direction of Jodi and the tree.

Something wasn't right with this story. First of all, if Santa had seen how drunk she was, then why didn't he immediately fly over to our house and pick us up. I always knew in my heart that if Santa had known how much Mom drank then certainly he would come and rescue me and my sister taking us up to the North Pole to live with the elves and reindeer.

I looked at her with all the skepticism I could muster and tried to get to the bottom of this, "And you actually *talked to him?* He saw *you,* and you talked to him?*"

"*Yeah!* I told you already," she said, trying to focus on my face with one eye closing. "He asked me to bring this stuff home for you kids. He was parked right in the middle of the street with his sleigh and everything. He caused a huge, goddam traffic jam." She sat up a little straighter and took a drag of her cigarette, dropping the long ash on her suit.

In that moment I knew; Santa Claus was bullshit. Santa Claus was my drunken mother who had tied one on after work and waited until the last moment to go Christmas shopping. My suspicions were confirmed when out of the corner of my eye I saw Jodi reach into one of the plastic bags and pull out a pair of scissors, a bag of bows, and Scotch tape. She shrugged, shoving the items back in the bag. That's why Mom took so long to come inside. She was out in the car wrapping the last of the presents and concocting this sham. Santa Claus was never coming to rescue me. All that letter writing and list-making was for nothing.

Jodi popped her head up for the first time since this conversation began, and said in a matter-of-fact tone, "We got 21 presents each." Always the practical one.

I had a decision to make. Call my mother out on her lie, or play the part of an excited child on Christmas Eve who had just struck gold. I opted for the second choice, pretending to believe the lie so I could get the gifts. I danced around the living room in my footie pajamas singing, "Santa came! Santa came!"

Joining my sister under the tree to shake and rattle the various shaped boxes, I turned to my mother, realizing two could play this lying game. I asked, "So did Santa say we could open some tonight?"

"Sure," she replied, as she lifted herself up and headed into the kitchen to get another beer. Then she poked her head back out. "But he said only one.

Abbeville, Louisiana

Chris and I, energized to be headed to Louisiana, had loaded up the new F150 with what was left of my possessions. I was beyond excited to start this new adventure. Restlessness was growing in me and I yearned for something different, anything different. I wasn't entirely sure what it was I looking for, but as long as it was completely foreign to what I knew, it was good enough for me. And Chris was the perfect man to begin this journey with: magnetic, fun and wild. I couldn't buy my ticket to board the crazy train fast enough.

Chris drove the entire way. I was content to gaze out the window and watch my past disappear in the distance. We covered a lot of miles very quickly, sleeping in the backseat of the truck when we grew tired. Normally I would have been too scared to sleep in a dark truck stop in the middle of nowhere, but with Chris's arms wrapped around me I felt no fear. If he had overcome years of war, survived numerous brushes with death, and lived on grubs in a South American jungle, then I could certainly tolerate a couple of nights with a seatbelt jammed in my back.

I felt free for the first time in my life. I didn't have to pretend to be anyone other than who I was. When I lived in Los Angeles there was constant pressure to prove my worthiness, to be something special. I'm a writer. I'm an actor. I'm a somebody! The big joke was that everyone scrambled around trying to prove themselves to a bunch of other people who were doing the same thing. No one ever bothered to stop and ask, what exactly are we trying to prove and who are we trying to prove it to? Pretending to be extraordinary was something I was never good at anyway, so the transition into anonymity was an easy one. I welcomed it.

After two days of traveling we arrived in Abbeville, Louisiana. My first thought as we drove down the main street through town was, *Oh, sweet Jesus, what the fuck have I done?* I was expecting a quaint small town with all the mystery and sexiness of the Louisiana I'd seen in movies. This was not it. Instead I saw lots of closed down businesses, a couple of run-down gas stations, a nasty torn-up hotel, and one gigantic Walmart. This wasn't sexy; it was just downright sad.

We quickly found the house, anxious to see for ourselves what kind of shape it was in. It was a simple brick house with three bedrooms and one bathroom. The ripped-out walls left the framing exposed, the floors had buckled from days under water, and the front door was boarded up after the house had been broken into. But it was easy for me to look past the damage to picture Chris and myself building a life together and calling this home. It wasn't fancy—certainly nothing in comparison to the homes where I'd snipped yellow flowers or scrubbed toilets. But I thought it was perfect.

Over the next few days we did our best to settle in. Jenn's brother Kevin and his girlfriend Jacqueline loaned us a bed and described the general layout of Abbeville to us. They said that since the new Walmart went in, most of the local businesses had closed. This meant that for the majority of things we needed, we'd have to drive thirty minutes north to

Lafayette. I didn't mind; it was fun exploring our new surroundings. Since we owned next to nothing, we had lots of excuses to get out of the house.

We were also blessed with the sweetest neighbors we could have hoped for. Miss B and Mr. Vic were an elderly couple next door, whose house had also flooded. Mr. Vic was doing the majority of work himself, so he and Chris were often had long discussions about home improvements.

Meanwhile Miss B was always feeding us, which was an tremendous help, since Chris could eat more than anyone I'd ever met. I soon found out that Louisianans placed a very high priority on eating. Having just come from a city where three lettuce leaves and half a carrot was considered a "binge day," I was going need some time to get used to this.

Of course, from the moment we arrived in Louisiana Chris fit right in. There was no period of adjustment for him. He spoke "swampbilly" and understood Southern sensibilities. Chris was able to charm everyone we met—the women with his good looks, the men with his wild tales. He was one of their own: a true-blue Southern boy and an American hero.

One night, a few weeks after we arrived, Chris and I were looking for something to do. We found a local bingo hall. Mom, Jodi, and I used to play together many years earlier in Los Angeles and it was always good for a laugh. Chris had never played bingo before, so I thought it would be a casual way to have some fun and relax. I was wrong. Nothing was ever relaxed with Chris. He was full throttle, high-octane all the time.

I had to bite my lip to keep from laughing as Chris swaggered into the bingo hall and checked out the crowd. I was used to him scanning a room whenever we entered; I suppose if I'd been shot in the Middle East, I'd be on the lookout for snipers too. But I hardly thought he would find one at the bingo hall.

I took his hand and led him to a woman sitting behind a foldout table. There we bought our packets of printed cards and daubers to stamp with, and found a couple seats. As soon as the caller announced the start of the game, Chris sat up at full attention, clenching his dauber as if it were a weapon.

" Beea-foour," the announcer drawled into the microphone.

Slam! Slam! Slam!

I jumped in my seat as Chris attacked the numbers on his bingo card with a vengeance. He pounded the sheet so hard it shook the table. Big splats of color oozed over the numbers and formed little pools of purple ink.

I could clearly see the veins in his neck bulging under the tight skin. "Babe, relax," I said. "Bingo isn't a contact sport."

He looked back with a wild look of joyful excitement. "This is great! We're coming back next week."

The announcer had only called the first number. How could he possibly be so thrilled so quickly? As our time together grew, I would come to learn that everything in Chris's life was met with this same level of adrenaline-fueled passion.

"Eeeeye siiixteeen"

Slam! Slam!

"Babe, seriously, you have to not hit it so hard. I think you might be scaring people."

His response was one I was growing accustomed to: a sideways glance with a twinkle in his eye and a crooked smile. "They should be. I'm 'bout to take all their money."

I reached out and placed my hand on his bicep. I'd seen this once on an episode of *Sex and the City*, where one of the women used this technique to get what she wanted from a man she hoped to marry.

Every muscle under his skin was flexed as he clutched the dauber in a death-like grip. I probably would have been more freaked out by his intensity if I hadn't been instantly turned on. Since meeting Chris my vagina had been on a mission to confuse me every time I tried to gain some perspective. It was winning. I dismissed my *Sex and the City* maneuver, kissed him on the cheek, and thought, *let him be who he is.*

"Geee Forty-niiine."

Slam! Slam! Slam! Slam!

I snatched my Diet Pepsi before it spilled.

A heavy-set woman who appeared to be in her mid-fifties, with greasy bleach-blond hair, too–tight holey sweatpants, and a stained tee-shirt, whipped her head around to see what all the commotion was about.

Chris met her gaze with a wide smile and a nod of his head. "Evenin', Ma'am. First time playin' Bingo."

"Ya all fired up?"

"Well, shoot yeah! I'm about to win me some money. What about you?"

She smiled shyly, showing a gap where an incisor should have been. "I hope so. Where you from?"

People were always asking Chris where he was from. His accent was thick but definitely not Cajun. And since he'd lived in so many different Southern regions it was hard to place. No one ever asked where I was from.

"I've lived all over the South—Texas, Mississippi, Alabama, and Florida.

"A true Southern boy!" She was positively beaming now.

"Yes Ma'am. Me and my baby just moved here. She's from Los Angeles."

"Hello," I said with a smile.

The woman barely flicked a glance of recognition in my direction. I knew later that night when she masturbated to memories of my boyfriend, I'd quickly be cut from the picture.

"Oh-sixty-niiine." The caller pulled our attention back to the game.

Chris stopped slamming the table quite as hard, but I noticed his muscles never relaxed, nor did his grip on the dauber. I could literally feel the intensity radiate off of him for the next two hours.

Bingo wasn't the only activity that pumped Chris up; even fishing became an adrenalin-fueled event. I'd always pictured fishing to be a sort of meditative activity: you sit with a pole in the silence while communing with nature. Peaceful. Quiet. But not with Chris.

I loved my boyfriend; I just sometimes wished I could slip him a tranquilizer.

It was late, well after midnight, one night when Chris couldn't sleep. He was out in the backyard fishing. I was in bed reading a book when I heard him yelling, "Babe, get out here! I caught an alligator!"

As I tried to grasp whether what I *thought* he said was what he *actually* said, I could hear him laughing and whooping. I begrudgingly set the book down, got out of bed, and headed outside to see what was up.

I pulled on my Wellies and wrapped a sweater around myself. It wasn't chilly, but the mosquitoes in Louisiana are disgusting when the sun goes down.

"What are you yelling about?" I whispered, hoping he'd catch the hint that some people slept at night.

"Look," Chris beamed as he shone a flashlight near the edge of the wooden deck.

I jumped back as two eyes glowed back at me. I had to blink a few times to adjust my eyes to the blackness that surrounded us. Sure enough, attached to Chris's fishing line was an alligator. Granted, it wasn't a huge alligator, but still, it was an alligator. Chris had managed to pull it out of the swamp and there it lay, shaking its head while snapping at the air.

Chris laughed, "Look Babe. You said you wanted to see an alligator. What my baby wants, she gets."

Yes, I had at some point mentioned that I hoped to see an alligator while in Louisiana. I think probably most people would say this if they had never been to a swamp before. What I didn't intend was for my boyfriend to catch one. In my mind, I'd pictured being safe in a boat, with a guide of some sort announcing, "Ladies and gentlemen if you look to the right you will see a native to Louisiana, the American Alligator." My fantasy ended with me ooohing and aaahing with some other tourists while we whipped out our cameras to take a photo. It didn't include trips to the ER for stitches in the middle of the night.

"It's a cool alligator, Babe." I said. "Now, let it go and come to bed. I'm lonely."

"Let it go?" Chris looked at me like I was the crazy one. "I ain't lettin' it go. We're gonna eat that som bitch!"

I'm from Los Angeles. This was way too much country for me. I needed to reestablish at least some minimal boundaries, and eating an alligator that my boyfriend pulled from the swamp crossed a line I never even imagined existed.

I sighed, "Will you please just let the alligator go? It's late. You're going to wake the neighbors"

Chris laughed again and shook his head. "I don't know how to let it go. Look where the hook is."

I took the flashlight from Chris and leaned a little closer—not much—but enough to see that the hook was attached to what I can only describe as the alligators arm pit. "Well, I don't know. Can't you just cut the line or something?"

Chris proceeded to flick and whip the fishing line, trying to unhook the alligator while keeping his distance. "I'm not cutting the line. That's my last hook, and the stores are closed."

"Just cut the line and come inside. You can buy more hooks in the morning."

Chris crinkled his brow like a child who isn't getting his way. "I'm not done fishing." He flicked the line harder. "It'll be easier to just cut its head off. Mmmmm mmmmm, fresh gator!"

Now I was annoyed. I'd spent sixteen years being a vegetarian, and even though I wasn't presently those feelings of compassion for animals—even snapping reptiles with razor-sharp teeth—were still there. To me this alligator had just been floating along under the moonlit sky minding its own business. It wasn't his fault Chris was an adrenalin junkie who never slept. I'd been with Chris for nearly four months now and I could relate to the alligator's plight; I too had been floating along lazily through life when I got hooked.

One thing I had learned in our short time together was that there were two ways to get Chris's attention. One was to get angry and act like a bitch. His response was always the same. He'd laugh, throw his arms around me, hug me tight until I relaxed, then give me my way. The other was to ignore him. His ego couldn't stand not being the center of attention, so the best way to get his attention was to not give him any.

I decided to use both tactics. "Do not cut that alligator's head off. Just let the fucking thing go. I'm going back to bed. You caught it, you figure it out."

I headed back toward the house, hoping this would work and I wouldn't wake up in the morning to find chunks of alligator meat in the refrigerator. I went back to bed but couldn't concentrate on my book. I tossed it to the side, sat up, and lit a cigarette. What was going on here?

More specifically, what was going on with me?

I'd started to feel an almost constant twinge of anxiety. Something wasn't right, but I didn't know what it was; I just felt it. Chris constantly went out of his way to give me everything I needed. He opened doors, carried the groceries, cooked me meals, and worked on the house. He was exciting and fun and, most of all, he was fearless. So why didn't I trust this?

I was in a constant state of conflict with myself. I longed for peace and quiet, and yet, I had to be honest: I loved the idea that I had a boyfriend who was capable of catching an alligator. Still I couldn't shake the feeling that Chris was always up to no good. I didn't know much about the military, but I imagined if someone spent the majority of their life in the Special Forces, there had to be things that went on that were morally questionable. I had no doubts that Chris had seen and possibly participated in events that I couldn't even imagine. I wondered what that did to someone's conscience.

Growing up I was afraid of everything: what my mother would do next, where we were going to live, constantly being the new kid. I was afraid of what people thought. I was afraid of being injured—or worse, humiliated. My adult life had become centered around overcoming my fears: learning to drive, performing on stage, allowing others to read my writing, having relationships, flying in planes, being alone; all of it became one test after another to overcome yet another fear. I went to Al-anon. I went to therapy. I meditated and was prayed for by anyone I could get to pray for me. I spoke with monks, ministers, and therapists. I was sick to my core of overcoming fears.

And then there was Chris, completely fearless in every way. I wanted that. I wanted what he had. I wanted to be the one out back in the dark catching an alligator. So why was I the one inside smoking a cigarette, chewing on my own anxiety?

The next morning I woke up early to find Chris had never come to bed. I got up and looked out the bedroom window. There he was, still fishing.

"What are you doing?" I asked as I came out of the house.

Chris swung his head around, looking thrilled. "What's it look like I'm doin' Baby? I'm fishin'."

"You stayed out here all night?" I asked rubbing the sleep out of my eyes.

Chris reeled in his line and began baiting the precious hook. "This is all I did when I was living in Florida. We'd take the boat out for days and fish the whole time. I live for this shit, Babe."

I looked around asking with reluctance, "What did you do with the alligator?"

"I let it go, Babe."

I sighed with relief. "Oh, good."

Chris laughed and added, "Then I snagged him again. I caught that som' bitch like six more times."

"Why?"

He could never understand why I couldn't understand the things he did. "Cause it was fun!"

"Not for the alligator," I mumbled with annoyance.

Why did this bother me so much? Chris was a grown man; if he wanted to stay up all night fishing, then why should that eat at me? I knew alligators had thick, hard skin, so I doubted very much that Chris's little hook was causing it pain. But why keep catching the same alligator over and over? What was the point? As I walked toward the house I had another moment where something felt off, but I couldn't place what it was.

****

Growing up in an alcoholic home, I'd learned certain behaviors, behaviors that as an adult I've had a hard time dropping. Although I'd discussed these behaviors ad nauseum with my therapist and in thousands of Al-Anon meetings over the years, they were so ingrained in who I was that I believed they would never leave me. Truth be told, at times they served me well. One behavior I had was that I studied people. I made mental notes about who they were, so I could adjust what I said and did—or what I didn't say and do—based on what I guessed their response would be.

I'd always been a slow decision-maker, in stark contrast to Chris, who had virtually no impulse control whatsoever. After realizing this difference in our personalities, I found myself constantly monitoring what I thought versus what I actually wanted to say out loud.

If we happened to be lying in bed at eleven o'clock at night and I casually mentioned, "I wish I had some ice cream," Chris would be out of the bed pulling on his jeans, saying, "Anything for my Baby," as he dashed out the door and tore off down the road in the truck.

Normally this would be great. Most women I know would be thrilled to have such an attentive man. The problem was, he'd be half way to the market before I'd finished my complete thought process. I knew me and I knew the way my brain worked, and typically it would have gone something like this; *I wish I had ice cream. Actually, no, I don't want to eat all those calories so late at night. Besides, I just brushed my teeth, and I don't want to get out of bed to brush them again. Mostly, I'm just tired and want to go to sleep.* Being able to complete my entire thought process, I'd skip the ice cream and just go to sleep.

But with Chris, I found myself on more than one occasion eating Ben and Jerry's because I felt guilty that he'd gone to the store after I said I wanted ice cream when I really didn't. I needed him to slow down. I needed to be able to take a moment to process what was happening before I made a decision. I understood that his life at times had depended on quick decisions and action. He hardly had time to weigh the pros and cons of whether it was better to dive for cover behind a boulder or behind a tank while being shot at.

I didn't think Chris would ever slow down, so I would have to be the one who adapted. Adapting was second nature. I'd been adapting to my surrounding since I was a child. So I started keeping more and more of my thoughts inside my head where they would safely remain ideas and not be instantly converted into action. Sometimes, though, I would still slip.

One morning I was leaning over the kitchen counter drinking coffee while flipping through a local Penny Saver. Chris and I spent a lot of time standing in the kitchen because we still had no furniture. We had our bed from Kevin and Jacqueline, two camping chairs, and a foldout table for my computer. That was it. The rest of the house remained empty. So, hanging out in the kitchen became a big part of our lives.

I was alone in the house, happy to be sipping coffee and looking at ads for things I never intended to buy, when I heard the truck pull up in the driveway. A few moment's later Chris's arms were wrapped tightly around my shoulders. I melted into the feeling of his chest pressed against my back. This was when I loved him most. Even if he had only been gone for ten minutes, he always made a point of making physical contact with me when he returned.

"Whatcha' doin', Baby?" he murmured into my ear.

"Reading the ads in this pa-per," I replied in a girly, singsong voice.

"Do you see anything you want?"

"A boxer pup-py," I chirped, while leaning over the counter pointing out an ad.

"Well, shoot Gal," he said, stepping away and slapping me on the butt, "then let's get you one." Chris went to the refrigerator and took out a bottle of iced tea. He closed the door and turned back to me. "Mmmmm Hmmmm... I love my Baby's ass."

I turned around to face him. "I don't know. Maybe it's not such a good idea."

Chris shrugged. "If you want a puppy, get one."

I sighed, "I don't know if I want to *buy* a dog. I feel bad that there are so many dogs at the shelter, but I really, really want another boxer. Those are my favorite, but I don't want to give money to puppy mills. Plus, they're expensive and it's not really practical to get a dog when we just got here..."

I could tell I had already bored Chris with my mental debate. My adult logic had sucked the fun out of getting a new puppy. He took a swig of his tea and headed for the door, his attention focused elsewhere. "Wait 'til you see what I bought at the store." And with that the puppy discussion was over.

A week later, I was once again standing in the kitchen while Chris was out running errands. Chris could spend countless hours running errands. A simple trip to the grocery store to pick up one item would turn into half a day of making his rounds. He took the truck to the carwash at least once—if not twice—a week. He would stop by the Ford dealership to talk about new toys for the truck or how much it would cost to lift the whole thing. I continued to slam my foot down on that idea. Boundaries.

He'd go to the local gun shop and shoot the shit with whoever was around. Usually it was some ex-military guy or current National Guardsman. They would swap war stories, or hunting stories, or just stories about guns and violence in general. *I had a cop friend once who told me about the time he shot....* I went with Chris on his errands once or twice; that was enough for me.

So, once again I was alone at home when my cell phone rang. It was Chris. It was always Chris. He called me twenty times a day.

"Hey, Babe, whatcha' doin'?"

"Nothing much."

"I'm fixin' to go to the store. You want anything?"

"No, I'm good."

Twenty minutes later my phone would ring again.

116

"Whatcha' doin?'"

"Nothing."

"I'm at the store. You want some ice cream?"

"No, I'm good."

And again on the drive home.

"Hey, Baby, whatcha' doin?'"

"Nothing. I'm not doing anything."

"I'm fixin' to pass McDonald's here in a bit. You want somethin'?"

"No. *Really*. I'm good."

So when the phone rang, I expected our usual drill. Instead Chris said, "Hey Baby, I'm turning the corner. Come outside."

Before I could even put my shoes on, I heard the truck pull up in the driveway. I really wished he wouldn't drive so fast. My phone rang again. "Where you at?" he asked.

"I'm right here." I hung up the phone as I opened the door to our driveway. There was Chris sitting in the driver's seat of the truck with a huge grin on his face. And then another face popped out the back window. The biggest boxer head I had ever seen looked from side to side with excitement, before disappearing again.

I froze in my tracks, a single thought swirling into a knot in my stomach: *Oh dear God, he stole someone's dog.*

Chris leaned out the window and laughed. "Well, don't just stand there. Get in."

117

"Where are we going?" I asked warily, approaching his side of the truck with hesitation. I wasn't sure I wanted to hear the answer.

"We got to take your dog to the vet."

I leaned closer to the back window to take another look; I was immediately met with big, sloppy, drooly kisses. "The vet? What's wrong with him?" I asked, rubbing his ears.

"We have to get his nuts chopped off."

"*Right now?* Wait… how did you… Whose dog is this?

"He's yours, Babe. Get in the truck. The vet closes in half an hour."

"Yeah, but…"

Chris was growing impatient. Lately, it seemed he was always impatient. And I was always confused. The more confused I became, the more questions I asked; the more questions I asked, the more impatient he became. "Babe, you said you wanted a boxer and I got you one. Now get in the truck."

I walked around climbing in the passenger's seat. As soon as I looked back at "my" new dog, I gasped, "Jesus Christ! What the fuck happened to him?"

It was the most heartbreaking thing I'd ever seen. This was a beautiful, brindle-colored boxer that was emaciated to the point where I didn't think it was possible for him to still be alive. Every bone was protruding from under his skin. His ribs, hips, and shoulder blades were all clearly defined. He was a skeleton with fur. If Chris had, in fact, stolen the dog, then I was glad, because whoever owned him was the

118

worst kind of person. They deserved not only to lose their dog but to be jailed for this type of cruelty.

Chris backed out of the driveway, whipped the truck around, and tore off down what was normally our quiet residential street. As I held on, he reached over grabbing my knee, "Do you like him?"

"Yeah... I guess... I mean... Of course I like him... Is he gonna live?"

"Heck yeah, he'll live. We just got to feed him that's all. This is a badass swampbilly dog. He's tough."

"Could you slow down? He's flying around all over the place back there."

Chris slowed down and the dog was able to get ahold of his footing. He inched his way forward, sticking his face up in the front seat between Chris and me. I took his head in my hands and kissed the side of his face. It was love.

I turned to Chris while the dog covered my cheek with kisses. "Where did you get him?"

He let go of my knee, then handed me some paperwork he pulled out of the console. "At the pound. I was in Lafayette and saw a sign, and I thought, you know what, my Baby wants a boxer, and I bet you there's one in there. An sure 'nough, there he was. They were gonna kill him tomorrow." Chris reached up with one free arm and wrapped it around the dog's head. "Ain't that right, boy? You was done for."

I looked over the paperwork and saw that it was mandatory to have an adopted dog fixed within forty-eight hours. Now I understood the rush to the vet. Under normal circumstances I would have thought it would be okay to wait until the morning. But this dog needed medical attention, so I was glad that Chris had pushed me to get in the truck.

I looked over at Chris and smiled. In that moment, I loved every wild, crazy, impatient thing about him. Although I had *said* I wanted a dog, that's where it had ended for me. While I debated the practicalities, and ultimately talked myself out of what I wanted, Chris just went forward. He didn't sit around thinking about life; he lived it. He went for it. Because of this he almost always ended up getting what he wanted. He made things happen out of his sheer belief that they would happen, and he never quit until they did.

We named the dog Beaux, partly to honor his Louisiana roots and partly because Chris and I had meet in Beaumont, Texas. For the next three weeks I cooked Beaux chicken and rice until he was healthy and muscular and ultimately huge. *Then* we had his nuts chopped off. The vet had taken one look at him the first day and said, "He'll never survive the anesthesia. Bring him back when he's gained twenty pounds."

****

Chris, Beaux, and I settled into a fairly regular routine. We worked on the house together; Chris did most of the work, while I assisted by handing him screws and nails. It was also my job to chase Beaux around the house and yank whatever he was ripping to shreds out of his mouth.

At night we would cook dinner together. Since we didn't have a dining table, we would either sit on the bed to eat or balance our

120

plates on our knees as we sank into the low-slung camping chairs. Sometimes after we ate, if we didn't go to bingo, we would watch a movie on my computer. But most nights I would read a book while Chris watched videos on the Internet.

He loved watching videos—the more violent and grisly the better. Too many times I fell for Chris calling me over to watch a video, only to be horrified by some brutal motorcycle crash or bloody fight that left somebody staggering around in a daze with a bloody head. As I covered my face in horror, Chris would throw his head back and laugh.

I'd taken to reading my books in the living room when he was on the computer, because I couldn't even stand the sounds of the violence. One night, I came into the bedroom to get something, and Chris called me over. Without thinking, I stepped over to him; I immediately turned away when I realized he was watching dead bodies being pulled from a car crash.

"You have to stop doing this to me," I snapped at him. "I am not into this stuff."

Chris shrugged, "It's interesting."

"No, it's not interesting. It's disgusting and horrifying, and to be honest I can't understand how you can just sit there and watch it like it's nothing."

Now Chris was irritated. "You think I haven't seen things ten times worse than this in real life? This *is* nothin'."

I took a deep breath. I wasn't naïve enough to think that after serving twenty years in the military, seeing what Chris had seen, he would suddenly embrace all things "love and light" just because we'd moved to our isolated little bubble in Louisiana. I knew there were things about him that would probably never change, but he needed to understand that there were things about me that would never change, and these things had to find a way to coexist.

"I know you've seen a lot of violence in your life but I don't want this around me. I think it brings negative energy, and I don't want to invite that kind of energy into my life. If I watch something like that, then for the next few days I'm thinking about car crashes, or violent awful things happening, and I honestly believe that what we think about we create." I sighed.

I knew once I threw "negative energy" into the conversation I'd lost him. Chris turned back to the computer rolling his eyes. "Whatever."

Chris watching these videos was also eating at me on a deeper level, one that was getting harder to compromise on. What kind of person found entertainment in watching other people suffer? I guessed the type who found pleasure in repeatedly catching the same alligator for no other reason than that he could. I tried not to think about it too much, focusing instead on the good and brushing the rest under the rug.

But most of our days went smoothly. We had fun, we had a few arguments, and we had lots and lots of sex. Living in a house under construction without television, radio, or furniture, can become extremely boring. Sex became one of the best ways for us to pass time. So it was no surprise that after being in Louisiana only two months, I found myself at the local Walmart picking out a pregnancy test.

I didn't tell Chris that I'd bought the test. I figured I'd find out the results first, and then decide the best way to handle it. I waited until

Chris left the house to go run some errands. I read the instructions on the box: pee on the end of the stick, and then wait three minutes for the results. One line: I was not pregnant; two lines: I was.

I had barely tinkled on the friggin' thing before two lines popped up. What happened to the three minutes? I needed those three minutes to think. I set the test on the side of the bathtub and pulled my jeans back on. I'd been promised three minutes and I was determined to take them. I told myself maybe the test would change, that I needed those three minutes to get the "for reals" answer. I glanced down at the two lines and knew it wouldn't change.

Hearing my cell phone ring in the other room, I ran to answer it.

"Hey, Baby, whatcha' doin'?"

I thought about my real answer for a split second, then went with the tried and true, "Nothing."

"Did I leave my bank card there?"

I looked around and saw the card on the kitchen counter. "Yeah, it's here."

"Damn. Alright, I'm on my way back."

I hung up the phone and leaned against the kitchen counter. I let my mind wander about what a child's experience would be with Chris and me as parents. From me he or she would learn compassion, patience, tolerance, and a love of the arts and other cultures. From Chris he or she would learn fearlessness, courage, and a sense of adventure.

Maybe this baby would even grow up to be the most perfect person: a Doctor who dedicated his life to Doctors Without Borders, heroically saving lives in some far off war torn country. Or—*Oh dear God*—what if this kid grew up with my deep-rooted fears and Chris's love of all things violent? We would bring into this world an antisocial recluse, who couldn't make a decision, refused to grow up, and stayed inside watching gory videos all day.

I was snapped out of my paranoid fantasy by the sound of the door opening. Chris entered and gave me a big hug, the way he always did. He was sweaty from working and smelled like a man. I wanted to hug him longer, breath him in, but he pulled away.

He lit a cigarette and tossed the lighter on the counter. "I'd got everything I needed at Lowe's, then went to pay and my card wasn't in my wallet."

He picked the card up off the counter and headed down the hall, calling out, "You want to play bingo tonight?"

"Sure, Babe," I called back.

A moment later Chris returned to the kitchen holding the pregnancy test I'd completely forgotten on the bathtub. "Is there something you want to tell me?"

My heart started pounding. I immediately felt like I was in trouble. I couldn't think. I couldn't speak. I just stood there. How could I be so stupid as to leave the pregnancy test just sitting there like that? I was so wrapped up in thinking about how jacked up my kid was going to be, that I completely forgot about it. Chris shrugged and motioned with his hands for me to say something.

"What does it say?" I asked.

Chris looked at the test. "That you're pregnant."

"Then I guess that's what I want to tell you."

We stood there looking at each other and it dawned on me that as fun as it had been playing house over the last two months, Chris and I were basically strangers. Chris finally broke the silence by pointing the stick at me, "You want this?"

"Um... no, not really."

He walked over and silently tossed the pregnancy test in the trashcan. I'd never seen him quiet before. Not just the fact that he wasn't talking, but that crazy energy he always had was subdued. I couldn't tell if he was defeated or just in shock. I couldn't read him at all. "Are you mad?" I asked.

Are you mad? Why did I ask that? I didn't do this all by myself, so why would I ask if he was mad and imply that I had committed some sort of wrongdoing that needed forgiveness? My mind knew that logically it took two people to make a baby. I didn't trick him or lie to him. I had committed no crime, yet I was filled with this childlike fear that he was mad at me.

I hate it when I feel like that. I hate when my emotions don't mesh with my logic. If any one of my friends came to me and said they were pregnant and the guy was mad about it, I would immediately jump on a soap box: *You tell him that if he wants to go around sticking his dick in places, then he needs to take responsibility for the consequences. How dare he blame this on you. You tell him that it's time to pull up his big boy pants and take responsibility for...*

Yes, I was very tough indeed in my fantasy world of this happening to someone else. But it wasn't happening to someone else; it was happening to me. And I faced the moment not as a brave feminist but as a needy girl waiting for her boyfriend to let her know she wasn't in trouble. I didn't have to wait long. Chris looked over and grinned. "No, Babe, I'm not mad."

"Are you freaked out?"

Chris looked at me like I was nuts. "What? Shoot no. I ain't sweatin' this." He came over and tightened his arms around me; just like that the cockiness and swagger were back.

"I'm sweating this," I mumbled into his shoulder.

He stepped back and looked at me. "Why?"

"Cause it's a *baby?*"

Chris shrugged, "Babies are cool." He walked over and opened the door to the refrigerator, looking inside. "What should we make for dinner?"

"I don't know. Whatever." Was this conversation really happening? I had never had a conversation about having a baby before but, this didn't feel normal, and I didn't know how to change it. *I ain't sweatin' this. What's for dinner?* I figured it was good that he wasn't screaming through the house frantically searching for the number to an abortion clinic, but *I ain't sweatin' this* felt bizarrely disconnected. Once again I was left with a feeling of not knowing how to feel.

Chris closed the door and came over to me again. He placed his hand on my stomach and rocked his butt back and forth while singing, "My Baby's havin' my baby. My Baby's havin' my baby..."

I had to laugh. Somehow he always managed to snap me out of my overthinking and make me not take life so seriously. Maybe it was

126

because he'd witnessed so much death that he just accepted life on life's terms. Whatever it was, with Chris I was able to push my fears aside—along with my rational thinking and intuition—and jump in with both feet.

Chris stopped his song and dance abruptly, and looked up with excitement in his eyes. "We should call my Mama!"

"Oh, uh, maybe not *right now*."

I'd only had a couple of brief conversations with his mother in the past and was really not prepared to have another one anytime soon. After Obama had been elected President she informed me over the phone that I needed to prepare for Armageddon now that the Devil was in the White House. This, she assured me, was prophesied in the Book of Revelations. On that occasion I threw the phone to Chris, saying, "I can't deal with this."

Before I could stop him, Chris was dialing his mother's number. He put it on speakerphone and I heard her pick up.

"Hello." A tired voice, sighed on the other end.

"Hi, Little Mama."

"Hi, Honey. How are you?" Chris's mother always sounded beaten down by the world.

"Jonna's here with me Mom."

"Oh, hi, Jonna."

"Hello, Angie. How are you?"

"Well, you know, okay, I guess. Tom's not working, so things have been tough—"

"Guess what, Mama!" Chris cut her off before she could continue on with what would inevitably become one of her long list of hardships and complaints.

"What's that?" she replied.

"Jonna's pregnant. We just found out."

"Well now, Christopher, you listen to your Mama. You know what you need to do. You do the right thing and you marry this girl."

What the fuck? Where did that come from? *Marriage?* I wasn't ready to get married. I wasn't ready for any of this. I wanted my three minutes back. I needed time to think. To process. I needed to ground myself in something real. I needed to connect with how I was feeling. I needed to not be having this conversation with this woman.

"Um, well, Angie, we're not really there yet," I explained as gently as I could. "That's something Chris and I can talk about at some later date."

"Well, don't wait too long. It's not fair to bring that poor little innocent baby into this world without a proper name."

I got the message loud and clear. Of course it wasn't the poor little innocent baby's fault that it's mother was a dirty unmarried whore that would most likely rot in Hell along with the "Devil in the White House." I made the sweeping cut motion to my neck to let Chris know I was done. He took her off speakerphone as I left the room.

The next morning I woke up to find Chris gone. I figured he was at the hardware store, but when he didn't return an hour later I called him.

"Hey, Baby!" He sounded particularly happy.

"Where are you?" I asked as I lay on the bed in the back bedroom.

"I got a surprise for you."

"What is it?" There was silence on the line. "Hello? Chris?" There was no response.

I figured we got cut off and was about to hang up when Chris suddenly hollered from the doorway as he leaped into the room, "Come outside and see!"

I nearly came out of my skin. I hated it when he snuck up on me like that. "Don't do that!" I shouted, hanging up the phone.

"Come on. Come see what I got you." He pulled me out of bed. With him wrapped around me in a bear hug from behind, he half pushed, half walked me out the bedroom and down the hall. As we reached the kitchen door leading to the driveway he said, "Close your eyes."

He opened the door, led me outside, then said, "Okay! Open them."

I opened my eyes as Chris let me go. All I saw was the truck parked where it was normally parked. I shrugged looking back at him blankly. "What?"

"Look Babe." He indicated toward the truck.

"You washed it?"

"I wash it every week. *Look.*"

I looked again at the truck. It looked like it always did. Big. White. Shiny. "Is it *in*side?" I asked.

"Baby, walk around and *look at the truck.*"

I did as he instructed making a full circle around the truck while saying, "*I am looking at the truck.* I'm sorry but I don't see what you're talking about. It looks like it always does."

Chris took my hand and pulled me to the driver's side. He pointed down to a silver bar that you step on to climb into the truck.

I shrugged, "I don't get it."

"They're side-steps. You step on them to get in the truck."

They looked really shiny, so I asked, "Are they new?"

Chris shook his head. I could see his frustration with me being a girl and not appreciating the beauty of the magnificent, spectacular sidesteps. No doubt he wished Jodi were here. She would understand the significance. "Yes, they're new," he groaned. "I just had them installed this morning. I got them for you, Babe."

I bent down taking a closer look, and then looked up to Chris, "How is this for me?"

"Because, Baby, with you being pregnant I didn't want you to have to struggle to get into the truck."

I stood upright, glaring at him with total disbelief. "We've known about this baby for a day," I said, holding up a finger to make my point.

"One day. One! You got these step things because you wanted them. Not for me. Let's be really clear about that."

I knew I was right when he hung his head and didn't say anything. I could see his mind ticking away, thinking *how do I get out of this or at least get her to shut up.*

I sighed with resignation. "How much did you spend?"

This immediately perked him up. "I got a great deal. Three-fifty. That included the install and I got the window deflectors," he added, while pointing at some plastic curved shades attached to the tops of the windows.

"You bought those *too?*" I cried out.

Chris turned to me with a total look of absolute perplexity. "Well, *damn, Girl,* have you not seen this truck before?"

I was frustrated, and it frustrated me more when he said funny things that made me laugh. I shrugged and reluctantly giggled. "Well, I don't pay attention that kind of stuff."

"You know we got a dog, right? He's that big brown thing that tears everything up."

I rolled my eyes in response.

Chris just laughed and pulled me tightly to him. "My baby lives in her own little world." Then he lowered his chin and murmured into my shoulder, "Next time I jus' won't say nothin' and you won't notice."

So I wasn't the only one observing the other and making mental notes on how to behave. I had the feeling I'd just exposed a secret to the wrong person; one that would come back later to bite me on the ass. It's true that I am not the most observant person when it comes to material things.

With people, conversations, situations, I am hyper vigilant; with stuff, I simply don't notice. I'm the girl who leaves the pregnancy test she's trying to hide out in the open. Over time, as our relationship continued, Chris's knowledge of this shortcoming of mine would nearly drive me insane. I would constantly find new things (at least new to me) around the house or in the truck then wonder where it had come from, how long it had been there, and—most importantly—how much had he spent.

I tried to push Chris away, but once he had his arms locked it was like pushing on concrete. As always, he found this amusing and waited patiently for me give up, which I did. I stared straight ahead, defeated. "You have got to stop spending so much money. Seriously. We have to finish this house, and there's not that much money left. As soon as the house is done, we'll need to find jobs."

Chris let go of me stepping away. "Jonna," he only used my name when he was getting angry, "I got this. All the materials I need to finish I already bought. All that's left is the paint, and put the floors in and we're done."

"Yes, then we need to get jobs," I stressed again. "Who knows how long that could take. We need to save the money we have."

Chris gave me his signature "you're crazy" look. "Why you sweatin' this stuff?"

I mimicked back his "you're crazy" look. "Why are you *not* sweating this stuff?"

"Shoot Girl, gettin' a job is easy. I can go out get one right now. I told you, if you don't want to work, you don't have to. Baby, I got this covered. I ain't sweatin' this." He pulled me close, hugging me tightly from behind as we both faced the truck. "Come on now, admit that's a pretty truck."

"Yes," I sighed, "It's a very pretty truck."

A week later I miscarried.

****

Since I'd only knowingly been pregnant for a week, it wasn't a crushing blow to miscarry, but I was definitely disappointed. I didn't think that at my age I would ever have children, so when this came up, I felt that I had been blessed. It was a surprise, but once I'd had a few days to let the idea settle in, I started to get excited by the idea of being a mother. But as quickly as the blessing came it went away.

When I knew something was wrong I told Chris and he drove me to the emergency room. There was nothing they could do. It was so early in the pregnancy, the doctor treating me basically said, "Maybe you'll miscarry. Maybe you won't." Then he sent me home to wait.

Chris, of course, was the perfect attentive boyfriend. He put me to bed, brought me anything I needed, and when the cramps became severe, he lay beside me rubbing my pelvis. But just like the day we found out about the pregnancy, I was once again confused by his reaction. He *did* everything right, and yet I had no idea how he *felt.*

Cracks were beginning to form in our relationship. On the surface, all seemed well. We didn't argue or fight, but our distance began to show itself in the long silences. I still believed in us, I just stopped believing it was all sunshine and flowers. I grew resentful each time I climbed into the truck and was reminded that the only result of my short pregnancy had been Chris spending a lot of money on unnecessary gear while I got a week of pain and bleeding.

I understood that Chris had not led a conventional life, but his constant need for stimulation was becoming exhausting. I wondered if a "regular life" would ever be exciting enough for him. By default I became the representative of that regular life and I felt his resentment each time I pointed out things like the house needing to get done, or that some new toy was too expensive, or, *no*, we couldn't take off for a weekend because we had a dog to take care of.

Maybe it was natural that two people who spent all their time alone together would start to get on each other's nerves. Maybe our differences had stopped being intriguing and had become simply annoying. All I knew was that I was ready for a break. He was so high energy I felt it was draining what little energy I had.

One night his mother called to tell Chris that a guy they knew, in the town that Chris had grown up in, had passed away. Chris was sitting on the bed, which was now in the living room. We were tired of moving the bed from room to room as he worked, so now we slept in the living room. He hung up with his mother and told me he wanted to go to the funeral. I couldn't tell by Chris's reaction if he was close to this guy or not. I felt I was watching an actor *act* sad as opposed to watching a sad person *be* sad.

"I think if you want to go, then you should. I'll stay here and take care of Beaux." I squatted down in the kitchen and hugged my knees. I was at the end of the miscarriage and this was the only position that helped with the random cramps I was still getting. I wasn't up for a trip. I just wanted a few days to be alone and relax. I'd had my fill of surprises and excitement over the five months since meeting Chris; I needed time to breathe.

That night I helped Chris pack a small bag. It was going to be a short trip to Texas and he would be back in a few days. The next morning when we said goodbye it was quick and distant. We'd had longer goodbyes when one of us was going to the store. This time it was like he couldn't get out the door—and I couldn't close it behind him— fast enough.

I came back into the kitchen and petted Beaux as I heard the truck start up and roar off. Something in my gut was telling me this relationship may not last much longer. It was the same feeling I'd get when a guy I really liked said he would call, but I knew deep down he wouldn't. It's a longing surrounded in questions that would forever remain unfulfilled.

Since I would be without the truck, Chris and I had gone to the store the night before to make sure I had everything I would need for the next few days. While there, I picked up the first book in a series about a girl who was in love with a vampire. Everyone was talking about it and I was curious to see what the big deal was.

I went to the pantry to get Beaux's food and realized we had forgotten to get another bag the night before. Estimating I had enough for a couple of days I hoped Chris's trip would be a quick one. The idea of lugging a bag of dog food back from Walmart was not something I looked forward to.

Beaux wiggled around the kitchen waiting for his food as I held his bowl and said, "Sit down, please." He stared at me. I repeated, "Sit down, please." I was trying to train him to sit only after hearing the word "please." At the moment he wasn't sitting after anything I said. "You are by far the worst dog ever. Do you know that? Do you even care?" I asked in a sweet gentle voice. His shaking butt and lack of focus told me he did not care; he only wanted the food. Once more I tried, "Sit down, *please*." Finally, Beaux sat and I slid the bowl in front of him.

With Beaux taken care of, I grabbed my new book and lay down on the bed in the middle of the living room. I stayed there all day, only getting up to take Beaux out or get something to drink. I allowed myself twenty-four hours to completely check out of my life and enter a world of make-believe bloodsuckers.

When I woke up the next morning, I thought it was out of character that Chris had not called, but at the same time I understood. We'd been joined at the hip for the last four months and I figured we both could use a break. Besides, I hadn't called him either.

As much as I would have loved to spend another day in bed reading, I also knew there were better things I could be doing with my time. Beaux was whining to go out, so I got up to take him for a walk. I didn't bother changing out of my sleeping attire, just pulled on my red plaid Wellies. In Abbeville, Louisiana there wasn't a single reason to be concerned with how I looked.

As soon as I picked up the leash he went nuts, leaping in the air and barking at me. Walking Beaux was always a struggle. As much as I

136

tried to control him, it was impossible. He just wanted to run fast and run free. I could totally sympathize. Isn't that exactly how I had ended up in Louisiana in the first place?

One of my favorite things to do on our walks was to stop at a field a few houses down and watch the horses there. If I stood by the fence long enough they would eventually make their way over and allow me pet them. It was the only time on our walk when Beaux settled down. He would lie quietly on the grass watching the horses. I think Beaux realized he was small in comparison, something that didn't happen often for him.

After about an hour, we headed back to the house. I wasn't entirely sure of what to do with myself. I figured I could finish painting one of the bedrooms or I could get on the computer and continuing looking for a job, something I had done on and off without much effort since we arrived. I had to admit that if Chris meant what he said, then I liked the idea of not having to work. I've never been career driven. Having a job has always been a drag. I'd much rather spend my time piddling around the house, writing, reading, or doing arts and crafts. I could spend an entire afternoon rearranging my iTunes playlists or painting little stools with my nieces' names. Unfortunately, we had already spent all the money we needed to finish the house and what was left for us Chris was rapidly blowing through. To be fair he was doing the majority of the work, so I felt like most of it was his to spend. Not all of it, but most of it.

I decided to go online and take a look at what was left in our account so I could try to put together some sort of budget for us. I doubted Chris would ever follow a budget, but it would make me feel better to have a timeframe for how long we had until we really, really, really *had* to get jobs. My online account popped up and I immediately noticed numerous withdrawals over the past twelve hours, plus a charge for a motel room in Chris's hometown of Terrell, Texas. I wasn't concerned about the motel room. I figured he probably didn't want to sleep at his Mom's because, from what he said, it was really small. What set my heart racing was the *minus $60, minus $60, minus $60, minus $60, minus $60...* I knew in a flash exactly what that was.

A knot formed in my stomach and my heart pounded so hard I could feel my chest vibrate. I had done a lot of drugs in my early twenties and knew that what I was looking at was withdrawals of cash to buy drugs. There was no doubt in my mind, but it didn't make sense. Chris didn't do drugs. He barely even drank alcohol. I had been with him every single day for nearly five months, I'd have known if he was high. Growing up with my mother had made me an expert at spotting changes in someone's personality.

I called Chris. When he didn't answer I left a message in a shaky voice, "Chris, you need to call me back right away. There are a lot of withdrawals on the account. I need to know if you have your card. Call me back."

I hung up and called his mother.

"Hello?"

I forced myself to stay calm. I was sure there was an explanation. He must have lost his card, although I couldn't figure out how someone got ahold of his pin number. "Hi, Angie. It's Jonna. Is Chris there? He didn't answer his cell."

"No, Honey, he's not here. He never showed up last night," she said casually.

I was surprised that she wasn't more concerned that her son hadn't shown up when he was supposed to. I didn't want to scare her, but I had to tell her that something was wrong.

"When you see him, tell him I need to speak with him right away. There's money missing from the account and I need to know if he has his debit card on—"

Angie cut me off, "Hang up the phone, go to the bank, and close that account. Then call me back. He's done this before."

My mind started spinning so fast I was having a hard time grasping the situation. I finally managed to blurt out, "What? What does that mean? He's done what before?"

"Chris has had drug problems in the past. We all thought he was past it. You just need to close that account. Once he realizes the money is gone, and he has nowhere to go, he'll come back."

"Okay, let me figure out the banking thing and I'll call you later." I hung up, lit a cigarette, and began pacing the kitchen. *What do I do? What do I do? What do I do? Think. Think. Think. What do I do? What do I do?*

The nearest bank was miles away and Chris had the truck. I went back to the computer to get the phone number for my bank. I figured I could call first to see if I could close the account over the phone. When I looked at the screen, my heart sank. In the time I had been on the phone with his mother, Chris had taken another $100 out of the account.

"*Fuuuucckk!* Are you fucking kidding me?" I shouted at the screen so loud that Beaux jumped up and ran out of the room.

I quickly found the number and called the bank. By the time I finally got in touch with a human, I was frantic.

"Customer service. Can I get your account number, please?" the voice drawled. She was the slowest speaking person I had ever encountered in my life. It was as if every word coming out of her mouth was being dragged through mud.

"Oh Jesus, hold on." I ran to get my checkbook and quickly read off the numbers.

"And who am I speaking with?"

"Jonna. I need to—"

"Can I have your last name, please?"

"Ivin. I need to—"

"Hello, Miss Irving. How may I—"

"It's Ivin. I need to close my account," I blurted out.

"I'm sorry, Miss Irving, in order—"

"Ivin. I really need to close the account immediately."

"Yes, I heard you, Ma'am," she said giving up on my name. "I'm sorry Ma'am, in order to close the account you need to go into a bank. If you need help finding a local branch you can visit our website at www—"

"Can you see all those withdrawals from last night and today? Sixty dollars, sixty dollars, sixty dollars?"

"Yes Ma'am, I see—"

140

"Apparently my boyfriend is on some sort of drug binge and according to his mother he won't stop until he runs out of money. You have to close this account now!" I was spitting out my words as fast as I could to make up for the time lost by the words crawling out of her mouth.

"I'm sorry, Ma'am, but with his name being—"

"Oh my God!" I cried out in frustration. "Please don't say you're sorry one more time! I don't want you to be sorry, I want you to tell me what to do. He has my truck. He is in Texas and he is emptying the account as we speak. I have no way to get to the bank. So fine, don't close the account, just shut it down, put a hold on it, freeze it, or whatever the fuck you have to do to stop the money. I need you to help me. Do you understand?" I stubbed out my cigarette and lit another.

I think what she actually understood was that she was dealing with someone who was near hysterics, and there was nothing in her manual that was going to help her. I was just thankful that she picked up the pace when she spoke again, "Hypothetically, if the card was *lost or stolen* then I could cancel his card."

I picked up on the hint she fed me and knew we were on the same page. "Yes. Thank you! That's what I meant to say. The card was lost or stolen."

"Which one?" she asked.

"Which one what?"

"Lost or stolen?"

"I don't know… whatever… stolen. It was stolen."

She went through the process of canceling Chris's card, and before getting off the line she asked, with what I felt was genuine sincerity, "Is there anything else I can help you with today?"

We both knew there wasn't. I was in this mess alone, but I appreciated the thought. "No, but thank you." I sighed, "Thank you for helping me."

I sat down on the bed just to stand back up again. I couldn't sit down and I couldn't stand still, so I paced. For the rest of the day I paced around the kitchen chain-smoking and thinking. Thinking. Thinking. I didn't have a clue what to do. I felt like I should call someone, but who? I couldn't call Jodi and Jenn because, one, there was nothing they could do from California, and two, if what Chris's mother told me was true, once he realized there wasn't any money available he would probably show up at her house or call me.

I didn't know if this was his way of breaking up with me, but he had left all his stuff here so I assumed he planned on coming back. His mother had said he'd had a drug problem in the past, so maybe going back home or the death of his friend triggered something in his head. It was my personal opinion that if someone had a drug problem in the past, they still have a drug problem. Drug and alcohol problems don't typically dry up and blow away. They stick around.

I thought about how it was when he left and how quickly we said goodbye to each other. I knew why I had been so quick to shut the door; I needed a break, not a breakup. But why was Chris in such a hurry? Did he know the whole time that once he got back to Texas his first stop would be to shake the hand of the drug dealer? Angie had only called the night before; did he make the decision that quickly? And who sees the drug dealer before seeing his or her own mother? Well, I knew the answer to that, a drug addict does.

I called Chris's cell. After it rang six times the voice mail picked up. I hung up and called again. I repeated this process three more times until finally when I called the phone went straight to voicemail without ringing. Okay, so now I knew he had his phone with him, because he had just shut it off. I fired off a text message. *If you want to end this relationship, that's fine. I don't know what is going on with you, but that truck you are driving around isn't yours. You need to bring it back.*

I hit send knowing that this text would be ignored just like my other messages. He had taken out over $340 in a 24-hour period. My guess was he had enough to keep him high for at least a little while, so I knew I wouldn't hear back from him anytime soon.

At some point in the evening I spoke with Chris's brother, David. I didn't know him very well, but I told him what was going on, and he assured me, just like their mother had, that Chris would show up eventually. We kept the conversation brief and David let me know that he would continue to call Chris and then call me if he spoke with him. David had been just as casual sounding as Angie; I thought it was disturbing that I was the only one flipping out. Is this how people were after living with Chris for a long time? If somehow Chris and I managed to stay together would I find myself one day saying, "Oh gee, you caught an alligator. *Sigh.* Big deal."

Long into the night my mind continued to jump around from one dark question to another. Was Chris having some sort of post-traumatic stress disorder breakdown? Was he suicidal again? Was he unable to cope with regular day-to-day life without the excitement of the Special

Forces? Was life with me just too boring? Was that why he watched all those disturbing videos? Or was he just an asshole?

Around 3 AM, after not eating all day and pouring four or five beers, three shots of tequila, and smoking two packs of cigarettes on an empty stomach, I crawled to the bathroom, threw up and passed out on the floor. About an hour later I woke up to the sound of the message alert going off on my phone. I grabbed my phone and by covering one eye managed to read a text from Chris.

I'm sorry babe I fucked up i love u so much i cant believe i hurt you like this. Dont worry about truck i promise 2 bring it back i love u

I managed in my drunken state to tap out a reply something like, *Just come back. We'll figure out what to do when you get here.* I hit Send, then pulled myself up off the bathroom floor and stumbled to the bed, breathing a sigh of relief that at least the worst was over.

I didn't know if Chris and I would stay together when he got back. A broken heart I could deal with; him missing in another state while on drugs in a truck my sister had signed for, I couldn't deal with. Once I had the truck keys safely in my hand, I would think about what to do with us.

I didn't want a man in my life that came home by default because he had nowhere else to go. I had definitely felt the distance between us in the last few weeks, but in my mind it was a rough patch. You bicker for a week and you get over it; you don't drive 400 miles away to smoke crack. I loved Chris, but I had to realize that maybe he was just too damaged. Did being in a relationship with him mean that anytime things got tough he would have an episode like this and disappear?

144

I woke up late the next morning, with a pounding headache and a churning stomach. I called Chris but it went straight to voicemail. I called his mother again and she said she still had not seen him. I sent Chris another text. *Call me when you wake up.*

After I fed Beaux and made coffee, I decided to check the bank account and see what the final damage had been. As soon as the balance popped up, I screamed, horrified by what I saw. *Minus $100. Minus $100. Minus $100...* Throughout the night he had continued to withdraw money. I immediately picked up the phone and called the bank.

I didn't give the woman on the other end a chance to speak before I started ranting, "I reported a card stolen yesterday and now there are all these withdrawals on the account! That card was supposed to be canceled!"

I was physically shaking as she explained to me that, yes, I had reported the card as stolen, but that Chris had called later and reinstated it. Since his name and Social Security number were on the account, it was simple for him to just say he found the card. Just like that he was back to emptying our account.

"Well the card was stolen again! Please cancel it right now!" I should have felt terrible that I was yelling at this anonymous woman, but I had no control at that point of my emotions or rational thinking. As soon as the card was canceled, I hung up and called Chris. It rang a few times and then I heard his recorded voice.

I was hysterical, frantically pacing through the house, sobbing uncontrollably. I felt like a caged animal and didn't recognize my own voice when I began screaming into his voicemail. "Why are you doing this? You have to stop! If you don't ever want to see me again, it's fine, but stop stealing the money!" I couldn't breathe. Between the crying and the shaking and the screaming I couldn't get any air. I started to hyperventilate; I just repeated over and over into the phone, "Why are you doing this? Why are you doing this?"

I hung up the phone and knew I needed to calm down. I had to figure out what to do and in this state I couldn't think. Picking up a pillow, I began swinging it wildly against the bed as guttural screams like I'd never heard before came out of me. I didn't even know I was capable of making these sounds and I was starting to scare myself because I couldn't stop. I wasn't screaming about six or seven hundred dollars. I was screaming about my life. I was screaming at God.

Eventually my body started to grow tired and I was able to stop swinging the pillow. The screaming subsided, but the crying continued. I looked up and saw Beaux sitting pushed up against the front door shaking. This made me cry harder; I had terrified my innocent dog.

I sat on the floor and wrapped my arms around him, petting his head until he stopped shaking. "It's okay," I cried. "We'll be okay. Don't be scared. It's okay. I'll fix this. I'm gonna fix this."

I was able to pull myself together but was barely hanging on by a thread when I got up to go see Miss B and Mr. Vic. Chris had told them the morning he left that he would be out of town. Mr. Vic agreed to look out for me. As I knocked on the door, I tried to put a smile on my face, hoping they had not heard my screaming earlier.

Miss B answered the door to let me in. She said she could take me to the bank and went to find her purse. Mr. Vic was in the kitchen installing cabinets.

"Hey, girl. When' da boy gettin' back?" he asked in his thick Cajun accent.

It took every ounce of energy I had to not burst into tears. I physically forced all that emotional energy into my chest cavity and held it there. I wasn't ready to let anyone know what was going on when I still didn't know. Smiling the best I could, I forced a reply, "In a couple of days."

"You tell him dat I said it's a damn shame to leave a woman all alone in da empty house like dat." He laughed. Chris and Mr. Vic always joked with each other in this way. "What kind o' man do dat, eh?"

I don't know Mr. Vic. I don't know. "Well, he knew you were here so I would be okay." I answered.

Miss B found her keys and we set off for the bank. Everything was moving in slow motion. If felt like I could have jumped out of the car and run faster. I held my hands together tightly so they wouldn't shake and pressed my feet as hard as I could against the floorboards. I was grateful that she didn't talk. Finally, we made it to the bank and I jumped out. I was desperate to get that account closed before Chris reinstated his card again. This back-and-forth game could go on indefinitely and it needed to end now.

I grabbed hold of the front door and pulled. It was stuck. Pulling harder, I shook the door. Why wasn't it opening? And then I saw the sign:

Closed for Martin Luther King Day

I went to the ATM thinking I'd take out as much money as I could. I put the card in the slot, only to have it spit back out. I did this three or four more times with the same result. The machine was broken or out of money or something. I wanted to drop down to the ground and cry. I wanted to hold my head in my hands and curl up in the fetal position. But more than anything else, I wanted my mother.

I knew Miss B could see me standing at the ATM. So I swallowed the feelings, stuffing them on top of the rest before heading back to the car. Opening the car door, I said casually, "Martin Luther King."

"Oh well," she said, "I'll bring ya back tomorrow."

At the rate Chris was going there would be nothing left by tomorrow.

When Miss B pulled up to the house I thanked her and went home. The moment I was safely alone, the pacing and chain-smoking started up again. I logged onto my bank and wasn't surprised by what I saw. Another withdrawal for $200. I needed to throw up but I hadn't eaten in two days so there was nothing there. I looked over at Beaux, "I'm not going to scream again. I promise." I said.

Taking a deep breath, I stared at the screen. I had to get that money before he did, but how? There was only around $1300 left. In three days he had taken nearly $800. Another day or two and the rest would be gone. He'd started taking larger chunks at a time since he most likely figured out that it was me canceling the card. He also knew now that he could just as easily reinstate it as quickly as I could cancel it. I called Chris. It went straight to voicemail, so I knew he'd heard my last message and his response was to shut off the phone.

Turning back to the computer, the answer came to me. The fasted way I knew to empty an account was to pay bills. I quickly went to my bill-pay to fill out my own name and address as the payee. Then I typed

148

in the amount—down to the penny—that was left in the account. I emptied the account by sending the money back to myself as a bill payment. It was going to take ten days to get my own money, but that was fine. I smiled with relief when I looked back at the balance reading zero.

The phone rang; I saw that it was David.

"Hey David," I sighed.

"How you holding up, Jonna?"

I'm fine. Did you talk to him?"

"I did," David said. "He finally called me back about an hour ago. He said he got a message from you and you sounded upset."

"Upset?" I asked in bewilderment. "He used that word? Upset? Like I'm sitting here being cranky? I'm losing my fucking mind David, *upset* doesn't come close to describing how I'm feeling."

"Yeah, I know Jonna." He said. David didn't have a thick Southern accent like Chris. But he spoke in a slow drawn out way, as though everything were said with a sigh. "Chris said you were real upset. I feel so bad for you. I just don't know what to say."

"Did he say he was bringing the truck back?"

"Oh yeah, he said he felt really bad and he was embarrassed, but he was going to call you and bring the truck back. You know, he's done this before and he always comes back. He told me how much he loves you."

"To be honest with you David, it doesn't really matter whether he loves me or not. At this point, if he doesn't get that truck back here, I'm going to have to call my sister, tell her what's going on and have her report it as stolen. I don't have a choice. I can't just sit here and do nothing."

David sighed, "Yeah, I know Jonna. I don't want to see my brother go to jail, but he has to take responsibility for what he's done. Just give him today to call you. I'm sure you guys can work this out. He'll come back. I know he will. He just does this stuff and I don't know why."

I knew Chris had been married before and had other relationships with women he lived with, so I asked, "What did the other women he was with do? Did his wives and girlfriends just take him back? I can't do this. This is too much for me."

"Chris has had a lot of good women in his life—just like you. But he always pulls stuff like this and messes it up." I could picture David shaking his head as he spoke, "You know, I love my brother, but I've never understood him. He does a lot of things I don't agree with, but I just try to stay out of it. Chris has always been wild. Even when we were kids he was always like this. He does what he wants and…"

David continued to talk, but I had stopped listening. All I could hear in my mind was, *even when we were kids he was always like this.* When they were kids? He didn't have PTSD as a child.

I was instantly transported back to Texas, back to the little Baptist Church, back to when I first met Chris… *she got hit by a train… he lost his wife and his baby… What's the tattoo? Special Forces Airborne… How many did you lose? All of them… I saw the guy right before he fired off the shot… the guy died and fell on top of him… all the teenagers were killed… he was suicidal… You're some crazy motherfuckers… We can be… fiancée… fiancée… fiancée… Black… Hawk… Down…"*

And then I remembered my own words, spoken before ever meeting him. *What a load of bullshit. No one's life is that dramatic.*

"David," I interrupted him abruptly, "Chris was never in the Army was he?"

My question disintegrated into a long silence of truth that gave me my answer long before he spoke. It was a suspended moment of nothingness and within that empty space I felt my faith, my heart, and my spirit splinter and break apart. My body remained standing in the kitchen as the deepest part of me fragmented and drifted away.

I heard a deep exhausted sigh followed by, "He isn't still telling that story, is he?"

I looked around the empty house where I stood in the swamps of Louisiana, 1700 miles away from everything I knew, completely disconnected from who I thought I was. "Yeah, David, he's still telling *that story*," I sighed.

I wanted to stop time. I wanted to go back and swallow the question so that I didn't have to face the answer. The man that I had prayed into my life didn't exist. Nothing about Chris was true. He was a fictional character created in his own mind and my instincts had sensed it. The lies he told began to unravel before me. There wasn't a teenage bride who was hit by a train. There wasn't an accident with teenagers. There wasn't a sniper. There were no friends and brothers lost in battle… but there was a tattoo. He had a *tattoo.*

"David, I snapped, "Why the fuck does Chris have a Special Forces tattoo? He was never in the military and he has a Special Forces tattoo! Who does that? What kind of person gets a fucking tattoo… *a tattoo! A motherfucking tattoo!*"

David listened in silence as my rant began to feed upon itself, growing in strength like a hurricane as I paced in circles around the kitchen. "Are you fucking kidding me? Are... you... seriously fucking... kidding... me? *A goddam, motherfucking tattoo!* That piece of shit! That low-life, motherfucking piece of shit. *God damn it! Fuck!*" Being articulate was not at the forefront of my mind. Expressing raw rage was. I was doing a good job.

I stopped venting long enough to light a cigarette and slam the lighter down on the counter. David took advantage of the pause, "I'm really sorry, Jonna. I hate that he does this. I've never understood it."

I shook my head, "I can't believe this is happening. A tattoo. I can't believe   it."
"I'm so sorry."

"It's not your fault. I gotta go, David. I can't even... I just... Fuck. I'll call you later."

"Okay, Jonna. You take care of yourself. It's gonna be okay."

"If you speak to your brother, tell him to bring my truck back."

I hung up and texted a simple message to Chris, *I know the truth.*

Driving I-5 North

Somewhere in California

I can't count the number of times I've been in a car traveling this highway, but this is the first time I am doing it alone. It feels the same. Running. Always running. I hate this section of the I-5 freeway. It feels endless. The wheels keep turning, but am I really getting anywhere? At least this time it is my choice to run. When I was growing up, it was my mother who ran and I felt dragged along like a brick weighing her down.

It was the middle of the school year in the fifth grade. Mom had just told us we were moving once again. Time to pack up. Time to say goodbye to friends and pretend we'd keep in touch. But even at twelve I had enough moves under my belt to know it never happened.

Half a grade here, half a grade there. We moved so often the teachers never knew what to do with Jodi and me. This was a time before computers and instant communication. Back then, the old school had to Xerox copy and mail transcripts to the new school. By the time our transcripts arrived we'd already moved on. The confused principals and teachers simply didn't know what to do with us.

I would be given a desk in the back of the class and told to follow along as well as I could. I learned to stay quiet, become invisible, and slide through the system. My education was built on "pity C's" written on report cards by teachers who didn't know enough about me to give anything else.

The teachers were easy; the kids were a complicated, often confusing, social maze. I never knew from town to town how I would be received. What I did know was that the first day set the tone for the rest of my time there. I'd leave one school on a Friday as a popular, well-liked kid with lots of friends, only to arrive at a new school on Monday to be treated like a freakish outcast.

There was no rhyme or reason to it. Nothing had dramatically changed about me from Friday afternoon to Monday morning. I was the same person. So why was I treated so differently from place to place? The answer was simple: Tween girls. The most popular girl in the class determined my popularity or lack of it. A baby seal swimming with sharks stood a better chance of survival.

If she decided to be nice to the "new girl," then I entered into an established circle of friends and was set for the remainder of my time. But if she decided I was weird, or she didn't like my shoes, or I looked at her funny, or any other number of reasons girls have for not liking each other, then I was toast. I'd be left to spend lonely lunches in the cafeteria, avoiding all eye contact and wishing to be invisible.

So after our latest move I entered my new fifth-grade class hoping for the best, but prepared for the worst. I'd dressed carefully that morning, putting on my favorite corduroy pants—that went *swish,*

swish, swish when I walked—and an iron-on T-shirt with the Fonz testifying to my coolness with a thumbs up and an "Aaaayyyyy."

As I took my desk I gave my best non-threatening smile to the kids sitting around me. I hoped it relayed *I'm fabulous enough to hang with, but not in any way stuck-up.*

I'd been in class for less than an hour when the boy behind me and one row over passed a note. I glanced over my shoulder to take a peek and my heart sank. At best he was the class nerd, at worst, the special-needs kid. It was hard to tell under his big geek glasses and bowl haircut. I glanced around and saw a couple of snickers and headshakes. I was doomed. I reluctantly opened the note and read:

Will you be my girlfriend?

Yes or No

A pretty blonde girl next to me leaned over and mouthed, "What does it say?"

I passed her the note without regard for the boy's privacy or feelings. The future of my popularity was hanging in the balance and might be determined before the recess bell rang. Giving the girl the note was a risk. I had no way of knowing if she was a popular kid or an outsider.

The blonde tapped the shoulder of a dark-haired girl sitting in front of her and handed her the note. The dark-haired girl glanced over her shoulder, taking me in, then picked up her pencil and marked an X on the note. So now I knew, Dark Hair was the popular girl and Blondie was her sidekick. I couldn't see if she had marked yes or no, and this had me worried.

Dark Hair handed the note back to Blondie who opened it and smiled. The smile told me nothing. Was she laughing at me? Was it a smug smile? Was it a smile of agreement at the decision of Dark Hair? These stupid girls had no idea of the power they held over me? If the note was marked "Yes," then I was guaranteed months of relentless teasing that the special needs kid was my boyfriend. Or even worse be shoved together in a closet or bathroom to kiss.

Blondie waited for the teacher to turn his back before tossing the note on my desk. My mouth went dry and my palms sweated as I opened it. To my great relief I found a large dark X marked over the "No" box. Dark Hair looked back at me and we exchanged, "what a loser" smiles before I tossed the note back to the geeky kid. I was in.

I spent the next year blissfully attending skating parties, putting on makeup we'd stolen from our mothers, and learning to French kiss behind the cafeteria. I had a boyfriend whose name I can't remember and a group of best friends whose names I also can't remember. My pre-teen world was complete.

And then we moved again.

On the first day at my new school, a group of girls approached me as I stood outside my classroom door. One of them looked me over with contempt before saying, "Nice shoes. Are you trying to be Mexican?" With that, the gaggle of girls burst into laughter while sauntering off down the hall. I had no idea what "trying to be Mexican" meant, but I knew the popularity I'd recently enjoyed was over. As I watched them walk away I thought, *nothing good ever lasts.*

It never occurred to me to ask myself if I actually wanted to be friends with these girls. I didn't make choices based on what I liked or didn't like. I simple accepted what they chose for me. My role had

156

always been to react and adapt to what was decided by other people, by outside circumstances, or in my mind, by God. My voice went unheard in my own life.

Abbeville, Louisiana

I didn't understand at the time why I was so fixated on the one detail of Chris's tattoo. Now, as I sit here reliving that day, it has come to me. Seeing the tattoo for the first time was the excuse that allowed me to disregard the voice inside telling me the truth. The tattoo gave me permission to blindly enter a fantasy world created by his sickness and my unfulfilled desire to be loved and taken care of.

Whenever my doubts tried to crack open the fictional bubble we lived in, I quickly chased them away by telling myself the tattoo proved he was the real thing. I had learned in Al-Anon that children of alcoholics were always waiting for the other shoe to drop and that I needed to put my trust into a Higher Power. I had learned in therapy that I was addicted to being unhappy and that when good things came into my life my mind would try to sabotage me. I had learned from my spiritual practices that my thoughts created the world I lived in and I needed to embrace the love that had come into my life. I twisted and used all of these principles in order to give myself permission to swallow the lies. I'd been willing to go to any lengths to ease the loneliness that had been choking me since childhood.

But I didn't know any of this when I pressed the send button on that message. All I knew was that I was gripped in fear, broken by betrayal, and filled with blind rage. And I knew just who to direct all the rage at: God.

I lit another cigarette as my anger turned to bitter tears. I looked up and said, "I prayed for you to bring love into my life. For years I've begged you to reveal my highest path. I surrendered to your will, not mine, and this is what you delivered? I hate you."

I picked up the bottle of tequila that was sitting in the counter and took a swig. I closed my eyes and repeated, "I really hate you."

I didn't know what to do. I knew I had to call Jodi and Jenn and let them know what was going on, but I couldn't bring myself to pick up the phone. I'd brought this mess into our lives and somehow I had to fix it. Somehow. I wracked my brain for a solution that never came. When I couldn't think anymore, I gave up.

I sat down on the kitchen floor, leaning against the kitchen cabinets with the bottle of tequila and a pack of cigarettes. For the second day in a row I followed in my mother's footsteps and tried in vain to drink my problems away. I didn't care that I knew it wouldn't work. It didn't matter that no matter how much my mother tried to get away she always ended up back in her own skin. And I would too.

As I watched the shadows sink lower on the walls, all I could think about was getting that truck back. With each sip of tequila, I gave up caring what was going to happen to me. It didn't matter where I went or what I did, but I couldn't stomach the idea of placing the burden of my life on Jodi's shoulders. How was I going to tell her that I had brought a liar and a thief into her home? That the truck that she had signed for was gone?

I don't know how long I sat there, but the house had grown dark. There was a knock on the door and I could see through the glass that it was Miss B. I thought about staying where I was and hiding, but I knew she knew I was home. I pulled myself up and opened the side door.

"Hi," I said, "come on in. Oh, here, let me turn on a light."

Miss B glanced around the dark house and asked, "Was you nappin'?"

"No, no, I was just..." I clicked on a kitchen light. "Let me let Beaux out." I left her standing in the kitchen as I walked Beaux out and clicked him to his tether. He immediately started incessantly barking the moment I walked back to the house.

As I closed the door behind me, Miss B handed me a foil-covered plate. "Dis here pot roast. We had us some extra from dinner so I fix dis plate for ya."

"Oh, thank you. That's really very kind," I said as a lump formed in my throat. I took the plate and set it on the counter trying to casually push back the opened bottle of tequila. I kept my back to her for just a moment and pressed my tongue against my bottom lip. It was an old trick someone taught me to prevent yourself from crying. I never knew why it worked but I was glad it did. I wanted her to leave. I wanted her to stop being nice to me.

I turned back around asking, "How are the cabinets coming along?" I wanted to keep the focus on her but she didn't bite.

"Dey good. Mr. Vic nearly finish dis afternoon. You okay, girl?"

I'm sure she could smell the liquor and see the puffy redness in my eyes, but I lied anyway. "Oh yeah, I'm good. You know, just tired."

I could tell she didn't believe me, but to my relief she let it go. "Okay den, you eat dat roast. I'll let you be." She headed for the door.

I followed her out to bring Beaux back in before he drove the whole neighborhood crazy.

Miss B turned back and asked over the noise of Beaux barking. "You feeling alright wit every-ting?" By the look on her face I knew she was talking about the miscarriage. Chris had told her and Mr. Vic about it when we first got back from the emergency room.

"Beaux, shut up," I said as I unclipped him from the tether. He yanked me toward the house as I held onto his collar and struggled to carry on the conversation. "Oh yeah, I'm okay. A little sad I guess."

"You be right soon," she offered.

"Yeah, yeah. I'm okay,"

"When da boy git back?"

"Oh... um..." I searched for an answer while my beast of a dog tried to dislocate my shoulder. "Goddammit, Beaux, sit!" He did as he was told and I was finally able to stand up straight and focus on and answer. "He's um... he's going to stay a little longer, but it'll be soon."

"Well, you take care and you need any-ting, me and Mr. Vic be right der," she said.

"Thank you." I answered, letting her believe that I was a woman suffering a bout of sadness due to a recent miscarriage while simultaneously missing my man.

I went back inside after Miss B left and took a beer out of the refrigerator. I opened it and took a long drink as I removed the foil off the plate. She had wrapped up a large piece of roast and some roasted potatoes. It was a beautiful gesture that was wasted on me. "Beaux," I called out as I slid the plate across the kitchen floor.

I knew I wasn't going to eat it and with the bank account cleaned out and no cash on hand I had no idea when I would be able to buy more dog food. I opened the freezer, which Chris kept stocked with meat, and took out a pork tenderloin, a couple of packages of hamburger and a few chicken breasts. I put them in the fridge section so they could defrost. Reaching down to rub Beaux's head as he swallowed hunks of roast without chewing, I said, "You're life just got really good."

And then I sat back down on the kitchen floor. It was where I was most comfortable. I drank. I smoked. I cried. Most of all I tortured myself by obsessing over every nitty-gritty detail of the last five months. I unraveled every lie. I broke down every story to the smallest detail making a mental timeline of his fictional life. My ego chewed up every bit of information I had, proving over and over that I was right and Chris was wrong. All of this was pointless. He lied. I already knew that. Regurgitating the lies over and over only succeeded in emotionally stabbing me in the chest and pouring salt in the wounds.

I knew I had to tell someone what was going on and I could only think of one person. Adam. He'd been there for the worst time of my life standing by my side when I lost Mom. Once again I needed his support so I picked up the phone and dialed.

The second I heard his voice, every emotion I'd stuffed down came rushing out of me all at once. I barely managed to get out, "It's Jonna," before I began hysterically crying. I couldn't speak.

I could hear the worry in Adam's voice, knowing that all he could hear on his end were my broken sobs and attempts to breath. "What's going on?" Where are you? What is it?" he asked.

I was scaring the shit out of him and I felt like an asshole for doing it but I couldn't catch enough air to speak. Eventually, I was able to say, "I'm okay, I'm okay." Once I started saying it, I couldn't stop. So I kept repeating, "I'm okay. I'm okay…" The problem was my voice didn't sound normal. I could hear the panic coming out of me but I didn't know how to control it.

"I'm okay. I'm okay." My attempts to reassure him were only succeeding in making it worse.

"You have to tell me what's going on." Adam now sounded panicked on the other line. "What is it? Is it Chris? Is he there?"

The mention of his name snapped me out of my verbal loop and I began rambling, "He's gone! It was lies. All lies! Everything. Everything was lies! He took the truck and I don't know where he is. He's been gone for days. Everything is a lie. All lies. All of it. He was never in the Army. He has the truck and I have to figure out how to get it back. I don't know what to do. What do I do? Tell me what to do. What do I do?"

Adam got that I was not in immediate danger and sighed, "I'm so sorry. I'm sorry this happened to you."

And then he stayed quiet allowing me the space to cry it out. When I was able to speak clearly, I told him everything that had happened. He was patient during the moments when I would melt down and sob. He said nothing as I broke off and angrily shouted a string of swearwords directed at a non-existent Chris.

Have you called your sister?" he asked, breaking into one of my rants.

"No. I can't. I can't. What am I going to say? I don't know what to do?"

Before I started looping again, Adam cut me off, "I think you need to call your sister. I'm worried about you. You don't sound right, like you're not all there."

"I've been drinking, that's all."

"Okay," he said his voice firm but consoling, "that's probably a really bad idea right now. You need to stop."

"I'm okay. I'm fine," I mumbled.

"Promise me you won't drink anymore tonight."

I picked up the bottle of tequila and took a final swig. "I promise I won't drink anymore tonight," I answered, as I put the cap back on.

I lit a cigarette and sighed, "I need to figure out a way to convince him to bring the truck back."

"I don't think you should," Adam said. "I don't like the idea of him coming back there and you being alone. You know he told me a really disturbing story that day he and I went hiking. He said that he was dating this woman and that they'd agreed to meet at a trail entrance to go hiking. He was really late and when he finally got there she'd been found raped and murdered."

"Oh Jesus," I groaned. "Why didn't you say anything before?"

"I figured you already knew and it was such a tragic story, I wasn't going to just blurt out randomly, 'Hey what about that time your girlfriend was murdered.' But now that I think about it, it felt—I don't know—like, a little creepy at the time. Like, why is he telling me this?"

"Can you hold on a second?" I asked.

"Sure."

I set the phone down and returned a few minutes later.

"Okay, I'm back."

"You were gone a long time. Where did you go?" He sounded concerned again.

"I had to throw up." This was not my finest hour.

"I'm really not feeling good about this. I think I need to call Jodi."

"No. Don't. Please, just don't call her," I begged. "I'm fine really. I just shouldn't have been drinking on an empty stomach."

"When was the last time you ate?" he asked.

"What day is it?"

"Monday."

"Right. Martin Luther King Day. Did I tell you the fucking bank was closed?"

"Yeah, you did. When did you eat last?" he pressed.

I thought about this for a second, "I ate something on Saturday. I don't remember what."

I could hear the stress in Adam's voice when he replied, "I really think I should call your sister if you aren't going to."

"I'll call her," I reassured him. "I'll call Jodi tomorrow morning. Promise. I'm sorry I dumped all this on you."

"No, I'm glad you called. I love you. I just... I don't know. I feel like I should do something. I don't feel right about any of this. You're sitting there by yourself in that empty house and he could be anywhere headed back. Plus, you just don't sound like yourself, and I don't want to be the guy who got the last phone call and did nothing."

This had not been my intention when I called and I needed to fix it. He needed to hear from the normal me, the me that didn't act irrationally, the me that didn't shout and scream and cry in hysterics, the me that stuffed everything down and presented a calm exterior. I had faked that me for most of my life; I could do it once more for a friend I loved deeply.

I took a deep breath pulling in my scattered energy, forcing myself to focus my thoughts and hold it together. "You're right," I said. "I promise you I am going to be alright. Chris knows I know the truth, so I doubt he'll be in any big hurry to come rushing back. I'll call Jodi in the morning and she can report the truck as stolen. After I hang up with you, I'll go to bed."

It worked—sort of. Adam was not completely convinced, but after I promised to call him in the morning, he reluctantly said his goodbye with a warning: "If I don't hear from you, I have to call your sister."

"Okay." A lump of barbed wire formed in my throat and I managed to croak out, "I love you," before I lost the fight and started crying again. I quickly pressed my thumb over the mouthpiece of the phone so he would not hear me.

"I love you too," he replied and I knew it was true.

I hung up the phone feeling drained. I felt beat up and broke down. But more than anything, what caused my stomach to turn inside out was knowing I had to call Jodi and Jenn in the morning and bring this stress into their lives. They'd given us everything to build a new life and this was what they received in return. I hated Chris for that and I was determined to set it straight.

Mostly I was pissed off that while I was sinking in emotional quicksand, he was out there somewhere getting high. I wanted him to be suffocating in fear and uncertainty the way I was. I wanted his heart to race with panic because he didn't know what was coming next. But more than all of that, I wanted him to feel what it was like to be lied to.

I typed out a text:

Chris, I don't know what I did to deserve this or why you have left me all alone. I have no one. I have nothing and I am nothing. Please make sure someone takes care of Beaux. He shouldn't suffer because I have failed at this life. I can't do this anymore.

"Let your cracked-out, paranoid mind chew on that, Motherfucker." I hit Send, then turned off my phone and went to bed. Was it a mature thing to do? No. Was it a smart thing to do? No. Was it an incredibly satisfying thing to do? Yes. Yes it was.

****

When I woke up early the next morning before the sun, I had a brief moment of peace before it all came flooding back. I just wanted to stay in bed with the covers pulled over my head, but I made myself get up. I made myself put on shoes and take Beaux out. I made myself turn on the coffeemaker. I made myself get in the shower and put clothes on that weren't pajamas.

I went into the kitchen, opened the cabinet to get a coffee cup, and saw the bottle of tequila. As tempting as it was, I decided Adam was right; this had not been one of my best ideas. I checked Beaux's food and there was barely half a cup left. I scooped it out and put it in his bowl, which I set on the counter. I went to the fridge and took out a package of hamburger meat. As the meat cooked in a pan, I leaned against the counter and lit a cigarette before turning on my cell phone.

The first smile in days came across my face when I saw all of the missed texts from Chris.

R U okay...

Text me let me no U okay...

Im sorry....

I promise 2 bring truck back...

U need 2 text me dont no whats going on..

It looked like he had been up worried most of the night.

Good. I didn't text him back. The way I saw it, I had been living this nightmare for four days now; he could stress for a little longer.

168

But there was one person who didn't deserve to live through this stress and that was Adam. I gave him a call and reassured him that I was still here and that I was going to call Jodi. Adam told me he thought I sounded better. I didn't feel any better, but I was relieved that he was relieved that I sounded better.

With a bowling ball sized knot in my stomach, I called Jodi. It was a repeat of the night before. As soon as I heard her voice my emotions overwhelmed me. But without Jose Cuervo slapping me around I was able to pull it together enough to speak in full sentences. Surprisingly, Jodi took the news pretty well. Of course, she was angry and pissed off at Chris, but she wasn't surprised, "Yeah, I kinda figured something like this might happen. When Jenn and I were there at Christmas, we talked, and both of us had an uneasy feeling, but couldn't put our finger on what it was."

"I know what you mean," I sighed, as I took the hamburger off the stove to cool. "I'm really sorry you guys got drug into this mess."

"It's not your fault," Jodi said. "He's the cocksucker. The fact that he made up a bunch of stories makes me like, 'whatever, you're stupid,' but lying about being in the military makes me want to hurt him. It makes me want to break every bone in his body and kick his teeth out and then watch as he lies on the ground in agony."

Jodi had always been more intense than me when it came to violence. She came from the school of 'you hurt me, I hurt you back twice as hard'; whereas I subscribed to the philosophy of 'you hurt me, I crawl inside myself and cry to God about it.' Different strokes, I guess.

"He keeps texting and saying that he'll bring the truck back, but then he disappears again and I don't hear from him," I said, "I've been talking to his brother and he swears he'll bring it back. But I don't know, I think you need to report it stolen at this point."

"I'll call Jenn and see what she thinks," Jodi answered.

"If we report it stolen they are going to impound the truck and the only person who can get it out is you; it's in your name. You'll need to fly out. It's going to be expensive."

"Do you think you'll stay there or come back here?" my sister asked.

"I have no idea. There's nothing there for me anymore: starting over, new job, new place to live. I might as well stay here." I started to cry again, "I don't know. I don't have a single clue what to do."

Like most men, my sister was uncomfortable with women crying. "Let me call Jenn and tell her what's going on so we can figure something out."

We hung up, but I didn't feel the relief I expected to feel once I had told her. I thought some of the pressure would be lifted from my chest, but it wasn't. Hearing Jodi's voice just made me more determined to "fix this" on my own.

As I kept running over different scenarios in my head, I put the cooled hamburger into Beaux's bowl. I heated the pan again and absentmindedly tossed in four chicken breasts. He was going to need to eat again. I got a pot and threw in a couple cans of soup and some brown rice. When the chicken was cooked and the rice was done, I chopped up the breasts and stirred them into the rice mixture. I eyeballed the concoction and figured at best it was two meals, maybe three.

I heard my cell phone ping, telling me I had a text.

Jonna i'm worried going 2 text kev and jaq and tell them 2 stop by house. Im sorry. hope u r ok love u

As much as it pleased me that he was still worried, I had no intention of bringing our friends into this sick little game. I texted back immediately: *I'm not dead. Jodi knows everything. Bring back the truck or she is reporting it stolen.*

It was time for people to know what was going on, so I started to make calls: first on the list, my younger sister, Judy, in Arkansas. She and her boyfriend Brett had driven down to Louisiana for a weekend visit when Chris and I first arrived.

At least this time when I told the story, I didn't cry. I felt this was an improvement.

"I knew he was a liar," Judy drawled in her Arkansas twang. "When we were there I told Brett, 'This guy is full of shit.'"

"Why didn't you tell *me* you thought that?" I asked.

"I figured you knew. You guys were all lovey dovey; I thought you didn't care." Judy laughed. "I mean, when he told that story about the woman driving off the bridge, I was like, *come on.*"

"What woman?"

"*The woman.* The one that drove off the bridge in Florida. Chris was in his boat and he saw the whole thing, so he dove in the water and tried to save her, but couldn't get the window open and he watched her drown."

"I have no idea what you are talking about," I said.

171

"You know what?" Judy continued. "Now that I think about it, whenever he told me and Brett some stupid story, you were never there. You'd be at the store or in the shower or something."

And this is how it went, over and over with each new conversation. I only called one or two people, then word spread and my phone started ringing off the hook. I became numb, checking out as I repeated the same information over and over, always with the same responses, same questions, same 'I knew it's.'

"He told me this crazy story about *blah blah blah*, do you think it was true?"

"No, probably not."

"I knew he was full of shit"

"You were right."

"Now that you tell me this, it makes sense. It did seem like he was always the big hero in all his stories."

"Yep."

"You know, there was something about him I didn't trust."

"Why didn't you tell me?"

"You seemed so happy, that I just… I don't know."

"I don't know."

"I don't know."

It was finally my best friend Jill who was able to explain her reasoning for not saying anything to me: "I know you and you've always been a really good judge of character, so I trusted that your instincts were right."

It was true. My instincts had been right, and I talked myself into being wrong because the other volunteers in the Red Cross *did* believe him. My friends and family dismissed their instincts because *I* believed him, and that's how he was able to get away with it. That and a motherfucking Special Forces tattoo.

I'd never been a person who snooped in other people's business. I didn't open the medicine cabinets while at a party. I wouldn't sneak a peek at an open diary. I never rummaged through drawers or closets when I housesat. I've always held personal privacy in the highest regard, with no desire to cross that line. Until that day.

As I was digging through Chris's personal belongings, I came across an old application for a job that he'd filled out while we were still in Los Angeles. On it were numbers listed for personal references. One was his friend Wes, who I'd heard him talking to on the phone once in a while; the other was for Pastor Randy, the pastor who had arranged for Chris to volunteer in Texas. I called them both. I figured since all my friends now knew the truth, his should too.

I first spoke with Wes, who I learned had met Chris in a yearlong Christian rehab program—a program Wes had completed and Chris had not. Wes hadn't heard the specific lies about the military, but he told me, "You know, Jonna, we all thought Chris was a great guy. He was fun to be around and worked really hard. But no matter how much we tried, we could never get through to him that he didn't need to make up these stories. All of us guys would tell him that he would never be free of his addiction until he could be honest."

I talked with Wes for a while. Before getting off the phone he said he would keep trying to call Chris and let me know if he was able to speak with him. I thanked him and called Pastor Randy.

Pastor Randy lived in Terrell, Texas where Chris was still hiding out. He agreed to keep a look out for the truck and ask around if anyone had seen Chris. He also said he would call Chris to try to talk him into bringing the truck to the church, where he could leave the keys so I could pick it up.

While on the phone with Pastor Randy I was simultaneously Googling his name and the church's to see if it was legit. Fool me once, you know. It was a small apostolic church at a truck stop. I had no idea what this meant, and didn't care. I'd never heard of a truck-stop church, but he was a legitimate pastor. I may not have agreed with his religion, but he was a safer choice to have my truck than Chris.

Before hanging up, Pastor Randy asked if it was okay if he said a prayer for me. I didn't have the heart to tell him that, given recent events, God and I were no longer on speaking terms. It seemed easier to just let him do his thing. The prayer went on for some time, but I couldn't focus on the words. Every few moments I heard, "In Jesus' name I pray, Lord... In the name of Jesus, Father, hear my prayer... Jesus, please come to the aid... Jesus... Jesus... Jesus...."

I'd never known much about Jesus in my life, so all I could hope for was that Pastor Randy had a better relationship with him than I was currently having with God. Maybe Jesus would step in on Pastor Randy's behalf and tell God to cut me some slack.

As another day came to an end, my head was spinning. I'd spoken to too many people, had too many opinions and too many voices swirling in my head. I'd been told all of the things I should have done,

174

could have done, and would have done if I were them and not me. I'd been offered a plane ticket back to L.A., a house to live in if I could somehow get to West Virginia, and had been told there was a woman who wanted to move into the house as my roommate if I stayed in Louisiana. I wasn't capable of making any of these decisions.

As it grew dark outside, I got on the computer to start looking for a job. I had to do something while I sat there in what was becoming my holding cell. I was about an hour into my search when I heard the familiar text message ping.

What r u doing? why ru calling people? if you want ur truck back tell everyone to stop bugging me. I've had enough jonna!

He'd had enough? He had had enough? *Seriously?* It wasn't any big secret that Mr. 'I ain't sweatin' this' had some big balls to match his big fat ego, but the gall it took to tell me he'd had had enough! I would have texted back *Are you smokin' crack?* But he actually was, so it was kind of a redundant question.

This message bugged me almost as much as the tattoo. It was the audacity. It was the complete and total lack of fear. Most people have told a lie at some point in their lives. Usually it's done with some guilt or at least a bit of fear at being caught. And when you are caught the normal reaction is to backpedal and wiggle out of it. We've all done it. But you can't backpedal out of a tattoo; that was a one-hundred-percent commitment to a lie. No wiggle room.

And if you can't wiggle out of the lie, if you are absolutely caught with your pants down and the nanny on your face, then you humble yourself. You hang your head, look as close to a scared puppy as you can, and beg forgiveness. This is the acceptable response. Never is it okay for the liar to announce they have had enough.

But the biggest kick to the head in all of this was that as soon as I read his text, my immediate gut reaction was to feel as if I'd done something wrong. Like I was the one in trouble. Me. Not him. *Me.* After all he had done—and was continuing to do—it sickened me that at my core I was still willing place his feelings in a higher position than my own. It only lasted a moment, but that moment spoke volumes.

****

On the surface this drama was seemingly about finding out my boyfriend was a compulsive liar, but for me it went much deeper than that. It went to the very center of the sadness I had carried with me most my life. There wasn't any religion in our home growing up, but somewhere along the line, as a very young child I came to believe in God. I believed that God would protect me, would always love me and look out for me.

In my child's mind God replaced the role my absent father could not fill; I went to Him with everything. Every day I prayed for God to help my mother quit drinking. I kept coming back with the same open heart, just knowing one day he would answer. He never did. And she never stopped.

As I grew into my teenage years my love for God began to fade. I began to believe that God simply didn't like me. I told myself don't ever get too excited about anything, because He will be right there to snatch it away. Always remember, good things don't last. I believed in my heart that God only showed up in my life to cause pain. So I went on without him.

In my mid-thirties, after the death of my mother, I felt alone in the world. It was then that I thought it was time to reconnect and repair my relationship with God. My mother was gone; I was no longer that child praying for her to not be an alcoholic. I thought if I was willing to put in the hard work, then maybe God would be willing to meet me halfway. I could once again be filled with the trust and love I had as a small child. And this was the beginning of the years I would spend on my spiritual path.

It was during this time, about a year before I met Chris that I reconnected with my father after more than twenty-five years. My sister Judy and I had found each other on the Internet and soon began communicating on a daily basis. It was her idea that I fly out to Arkansas to surprise our Dad on his seventieth birthday. I would also get to see my younger brother, Jake, whom I had never met.

It was a quick decision on my part to say yes. It felt right. It felt like it was time. I'd grown spiritually, and had surrendered my life over to the care of God. I was ready to have my father back in my life, to let go of any negativities of the past and move forward into a peaceful future. Yes, it was a lot of touchy-feely bullshit, but it was touchy-feely bullshit that I completely embraced.

I told Jodi about my plans, but she wanted no part of it. She had written our father off years ago and had no intentions of opening a door to the past. I respected her decision but felt differently. In order to open new doors I needed to go back and clean up the past. Within a week I was flying to Arkansas.

My life didn't change dramatically after meeting my father. The skies didn't open up. Everything in my life didn't suddenly fall magically into alignment with my highest purpose. But it was pleasant—weirdly polite and distant—but pleasant. I felt I was moving in the right direction, that my re-found connections with God and with my father would bring peace into my life.

After reuniting with my Dad, I returned to Los Angeles and decided I was ready for love. Adam and I had broken up soon after my mother passed away, so I'd been single for more than six years. It was time. I had the tools I needed and I got to work using them. I meditated on love. I prayed and visualized being surrounded in love and what the perfect man would look like to me. I made a "God-box"; I wrote down all the qualities I was looking for in a partner, then put the list into the box and surrendered it to the will of God.

Two months later I was on my way to Texas with the American Red Cross. After meeting Chris, I told myself it was okay that I had lost my job, because that is what it took in order for love to enter my life. And I thanked God. When things didn't work out in L.A. and we moved to a torn up house in Louisiana, I knew this had to happen in order for us to be together. And I thanked God. When I became pregnant after thinking I was never going to have children, I knew everything had a divine order. And I thanked God.

When I found out that the love of my life was completely based on fiction, that everything I'd been through was for nothing, I stopped thanking God. When I uttered the words, "I hate you," I meant it from the deepest part of me. Sure, I was angry at Chris, but much bigger than that, I felt destroyed by God. In my mind Chris was just the instrument God used to remind me once again that it was His world and I had never been welcome in it.

****

Im at a gas station and see Randy. im so tired and so sorry jonna i'll leave truck and give key to Randy so u can come get it.

I received the text from Chris six days into his run. Of course I didn't believe him, so I called Pastor Randy. When he answered I asked, "Are you at a gas station?"

"How did you know that?"

"Chris texted and says he's there too. Do you see him?" I was twitching with the anticipation that this might actually be coming to an end.

There was a long pause as I assumed Pastor Randy was looking around. "Yep, there he is. He's parked over on the side lot. Big white F150?"

"Yes!" I nearly shouted.

"That's him."

Finally I could breathe. All Pastor Randy had to do was get the keys. Once I knew he had them in his hand and Chris was out of the truck, it was just a matter of arranging a six-hour drive to Texas. The nightmare was over.

"I can't believe it." I exhaled with relief. "Thank you so much, Randy, for doing this. Chris said he'd give you the keys and then—"

"Oh, I'm sorry, Jonna," he said, cutting me off. "I'm not gonna be able to keep those keys for you. My grandmother passed away this morning and I'm heading to Dallas here in a few minutes. I don't know when I'll be back."

My stomach sank; as a reflex action I threw God the finger. "I'm so sorry for your loss," I sighed, feeling completely deflated.

"She's at rest with her Lord and Savior Jesus Christ," he assured me.

"Uh-huh." If Pastor Randy didn't get those keys now, Chris would change his mind and disappear again. *Fuck.*

"Let me go an' talk with Chris. See where his head's at. I'll call you in a minute."

I hung up the phone then looked up to Heaven to the one I blamed. "A dead grandma? Seriously? You're an asshole."

To pass time until I heard back from the pastor, I started slicing large pieces of pork tenderloin to cook for Beaux's dinner. I took the thick slices of raw meat and threw them in a frying pan. As the dog's dinner cooked, I paced the kitchen feeling so close to getting the truck back—and terrified it would fall apart.

When the phone eventually rang, I snatched it off the counter, hoping it was good news.

"Well, I spoke with Chris," Randy said with sadness in his voice. "He has a heavy heart for what's he's done to you and to himself."

I rolled my eyes. *Fuck Chris and fuck his heavy heart.*

Pastor Randy continued, "We had a long talk and I've prayed with him for the Lord to release Chris from the stronghold that this addiction and the lies he's told have on his heart."

I couldn't help but think that had the Good Lord really given a crap about this situation the smart thing to do would have been to let

Grandma live for a few more days so I could get my truck back from the crack-smoking liar who took it.

"Did he give you the keys?" I asked.

"Well now, like I said, I can't take those keys. But I have agreed to give Chris the gas to get the truck back to you."

"Don't give him any money!" I exclaimed as I flipped Beaux's tenderloin before it burned.

"No, I don't intend to do that. But I will fill the tank. He says he can make it back."

"Thank you, Pastor Randy, for everything you've done. I'll never forget it." I meant it too. I may have been angry at God, but I could still recognize the thoughtfulness of a kind man.

"I just let the Good Lord work through me."

I sighed and asked, "Is Chris standing there? Let me talk to him please." I flipped the tenderloin slices on a plate then began cutting them with a carving knife into smaller squares so they would cool faster.

"Yes, here he is. Hold on. May the Lord be with you."

"Thank you."

I heard the phone being passed, then for the first time in nearly a week I heard Chris's voice. "Hey, Babe," he said sounding sad and pathetic. "I miss you and I want to come home. Do you still want me to come back?"

I didn't buy the sorry act for a second, but felt backed into a corner to make a decision. What could I do? Tell him, no don't bring the truck back, just go ahead and keep it. So instead I said "Look, I'll make a deal with you: you get the truck back to me by tonight and I'll help you check into rehab. That's all I can offer you."

"Okay, I'll do that."

"I'm serious. If you come back, you have to go into rehab immediately."

His voice cracked, "I'm sorry, Baby. I never meant to hurt you."

"Do you really think you can get back here on one tank of gas?" I asked.

"All I can do is try. I'll keep it under 60 the whole way, and get as close as I can."

"The truck is reported as stolen. I can't call Jodi and ask her to cancel the report unless I have a guarantee you're really bringing it back."

"Jonna, I said I'm bringing it back, and I will." He actually copped a little attitude, like, how dare I not believe him at his word.

"You need to take pictures of signs saying where you are and text them to me. When I feel okay that you're actually in Louisiana headed this way, I'll call Jodi." I stopped cutting pork and waved the knife at an empty kitchen. "For the last three days you said you'd bring it back then you take off again, so I can't trust you."

"Okay," he sighed." If that's what you want. I need to do right by you for everything I've done."

"You realize you could still get pulled over and arrested, right?"

"If that's what needs to happen, then that's what will happen. But I'll do whatever it takes to get this truck back to you."

It was unbelievable to me, after everything that happened, how he was still able to paint himself as the big hero.

"Okay, well I guess you'd better get on the road. Be careful."

"You know, I really do love you."

"Don't forget to send the pictures," I mumbled in response.

We hung up and I looked down at Beaux's dinner. It was a chopped up shredded mess. Well, he never chewed his food anyway. "Beaux," I called, "come get your dinner."

And then I waited to see what would unfold.

I called Jacqueline and she came over to the house to wait with me. We were both content to sit in camping chairs and chain smoke. I listened as Jaq told me about her problems. She was tired. She and Kevin had two kids together, and they were going through a difficult time in their relationship.

"I just hate living in Abbeville, and Kevin won't move to Lafayette. I'm just going crazy in that tiny little house," she said.

I glanced at my cell phone for the hundredth time. No message. "So what are you going to do?"

"Well, I already rented an apartment in Lafayette. I signed the lease yesterday. Kev just got back today; then he leaves again in a couple of days, so I have to tell him tomorrow."

Kevin's job took him out of town most of the time. He was away more than he was around, and I knew Jacqueline would get lonely. Abbeville was so small that in order to do anything you needed to drive into Lafayette, so she was spending all her time alone driving back and forth.

"You rented a place already and never told him?" I asked in shock.

"I know, I'm bad," she said, "but I keep chickening out. It's not like we would be breaking up. During the week the kids and I will stay at the apartment, and on the weekends we'll come stay with Kev at the house. I mean, he's never home anyway!"

I laughed again, "You don't have to convince me."

Jaq laughed along with me. "Girl, I'm trying to convince myself so I don't chicken out again."

It felt good to be thinking about someone else, even if it was only for a moment. It had been a couple of hours since I had spoken to Chris, and so far there was no message. When my cell phone did beep I nearly jumped out of my skin. It was a picture of a freeway exit sign showing the name of a town. I showed it to Jaq.

"Do you know this place? Is it Louisiana?"

She squinted at the blurry photo. "I'm not sure."

I went to the computer and Googled the name of the town. It was a relief to discover he'd crossed the state line into Texas. My phone rang a moment later.

"Did you get it?" Chris asked.

"Yeah, I did."

184

"It's kind of hard to take pictures while I'm driving," he said, sounding rather happy.

Was he actually having fun on this journey? Where was the sad little puppy that I had spoken to in Texas? Maybe I was reading too much into it. Maybe he was just trying to be polite.

"Just do the best you can," I replied.

"Well, shoot, girl, it's getting dark. They won't show up," he laughed.

He laughed. He was laughing. He'd just been busted making up an entire life that was untrue. Everyone knew he was a liar. He was exposed as a total and complete fraud. How the fuck did he manage to sound happy? Normal people would be mortified. Normal people would be so humiliated they would want to crawl into a hole and die. And there was my answer. Normal people wouldn't have made up the stories in the first place.

"Then I guess you'll need to pull over to get the photos," I refused to lighten my monotone voice. "Two hours outside of Terrell isn't good enough. I need to know you're on your way here." I was determined that at least one of us was going to stay committed to the severity of the situation; clearly it wasn't him.

"Okay, okay." He said. "If that's what you want, then that's what I'll do." He was using his old "wrap his arms around me and pull me close to appease me until I wasn't mad anymore" voice. He stopped short of saying, "What my Baby wants, my Baby gets," but it was the same tone behind the words.

"Well, be careful." And then to put a little fear back into the moment, I threw in an extra, "Don't get pulled over."

He tossed off a dismissive reply. "It's all good, Babe. I ain't sweatin' this."

I actually thought I felt a small aneurism pop in my brain, so I hurried off the phone. I ain't sweatin' this? Seriously? I mean... Seriously? Did he actually just say to me, I ain't sweatin' this? He was driving a stolen vehicle, after coming off a six-day crack binge, back to woman full of rage and he "wasn't sweatin' this"?

"How did he sound?" Jaq asked when I hung up.

"Oh, he seems jim-dandy. He's totally fine, as though nothing has happened," I said, shaking my head in disbelief. "It's like he just went for a little trip and now he's headed home. Totally normal. It's all good."

Jacqueline shrugged, "That's Chris though, isn't it?"

"I don't know. I have no idea who Chris is," I said as I lit yet another cigarette.

"I know what you're saying about that fact that he lied, but his personality is still going to be his personality, and Chris is always going to be that cocky, bigger-than-life guy."

"Yeah, I guess. I don't know what to think." I stood up and leaned against the kitchen counter. "A week ago this guy was the love of my life. Obviously it wasn't perfect, but I had never had a guy who—I don't know—took care of me the way Chris did. Like he's a guy's guy, you know? I never have to carry anything; he always gets the groceries and he always unloads the truck. I like that stuff. I don't want to be all 'I am woman, hear me roar.' I want a man who's a man. For my whole life I watched my mother struggle to do everything on her own; and then she died. Fuck that. I don't want that." Jacqueline was still in

186

the room, but I was no longer speaking directly to her. I was in my own world, talking to myself.

"I want a man in my life, you know? Chris opens the door for me. He mows the lawn, he takes out the trash; and he does almost all the work in the house by himself. I wanted a dog; he got me a dog. He tells me he loves me every single day, ten times a day even. He even likes my ass! No one in my entire life has ever complimented my ass. Ever! When he's out, he calls to see if I need anything. All the time! Like, all the fucking time! And he never looks at other women. He flirts, like, you know, in a funny way, but he always makes sure they know he's with me. I mean, what the hell? He even rescued that puppy that got hit in the road, and then, when it died at the vet's, he went and got it and buried it in the backyard because he didn't want it to just get thrown away. And remember… and remember when the kids flipped the four-wheeler? Chris was the first one to run over and make sure they were okay."

I finally took a deep breath and wrapped up my tangent with a sigh. "All of that stuff is good enough. I just don't get it. I don't understand. He could have said he was in construction. He could have said he was unemployed. Like, what do I care? It's not like I bring much to the table. I liked him for him. Why make up lies and stories? And the tattoo… the motherfucking tattoo. What the hell is that all about?"

I took another deep breath and looked at Jaq. "Sorry. Apparently, I had a few things to get off my chest."

"Girl, don't apologize to me. I don't know what I would do right now if I was you."

I smiled. "Kevin probably doesn't seem so bad right now."

Jaq laughed. "When I first found out about what Chris had done, I was like, Lord, thank you. My babies have a good daddy, and I have a good man in my life."

I nodded. "Yeah, you really do."

"But," Jaq said, "Chris is a good guy too."

I shot her a look that conveyed, are you out of your ever-loving mind?

"I know!" she said with a laugh. "But, I mean… I understand what he did was bad. It was really bad, but it's not like he killed someone. He didn't rob anybody or run them over. He didn't hurt anyone. I don't mean that. He hurt you. I get that, but I mean... yeah, he made up a bunch of stupid stories and he lied, but he didn't do anything to anyone. I don't know what I'm trying to say."

"No, I get it. I know what you're saying."

"I called Kevin when you told me about all the lies, and I asked him what he was going to say to Chris if he ever saw him again. And he said 'nothing.' He said, 'I'm going to treat him like I always did. He hasn't done anything to me.' I guess I kind of feel the same way. I still like Chris. I don't like the Chris that did this to you, but I like the Chris we hung out with."

Jacqueline had to get back to Kevin and the kids, so we said goodnight. I promised to call if I needed anything. I told her I would be fine. I was tired. I was confused, but I was glad that the worst of it was over. But before Jaq left, I took all of the banking information, the checks, and my ATM card, and put them in an envelope. "Hold onto this for me. I'll get it back from you after he's in rehab."

188

Chris sent a picture an hour later and called to say what town he had just passed. I looked it up on the map and felt satisfied that he was definitely headed this way. I didn't have any fight left in me. I was exhausted, so our conversation was short but polite. I asked how he was on gas; he told me he felt like he was going to make it. We agreed that if he was running out of gas that he would park the truck somewhere safe and we would deal with it in the morning, depending on how far away he was. If he had to, he would sleep in the truck.

It was going on about 9 PM Louisiana time, so it was 7 in California. I called Jodi to tell her she could call the police and let them know we had the truck back.

"Hey it's me," I said when she picked up. "Chris is on his way back with the truck. He's been sending me pictures along the way to show he's really coming. He's about two hours out. So he's definitely bringing the truck back."

"Um... okay," she said, implying that she was confused as to why I was telling her this.

"I just wanted you to know we got the truck back, so you can cancel the police report."

"I'm not canceling anything."

Now I was confused. "Why not? He's bringing it back. We know it hasn't been stolen."

"I don't care." I could hear the anger in her voice, "That son of a bitch took the truck without asking, so as far as I'm concerned, he can go to jail. I hope he does get caught. I hope he goes to prison and rots."

I understood she was angry. I was angry too, but I couldn't figure out why she was insisting on making this more difficult. Not for Chris but for me and for herself. If he was pulled over, sure they would arrest him and she would get her wish, but they would also impound the truck and I couldn't get it out. She would be the only one who could get it out. She would have to fly out from Los Angeles to wherever he got arrested and get the truck. It didn't make any sense to me.

"Jodi," I tried to reason with her, "I know I asked you to report the truck as stolen, but that was because I didn't know if he was going to bring it back. I knew he took the truck to Texas. We agreed he would go to Texas. He didn't like, take the truck in the middle of the night. I knew where he went. I just didn't know if he was coming back; that's why I called you. But now he's almost here, so he didn't really steal it. Do you know what I mean?"

"Yeah, I get it. I don't care." I could tell by her voice she had dug her heels in, not because it made sense but because she was pissed off.

I loved my sister very much, but when Jodi decided she was going to throw her weight around and prove how tough she could be, it was nearly impossible to get her to budge. So I gave up trying.

"Okay," I said, "Do whatever you want. I don't really know what to say."

"There's nothing to say. He's a piece of shit and I hope he gets arrested."

"If you're worried that if he knows it's not reported stolen anymore that he'll take off again, then I won't tell him. I'll let him think it's still reported but you and I will know the truth."

No, that's not it. I'm just not canceling the report."

I couldn't stomach this conversation any longer. I'd been in hell for six days. My nerves were shot, my brain was fried, and I was running on empty. I was cried out and exhausted to my core. This was the last thing I needed to deal with.

"Okay, do whatever you want. I'll call you tomorrow."

We hung up and I called Chris. "Hey," I said when he answered, "Jodi won't drop the charges, so if you do run out of gas, just make sure you park the truck somewhere where it won't be that noticeable. If you make it back here, pull it around back behind the house. We're going to have to hide it until she decides to drop the charges."

"Why won't she drop the charges?" he asked.

"Chris, really? I mean, come on, it's obvious: she fucking hates you."

"I don't care if she hates me. I didn't steal anything from her and you know it. You knew I was going to Texas. I didn't steal this fucking truck from anyone."

"I know that now," I explained. "But I didn't know that when you decided to disappear, empty the fucking bank account, and not return my calls. I texted you numerous times and specifically told you to call me, because I didn't want to call Jodi. I didn't want to involve her in this bullshit. But you wouldn't do it, so this is on you. You did this, not me."

"You know what, its fine. I know in my heart I never stole this truck, so your sister can do whatever she wants. It won't touch me," he said with a defiant arrogance.

I sighed for the nine hundredth time and said, "Just be careful and call me when you get closer."

"Oh, it's all good. I got this. That fucking bitch thinks she can put me in jail—"

"Hey," I cut in, "That's my sister. You can't talk about her like that to me. She's pissed off. You're pissed off. Everyone's fucking pissed off. I'm the one who should be pissed off, but now I'm stuck in the middle. Just drop it. All right? I've had enough."

Chris agreed to let it go and we got off the phone. I leaned against the kitchen counter and closed my eyes. The house was totally silent. I wanted the silence to last. I wanted to live in it forever. I wanted to wrap it around me and use it as a buffer between me and the rest of the world.

For days my mind spun out one question after another. Now that Chris was about to walk through the door, looking, sounding, behaving exactly as he left, but returning as a completely different person, I couldn't think of anything I wanted to say. I stayed in the kitchen, not thinking, not doing—just stood there passing time. I was numb.

Two more hours passed. I went to the refrigerator, figuring I should make Beaux's breakfast and try to take my mind off the situation. After taking out a package of thawed chicken breasts, I heated up the frying pan again and tossed them in. Smelling the meat, Beaux came into the kitchen with his nose searching the air. I looked back at him, "You know this isn't going to last forever, right?"

The chicken was nearly done when my phone rang. I picked it up.

"Hey."

"The gas light just came on," he said.

"Shit. Okay. Well, where are you?" I hoped Jaq would have the time the next day to drive me out to wherever he was.

"Hold on, let me see. Well, it looks like there is a gas station up ahead and I see a Blockbuster. I reckon, the best I can tell, I'm about a mile from the house."

Despite myself, I laughed. "Are you serious? I can't believe you made it back here on one tank of gas. You've got to be the luckiest person I have ever met."

"I should be pulling up in the driveway in about five minutes," Chris said with a laugh. I imagined he was feeling proud of himself for pulling one over on me and getting me to laugh.

"Okay, well I'll see—"

Chris cut me off. "What the fuck does this guy want?"

"What guy?"

"Hold on." He was no longer talking to me as I heard him muttering under his breath to an unknown stranger, "What are you gonna do, huh?"

"Are you joking with me? I'm not in the mood, like seriously, not in the mood," I told him.

"Okay, fucker. You want to do this? Let's do this," he said to the anonymous person.

"Do what?" I pressed harder.

"I'm being pulled over," Chris answered me. "Don't act like you didn't know."

Everything went fuzzy. It felt as though the floor had opened up and I was falling into a bottomless pit. My body released a flood of adrenaline and every nerve began to spark and fire. I was being electrocuted from the inside out.

This wasn't happening. This could not be happening. He didn't just get all the way from Texas, to be pulled over a mile from the house. How was this possible? It was supposed to be over. All I could hear was my heart pounding against my chest.

When I was able to find my voice I said, "I have no idea what you're talking about. I don't know anything, I swear."

He didn't respond to me as I heard him speaking with the officer, "Yes sir. How are you tonight?"

I could hear the cop's voice but couldn't make out what he was saying. I could only hear Chris's side of the conversation.

"Just coming back from Texas. Headed home. About a mile up the road on Pine St. Yes sir. Yes sir."

I could only take in quick shallow breaths. "What is he saying?" I whispered.

"Hold on," Chris whispered back. A moment later he added, "He's checking my license."

"Oh my God, I can't believe this is happening."

"I got this. I didn't steal this truck. This old' boy ain't gonna take me in."

A moment later I heard the officer return. This time I heard him ask, "Who's on the phone."

"My girlfriend," Chris answered. "She's at the house waiting for me."

The cop said something I didn't catch. Chris replied, "Yes sir." Then he said to me, "Baby I gotta go."

"Are they arresting you?"

"Don't worry. It's fine. I gotta go." And with that he hung up.

I frantically began pacing the kitchen. Jodi. It had to be Jodi. She must have called the Abbeville Police and told them Chris would be coming through town and to keep an eye out for the truck. It was the only explanation there was. A mile from the house? What were the odds? There was nothing I could do. The thoughts were racing through my mind faster than I could keep up. And then the phone rang.

"Chris?" I said as I answered.

"Hey, they want you to come down here."

"Who are they? Where are you?"

"At the gas station on Highway 14; you can't miss it. There are about five cop cars surrounding the truck with their lights flashing."

I heard a voice and then Chris said, "Hold on."

The phone was passed to someone else and a man's voice came over the line, "Is dis Miss Ivin?"

"Yes."

"Miss Ivin, do the man driving dis truck be ya'll boyfriend and do ya'll live together at 4586 Pine Street?

"Yes."

"Den I be needing' you to come on down here and bring you a picture ID."

"I have to call my friend and try to get a ride."

"Do whatever it is you need."

I heard the phone being passed back to Chris. "You there?" he asked.

"What is going on?"

"Just get down here, Babe." He sounded so calm.

"Alright, I'll call Jaq right now."

I hung up with Chris and dialed Jaq. It was after 11 by this time, but luckily she wasn't sleeping. "I'll be right there," she said. "Just let me get some pants on."

I needed to find some ID. My California driver's license had expired right before leaving L.A. I'd been trying to get a Louisiana license for two months, but there were hang-ups getting paperwork from the California DMV that the Louisiana DMV needed before they would give me a license. So, as it stood, I didn't have a driver's license from either state. But I did have a passport. I quickly grabbed it as I heard Jaq pull up outside.

I ran to get in her car, barely shutting the door, before she took off. "Oh my God, girl what is going on?"

"I have no clue. Look at me; I'm shaking." I held my trembling hands out for her to see.

"You need to calm down before you have a heart attack."

"I am so freaked out right now." I quickly relayed the story of Chris being pulled over, and then continued with, "and I don't know why they want me to come there. Police don't call people when they are about to arrest someone. I've never heard of that happening."

"Do you think Jodi and Jenn called the cops?" she asked.

"Maybe, I don't know. I don't know what to think. There they are." I said pointing to the truck surrounded by cop cars. It looked like a scene from a movie. By the amount of flashing lights going off, you would have thought they had a kidnapper or a serial killer trapped.

I have always been petrified of the police. I get absolutely panic-stricken at the thought of being arrested. There is something about the flashing lights, and being put into a locked back seat that fills me with anxiety. We pulled up just as one of the officers was cuffing Chris and putting him in the back of the squad car. He looked back making eye contact with me. The look in his eyes told me he thought this was my doing.

The officer in charge who had originally pulled Chris over approached me. He was a squat, portly black man who didn't stand much taller than me. "Did ya bring da ID?" he asked.

I handed him my passport. He looked at it, flipped it over, then looked back at me. "Why you give me dis?" he asked.

"It's my passport."

"Where da driver's license at, girl?" he snapped, as if I were playing games and wasting his time.

"I don't have one."

"Den who be driving dis truck from California?"

Technically, we had both driven but I wasn't about to tell the po-po that. I pointed to the cop car where Chris sat. "He did."

I have issues with authority figures, and the more this cop kept being so gruff the harder it was for me not to cry. I was already starting to do the heavy panting and knew it was only a matter of time before the sobs came.

"You be stayin' right der." The cop turned and went back to his car.

I could feel the ugly cries coming on and the more I tried to fight it, the more I shook. I thought he was going to get into the police car and drive away. Chris must have been thinking the same thing, because he turned back and looked at me. It was the first time I had ever seen him look worried. I completely lost it. I began to sob uncontrollably and to hyperventilate. I called out after the cop. "He didn't steal the truck. He was bringing it back."

I was more than aware that Chris was a piece of shit. I knew it in every fiber of my being. But when he looked back at me it still broke my heart. Yes, he had lied. Yes, he had done drugs. I was bitterly angry at him, but I felt deep down that he had never intended to steal the truck the day he left for Texas. Standing there looking at his face, I thought, he's a son of a bitch, but he didn't commit the crime he's sitting in the back of the cop car for.

198

I got my cell phone out and called Jodi. She picked up, her voice like stone. "Yeah," she said.

"Chris was arrested."

"I know. I talked to the cop."

"Can you please just drop the charges?" I cried. "He brought it back. We have it. It's right here."

"No, I'm not dropping the charges."

"Jodi, they're going to take the truck away. Just drop the charges so I can take it home."

"Jonna, whatever happens, happens. Chris did this to himself."

The cop looked over seeing I was on the phone. "Is dat your sister?" he asked.

"Yes." I answered.

He walked toward me with his hand out. "Let me talk to her."

I handed him the phone and he walked away. I couldn't stand up anymore. I bent over trying to catch my breath. Jaq came over to me and put her hand on my back.

Just then a tow truck pulled in and backed up to the truck. They were taking it away. Was it logical to be so distraught over a truck? No, of course not. Any rational person would have just thrown in the towel, admitted defeat, and surrendered to the fact that this was happening. It was a truck. It wasn't a child. It wasn't a loved one. It wasn't a pet. It was a truck. But none of that mattered to me. I was beyond any kind of rational thought.

I started yelling like a crazy person in between my hyperventilating and sobbing, "He didn't steal it! He was bringing it back. It's my fault. I called my sister. He didn't steal it."

A tall lanky cop standing nearby, looked at me like I was a piece of old gum stuck to his shoe. "You're not helping anything. Maybe you should just be quiet."

Jaq chimed in agreeing with him. "Honey, you need to calm down. You're gonna make yourself sick."

The original cop came back with my phone and handed it to me. "I give her da chance, but she don't want to drop no charges."

Before I could say anything, he went back to his patrol car and got back on his own phone. I bent down and put my hands on my knees to try to steady my breathing. It was then that I realized I'd finally snapped. A small part of my brain knew I was completely out of my mind, but it was no match for the bigger crazy part that was running the show.

Chris looked over again, and I just shook my head. There was nothing I could do. After what felt like ages, the cop who was running the show finally hung up the phone and opened the back door to the patrol car. He lifted Chris out, then turned him around to un-cuff him.

The cop motioned for me to join them. I walked over and stood in front of him, as he looked me over with total disdain. "Stop dis crying," he ordered.

I bit down on my lower lip to try and hold it all in, but the harder I tried the more I shook. The officer looked at Chris saying, "You be a lucky man."

200

Chris cocked his head with a chip on his shoulder and stared back at the cop. "Shoot, luck's got nothin' to do with it," he said. "I knew I didn't steal that truck."

"Dis what be happening," the officer turned his attention to me. "You're sister still be refusing to drop da charges, but she say dat ya'll were given permission to drive dis truck from California to Louisiana." Nodding toward Chris he continued, "He be in Louisiana so I can't see how he be stealing somethin' dat he be havin' permission to bring here. Since da owner of da vehicle be sayin' it stolen, I'm gonna impound it as such, but since he don't be stealin' it, he free to go."

Then the cop zeroed in on me. "I could be arresting you right now, for filin' dat false police report. You understand dat? I don't mean no joke. Next time ya'll be fightin' you best be thinkin' twice 'fore you pull a stunt like dis. I tell you now, I get any call for a disturbance comin' from ya'll address, you can bet I be comin' and arresting you. You got dat?"

I was frozen in fear. All I could manage was a nod.

"And I already be tellin' ya to stop dat cryin'."

"Sorry," I squeaked out.

Chris moved behind me and wrapped his arms around my shoulders while placing his face near my neck. I wanted to reach back and rip is face off. It's true, I didn't want Chris to go to jail, but I sure wasn't prepared for him to be painted as the victim while I was being chastised for being a troublemaker.

When the cop turned to open the trunk of his car, I used the opportunity to jerk my shoulder to let Chris know I didn't want him touching me. He ignored the gesture and answered by squeezing me

201

tighter. The cop motioned for us to follow him to the trunk. He pulled out a few forms from a box and handed them to Chris saying, "If you be wanting to file charges against her"—he practically spit the word 'her'—"den call dis number and dey tell you what you need to do."

Chris smiled and turned on the charm by putting his arm over my shoulder and pulling me close. He was putting on a show for the cop, playing the kind and forgiving boyfriend. "No, sir, I'm not gonna to do that. We had a little fight and she got upset, but this little gal right here is a good woman."

I was disgusted. More with myself than anyone else.

"Well hang onto dat number just in case," the cop said, then glanced at me with annoyance before adding, "I hope you be learnin' a lesson."

The truth was when I saw Chris sitting in the back of the cop car, I felt sorry for him. Even after everything that he'd put me through, I still felt this need to protect him and keep his secret. I could have easily told the police that he'd been on a drug binge and that's why I reported the truck stolen, but I didn't. When Chris had looked at me from the back of the police car with his hands cuffed behind his back, I knew he thought I'd set him up, and I felt guilty. I felt guilty. Chris had lied about every aspect of his life, and I felt guilty for a perceived lie that I didn't even tell. Once again, I was willing to put someone's needs ahead of my own, even someone who was clearly showing me he put himself first. Had I been arrested, there's wasn't a doubt in my mind that Chris would easily have waved bye-bye to me as I was driven off to the pokey.

Chris turned to the officer and said, "I'm gonna grab my stuff out of the truck before they take it away."

202

"Yeah, sure," the cop causally responded.

I walked over with Chris to help him get his bags. He opened the door, and I got my first look inside. The stereo had been ripped out. The GPS was gone, along with the Sirius radio. I opened a box that had once held my brand new camera. Chris had bought it for me as a Christmas present and then borrowed it for the trip. I wasn't surprised to find the box empty. Now I knew how he'd managed to stay on his drug run after the account had been frozen.

There was one item that had not been pawned. A few weeks previous, Chris had bought a remote control helicopter. It had cost few hundred dollars; every night he practiced flying it. This he kept. Everything else was pawned for drugs—but this he kept. If I'd had any emotions left, I probably would have been livid.

We put his belongings into Jacqueline's van and she drove us back to the house. The drive was silent. It felt like we had just picked up a friend from the airport, yet no one dared ask, "How was your trip?" I stared out the window, mentally flogging myself. All I'd wanted was to get the truck back; instead the truck was on its way to the impound yard while Chris sat comfortably in the seat behind me. All my thinking and planning only succeeded in helping me to screw this up good.

Jaq dropped us off at the house. Before I followed Chris inside, she whispered, "Are you okay?"

"It's fine," I told her with a shrug.

"I'll call you tomorrow," she assured me before driving off.

I walked in the house and found Chris kneeling on the kitchen floor being covered in kisses by Beaux. Animals and children, forever being used as the great distracters. I lit a cigarette and leaned against the counter watching them. Eventually Chris stood up and lit his own smoke. We stood there, smoking and staring at each other. I had no words. I had a million thoughts and absolutely no words, so I lifted my hands as if to say, "Well?"

"What?" he responded.

"What?" I asked in exaggerated surprise that he could even pretend to not know.

"Jonna, I know there's a lot to say, but I ain't doin' it tonight. It's been a long day, and I ain't talkin' tonight."

As I stood there stunned into silence, Chris walked over to the stove. He looked at the cold chicken breasts lying in the frying pan and started to reach out to touch one. "That's for Beaux," I snapped. "They're his breakfast."

He raised an eyebrow and asked "All four of them?"

"Yes," I said, glaring at him with misguided defiance.

Chris smiled and shook his head. "Okay, I get it. Feed it to the dog if that's what you want to do, Jonna. I'm gonna take a shower."

He started to walk away, but I stopped him, "I need your bank card."

Chris turned around, then took out his wallet and handed me the card. "Whatever I need to do, Babe, to make you feel better, I'm going to do. I'll make this right. That's a promise." Then he reached up and kissed my forehead, before leaving me in the kitchen. My first thought was to look around the house for my spine because, clearly, I had lost it somewhere. Then I cut his bankcard into little pieces and threw it in the trash.

Chris emerged from the bathroom a while later and we managed to avoid each other. He went into the bedroom to change while I took the opportunity to slip into the shower. The hot water felt good. I didn't wash my hair, use soap, shave my legs, or do any of the normal things people do in the shower. I just stood there letting the water pour over me while I stared at the grout between the tiles. I'd never noticed all the little pores before.

When the water ran cold, I got out. I shuffled into the bedroom and quickly changed into a tee shirt and pajama bottoms. Chris was in the kitchen smoking a cigarette when I came into the living room and sat on the bed. Once again we stayed in the awkward silence, until I eventually broke it with, "I'm tired."

I crawled to the far side of the bed and curled up with my back facing Chris. After a while, he put out his cigarette and clicked off the kitchen light. I felt him climb into the bed. My eyes adjusted to the dark and I stared at the wall. I could make out the outline of the living room window as the moonlight seeped in. He stayed on his side. I stayed on mine.

After a while my eyes began to grow heavy. Just as I was drifting off to sleep, I felt Chris move over and spoon tightly against my back. His muscular arm felt heavy as he threw it over my torso to pull me even closer. I thought if he squeezes me hard enough, he could crack my ribs. Chris felt huge and I felt teeny tiny as if my body were going to continue to shrink until it disappeared completely.

A minute or so passed as I lay perfectly still; then I felt his dick growing hard as it pressed against me. I could physically feel it touching me, but at the same time it felt really far away. I had no emotional response to what was happening. It was as if I was an observer, not a participant. Thoughts passed through my mind, then disappeared and floated away. It's so quiet, I noticed, as Chris pulled down my pajama bottoms. My legs were pressed close together as I lay on my side and it took no effort on his part to push my knee up leaving me open to his will. I was a limp rag doll without an ounce of fight. I had no desire to fight. I simply wanted to stay where I was in this calm place.

Chris entered me from behind and I felt the motion of him moving in and out of my body. His weight pressed down on me; I felt as if I had no bones. I was transparent. You've taken everything else, I realized. You might as well have this too. I understood clearly that I'd finally received my childhood superpower: I was invisible.

I heard his breathing far off in the distance growing stronger, while simultaneously feeling the air moving back and forth across my neck and cheek. He was exhaling each time he thrust himself inside me. Thrust, exhale. Thrust, exhale. Thrust, exhale. I focused on the lyrical rhythm of his breaths. It sounded like a single Indian war drum growing faster and faster until he came, collapsing against my back and crushing me under his weight.

I couldn't breathe, but I didn't really care. It actually felt kind of good. The crushing feeling was keeping me connected to my body so that I didn't float away. When Chris's breathing returned to normal, he pulled himself up and I was finally able to inhale deeply. He reached down, took my ankle and placed it back through the legging of my underwear and into my pajama bottoms. He quickly pulled my pajamas back up and then wrapped his arm around my waist and yanked me close to him. I could feel the tension in his arm as he held me tight.

206

"I love you Babe," he whispered.

Slowly I felt his arm relax as he fell asleep. I continued to stare at the dark wall, trying to understand what I'd just allowed to happen. I replayed events of the last five months over and over in my mind, but it all felt so long ago. I could remember crying and screaming. I could remember the rage and the panic. I saw the look of disgust on the officer's face. I could remember it all, but I felt no attachment to the events. The most I could feel was this isn't normal life.

****

In the morning things were different. I was back. I woke up with a new plan and a new attitude. I had some fire back, and I was going to fix this. I was going to get Chris into rehab, but before he left, he would finish this house. All of the mental energy that had been thrown toward getting the truck back was now fixated on the completion of this house.

I got out of bed and got dressed. I tried to wake Chris, but he wouldn't budge. I stood in the kitchen, leaning against the counter, and watched him sleep. Why should he be allowed to sleep? I thought. He needs to feel bad. He needs to be remorseful. The longer he slept the more irritated I became. Fine, if he won't get up and work, I will.

The ceramic tiles in the kitchen needed to be removed before he could lay the new flooring. I decided to help the process along. I found a hammer and began smashing the ceramic tiles. It didn't take long for the bear to rise.

"What the fuck are you doing?" Chris barked as he rolled over and opened his eyes.

"This house needs to get finished now. You're going into rehab, so this needs to get done before you go. You spent the money, you need to finish the job."

I continued to hammer away. Crash. Crack. Smash.

"Are you fucking crazy?" he snapped.

"Yes, I'm crazy. You spend six days locked up in a house alone after finding out your boyfriend is a liar and see how fucking crazy you get."

This got him out of bed. He yanked the covers back and stormed off to the bathroom. After a little while Chris returned dressed in jeans and a T-shirt. Without a word, he took the hammer from me and began smashing the tiles with a vengeance. I didn't know if it was anger that was motivating him or a sense of doing the right thing, but whatever it was, he was working like a machine and that made me happy.

He worked all day, and we didn't speak much. Later that night, I was on the computer looking for a job when I heard a familiar whirling sound to my right. I whipped my head around and saw Chris playing with his helicopter.

"Are you serious right now?" I asked.

"What?"

"You pawned everything in the truck, including my camera, but you kept your helicopter, and now you stand there and play with it? Do you not see where I might find that a little bit irritating? That the sound of you playing with the one thing that you kept for yourself might get under my skin a little bit?"

"Okay, Jonna, I get it," he snapped. "What do you want me to do? You want me to just throw it away?"

I looked him directly in the eyes and answered, "Yes."

"Fine, I'll throw it in the trash if that's what you really want."

"Yes, that is what I want."

We were having a standoff and I wasn't going to budge. Finally Chris walked over to the door, opened it up and threw the helicopter outside. He slammed the door, pulled a cigarette out of his pocket and lit it. "You happy now?" he asked.

"Do I look happy to you?" I shot back. "Do you think any of this makes me happy?"

"Whatever you want, Jonna. Okay? Whatever you want." He walked over and snatched a book off the folding table, then sat in a camping chair pretending to read.

"Yeah," I muttered, "all of this has been about what I want." I continued directing my words over my shoulder as he sat behind me. "I wanted you to lie and I wanted you to do drugs and I wanted you to pawn all our shit because I'm just selfish that way."

"I threw the fucking thing away. What else do you want from me?"

"Nothing. I don't want anything from you."

And this is how our communication continued. We either completely ignored the situation we were in or we had petty fights about everything except the real issue. We were two middle-aged children completely incapable of dealing with the mess we'd co-created.

Over the next few days Chris worked on the house from the time he got up until it grew dark outside and I focused on getting him into rehab. I wasn't having much luck. The places I was calling kept saying he needed to go to detox before he could be admitted, but the detox place would not call me back. I left multiple messages every day, and not a word. At the pace Chris was working and sweating he'd already detoxed on his own.

I wanted Chris out of the house so I could take some time to decide what I was going to do. But before he left, I needed the house completed. I also knew Jodi was pissed off that Chris hadn't been arrested, so I was trying to force the situation to be better for everyone. I became a crazed cheerleader of positivity. I took a picture of every little thing Chris accomplished and texted it to Jodi and Jenn with messages saying things like, *The floors look great!! The walls are finished!!*

When I wasn't trying to convince Jodi and Jenn that everything was hunky-dory, I was sending emails begging for someone to take Chris into rehab. I poured out my story in an emotional email and sent it to every single person I could find in the Lafayette area that was in any way associated with drug recovery. I sent letters to commissioners, drug counselors, anyone serving on a drug committee. I didn't care. If there was a judge who presided over drug court, he got a letter. If a doctor spoke on a panel about addiction, she got a letter. I must have sent twenty emails in a couple of days.

It finally worked; I received a call from the director of a local rehab. After I explained that Chris had not done drugs for four days, he agreed to meet with us and consider skipping the detox. I made an appointment for the following day.

In the meantime I'd spoken with Jaq; who had found out that Jodi did not have to come to Louisiana to get the truck out of impound. Jodi and Jenn did, however, have to hire a lawyer to draw up an official document to give Jacqueline permission to retrieve the vehicle. Jaq called me the day she was going to get the truck. I told her not to bring the truck to the house. We agreed that she would take it to a friend's house and hide it there until Chris went into rehab. I told Chris it was still impounded.

I also knew the check I'd issued to myself when I emptied the bank account would be arriving any day. Every afternoon I checked the mail. When it finally came, I went to see Miss B and Mr. Vic. I gave Mr. Vic the check and asked him to hide it for me until Chris was out of the house.

In the morning, Jaq took Chris and me to the rehab center to speak with the director. He agreed to bump Chris to the top of the waiting list so that as soon as a bed opened he would be the next admitted. I don't know why the director did this when other people were waiting to be admitted, but when it came to Chris, I had learned to stop asking why things worked out for him the way they did. I was just incredibly grateful that it worked out.

Everything was coming together. The house was nearly finished. Chris was on his way to rehab. The truck was out of the impound yard. And I had a check waiting to go into the bank. Things were moving fast, but they were looking up at last. Finally I could begin to breathe again.

And then Jodi called.

I could tell immediately from her tone that she was still fuming.

"So what are you doing?" she asked. I could hear that she was barely able to control her anger.

I went outside to talk so that Chris couldn't hear.

"The house is almost done. Chris is set up at a rehab. We just have to wait a few days for a bed to open up. I'm hoping by the time he goes in, he'll have finished the house. The truck is hiding at Jaq's friends house and—"

She cut me off, "I know all that, but what are you doing?"

"I'm looking for a job and just trying to get everything taken care of."

"I can't believe that… that…" She was so angry she couldn't even find words. "…he is still there."

"I know, but he's working every day and the house is going to be done and then he'll be in rehab. We're just waiting for a bed. A couple days tops."

"He should be in jail."

"Jodi, there was no way that cop was going to arrest him. Once he found out you gave us permission to bring the truck to Louisiana, and Chris was in Louisiana, that was it. His mind was made up."

"Oh so this is all my fault?"

"No, I'm not saying it's your fault, but that's why they took the truck and let Chris go. The truck was considered stolen, but Chris had permission to drive it, so he couldn't have stolen it."

"I want that fucker out of my house."

"I know you do," I said. "He's going to be out in a few days, but in the meantime I want him to keep working."

"So what are you gonna do?"

I felt like we were just going in circles. I understood her frustration. I was frustrated too. I hadn't had a clear thought in weeks. I'd stopped making plans and was simply reacting to what was thrown at me each day. "I don't know what I'm doing," I stressed, my voice getting higher with tension. "I have no idea what I'm going to do. I don't know!"

"Well, this is what I'm doing. I'm flying down there in two weeks. I'm taking the truck and bringing it back here. I want you and that piece of shit out of the house by the time I get there. I don't care if he finishes. I'll finish it myself." I could hear in her voice that if she could have reached through the phone and shaken me by the throat she would have.

I knew my sister well; I knew when you could talk to her and when you couldn't. There was absolutely nothing I could say at that time that would have any effect. I sat down on the little wooden deck in the backyard and looked up, as the sky grew dark with storm clouds. I had come to understand this about Louisiana: one minute it could be bright and sunny, and in the next moment it could be pissing rain on your head.

213

"Do you understand that I want you out?" Jodi asked.

"Yep," I answered.

"You want to fuck up your life, go ahead. I don't care, but I don't want any part of it. Leave the truck parked in the driveway and the keys on the counter and I better not see either one of you."

"Okay."

My sister and I had never in our lives—until that moment—spoken words of hatred to each other. "You're a stupid fucking bitch with stupid written all over your forehead," she said.

I stood up and headed back toward the house as big fat rain drops began to land on my head. This was the final blow that took me out. I'd been on a roller coaster over the last few weeks. I'd felt every emotion a person could feel; at times—numerous times—I even went numb. This was different. I wasn't angry. I wasn't sad. I wasn't checked out. And I certainly wasn't numb. Simply and plainly, I was over it.

"Okay." I said.

"You are. You're a stupid fucking bitch with stupid written all over your forehead."

"Yeah, I caught that the first time. Are you done?"

"Yeah, I'm done. I'm definitely done." And with that she hung up.

I opened the door and found Chris in the kitchen getting a glass of water. He was sweating from installing the hardwood floors all day. He obviously could tell something was up when he looked at my face. "What was Jodi saying," he asked.

"She's coming in two weeks to take the truck back," I said. And she wants me out of the house by the time she gets here."

Chris looked shocked. "What? She just said that to you?"

"Yep."

"You know what? That's fine." Chris was now defiant in his stance, "Let her come. Let her take the truck. I've been in worse than this. This ain't anything. And she's gonna throw you out? Her own sister? Fuck her. You don't need that."

All I could do was listen to him in amazement. As much as I appreciated the heroics of him jumping to my defense, there was one glaring flaw in his argument. He had been the cause of all of this.

Perhaps I should have stopped him from saying anymore about Jodi, but I really didn't feel like it. Stupid fucking bitch was still ringing in my ears and drowning out any thoughts of her redeeming qualities.

The thing that stood out to me, as I'd been berated by my tough talking sister and was now witnessing Chris's verbal retaliation, was that neither of the two bad-asses had yet to pick up the phone to call each other.

Chris continued, "You don't need to worry about anything. I'm gonna take care of this. If your sister thinks this is gonna break me, she ain't seen nothin'. I ain't sweatin' this."

"Well, that's good to know," I replied, as I sank down and sat on the floor.

"I'll have a job by the end of the week, and I'll find us somewhere to live."

"And how are you planning to do all this from rehab?" I asked.

He shot me the look I'd come to know so well. "What? I'm not goin' to rehab and leavin' you here by yourself."

"Chris, you have to go to rehab. That was the deal we made."

"Well, Darlin', things have changed. I'm getting a job."

"You know what? I don't care," I said as I lifted myself off the floor. "You do whatever you want. I'm going to take a nap."

"You're just going to lie down? Right now? In the middle of the living room?" he asked.

"If you can come up with a better idea, I'd love to hear it."

The house was so small—and without furniture—that my taking a nap meant there was nowhere for Chris to go. I suppose he could have taken a camping chair and sat in one of the empty bedrooms, but that was his problem. I didn't care where he went. After about a minute, I heard him go outside. I immediately fell asleep.

It felt as if I had just shut my eyes when I felt Chris lay down beside me. He put his face near my ear and I could hear him whispering, "Babe, wake up."

He shook my shoulder gently and I reluctantly opened my eyes. "How long was I asleep for?" I mumbled.

"About two hours."

I rolled over and looked at him. "Really? It felt like two minutes."

"My Baby was tired," he said and kissed my forehead.

I stretched and smiled at him. "Yeah, I was." For a brief moment I felt refreshed and peaceful; then I remembered everything: the phone call with Jodi, the fact that Chris wasn't my loving, protective, Special Forces boyfriend; and that in two weeks I would be without a vehicle or home.

I sat up abruptly and swung my legs off the bed. Chris sensed the "loving moment" was over and he got up too. "So," he said, "I decided I am going to go into rehab like I promised you I would."

This news didn't surprise me. I figured after he thought about the choices, living on the streets with me, or having a warm bed in rehab for thirty days, he'd pick the second option. I couldn't complain. It's what I had wanted. But after Jodi's announcement, everything had changed. Now I needed him. I couldn't do all this on my own. Where would I go? Where would I sleep? What would happen to Beaux?

The way I was seeing it, he got us into this mess, now I wanted him to fix it. I was in way over my head and just about to tell Chris that I'd changed my mind. He was right and it was better if he skipped rehab and got a job instead. I didn't see that I had many options, so I was prepared to pick the one standing in front of me.

Before I could speak, Chris continued, "I had a long talk with Jacqueline, and she told me that I had to do what you wanted and that meant going to rehab. She also said we could move into their house. Once we're working we'll pay rent. Did you know she got an apartment?"

"Yeah, she told me when you were in Texas. Is Kevin okay with this?"

"Yeah, he's said it was fine. I wasn't going to leave you, but if I know you're okay, then I'll go.

The new information gave me some breathing space. It was still going to be tough to find work without a vehicle. There was nothing in Abbeville, and the nearest city was Lafayette, thirty-five miles away without a single bus that ran between the two. But that was something I would have to worry about later. At this moment I was just incredibly grateful that I would have someplace to go.

"That's really cool of them," I said. "I wonder if Jodi and Jenn are going to be mad at them for doing this."

"Who cares," Chris said with a shrug.

"I care," I replied. "I don't want to cause problems between all them because of me."

"You need to stop thinkin' 'bout other people, and do for yourself. Your sister just threw you out. She don't give a shit about you, so what do you care what she thinks?"

It didn't escape my attention that I was getting advice on how to piece my life back together from the very person who tore it apart. But at this point I had to consider that maybe he was right. Maybe it was time I became a little more like him and lot less like me. The way I saw it, Chris kept gaining ground, and I kept losing it.

Later that day, the rehab center called and they had a bed for Chris. He was to check in at 8 AM in two days' time.

****

When the morning arrived for Chris to check into rehab, we woke up early and he packed a bag. Once we got there he filled out the required paperwork, we hugged, and he was gone. As I left, I wondered if this would be the last time I would ever see him.

I had two plans brewing. The first one required that I find a job immediately. The sooner I got my first paycheck, the sooner I could buy Chris a bus ticket back to Texas and drop it off at the rehab center. I figured as long as he had a way back home it would keep him from showing up on my doorstep.

The fallback plan would kick in if I wasn't able to find work. Then I would need Chris to get a job to help pay the bills as soon as he got out of rehab.

I filled out online applications for every place I could find. I emailed resumes and applied to every temp agency in the area. In the meantime I attended family therapy at the rehab center just in case I needed Chris to stick around.

Family therapy consisted of a class for friends and family where we learned how to deal with an addict and their behavior. After class we would meet up with our "addict" and have group therapy. It was during this time I started to think Chris wasn't a drug addict at all. It felt as if he was playing the part of a recovering addict.

While we sat across from each other in the center of the healing circle, Chris dramatically pulled up the sleeve of his T-shirt to flash his Special Forces tattoo to the rest of the room. With crocodile tears flowing he sobbed, "I've come clean to everyone here. They know all about the lies. I never thought I was good enough to just be Chris, but now I'm finally free to be the real me."

Chris glanced to his counselor, Adrian, who nodded in approval of the deep progress Chris made with this latest breakthrough. The other addicts gazed at Chris with glassy-eyed admiration for his bravery in admitting the truth of his deceptions. Once again he was being praised for his bravery.

I knew in my heart of hearts that Chris didn't get that tattoo to cover an addiction to drugs. He got that tattoo to support a false life. A life he used to manipulate people and situations for his own benefit. As easily as Chris had fooled everyone in the Red Cross, he'd done the same with the counselors and patients in rehab. The "real me" had to fight back the urge to smack the "real him" upside the head.

Adrian then instructed me to express my feelings. I looked at Chris and burst into tears. Not just regular tears but the ugly, snotty, gasping for air, deep sobs that came from some deep place that had nothing to do with the man sitting across from me. I managed to garble out something about being afraid to trust; thankfully, Adrian moved on to the next family in crisis.

The following week, during the question and answer portion of family class, I raised my hand and asked, "Do you treat compulsive liars here?"

The instructor gave me a knowing, gentle smile and answered with a canned response. "An addict is going to do whatever it takes to get the drugs and alcohol he or she needs. A lot of time that means lying to friends and loved ones. At some point in their recovery they'll need to make amends for that."

"Yeah, that's not what I mean. I'm talking about someone who tells lies just to tell lies."

He paused to think about his answer. "Well there are a lot of reasons an addict will lie, to hide their addiction, out of shame or embarrassment—"

"No, you don't understand," I said, cutting him off. "I'm talking about someone who just makes up stories and lies for no reason. I understand the lies like, borrowing money to get the car fixed but really spending it on drugs. I get that. I'm talking about making up an entire life that doesn't exist and has nothing to do with getting drugs."

He smiled and replied, "Well you know the old joke. How do you know when an addict is lying? When their lips are moving." He quickly turned away and picked someone else, "Yes, you had a question?"

This place wasn't going to be any help. Chris became the poster child of perfect recovery. He answered every question with the right answer. He followed all the rules to the letter. He completed his assignments and opened up with complete "honesty" about his past. In their eyes he was a success story.

While Chris stayed in rehab talking about his "feelings," I spent the remaining time packing up our belongings and moving to Kevin and Jaq's. Without any immediate job prospects, I gave up on the first plan to send Chris back to Texas and committed to the second. I needed to get out of this financial black hole. To do that I needed Chris's help, so I continued to drive into Lafayette once a week to attend fake recovery sessions.

At the end of the twenty-eight days it was time for Chris to come home. Jaq and the kids had moved out and Kevin was working out of town, so we had the place to ourselves. Chris walked in and tossed his duffle bag on the floor. He looked around. I could tell by the look on his face he wasn't too thrilled with our new living arrangements.

The house was tiny—teeny, teeny, tiny. It had four small rooms that each connected to form a small square. That was it. Two bedrooms and one bathroom. Square. Our bedroom barely fit a double bed and a dresser. Added to that all of the boxes I had brought over from the old house and it felt like we were living in a storage unit. I was just grateful to have a roof over my head. I thought perhaps in rehab Chris would have learned some gratitude. Apparently I was wrong.

"We have to get our own place. This ain't gonna work," he said as he looked into each of the rooms.

I sat on the couch looking up at him. "If you have some other great idea, I'd love to hear it."

"I thought you said Jaq moved out."

"She did," I answered.

"Then why is there so much shit still here?"

"She took some of the kids clothes and toys, but left a lot of it so they have stuff here on the weekends."

Chris looked at me with a huge question mark on his face. "Whatta ya mean the weekends?"

"Jaq and the kids will be here on the weekends, "I explained, though I didn't think he was in a position to be asking questions. "During the week they will be in Lafayette and on Friday nights they'll come here and stay with Kevin."

Chris looked like his head was going to pop off as he took in more information about the reality of our situation. "You're tellin' me that we're supposed to stay here with Kevin, Jacqueline, and two kids. In this little house?"

"Three kids," I answered smugly. I was starting to enjoy watching his crash into reality.

"Three kids?"

"Ashley," I reminded Chris of Kevin's daughter from a previous relationship. "He has her every other weekend."

Chris shook his head. "Fuck this."

I narrowed my eyes and glared at him. "If you don't like it, you can go right ahead and fix it, cause I'm fucking tired of trying to figure it all out."

Chris reached down and took my hands, then pulled me up into tight hug. "You don't need to worry. I'm back now. I promise you Jonna, it's all gonna be good. You don't worry about nothin'. You let me do that."

"You never worry about anything," I mumbled.

"Because I always know everything is going to be okay."

"But how do you know that?" I asked, genuinely interested in how a person could live life—especially the life Chris lived—and not be constantly worried about the future.

"Because, Little Mama, I know God is always watching out for me."

I didn't know whether to laugh, cry, or throw-up at that comment, but I had to agree it was true. From what I had seen, God completely looked out for him. With every event that had unfolded, Chris had come out on the winning end. He had come to Los Angeles with nothing but stories. He left with a new truck, a girlfriend who adored him, a place to live, and a job that paid really well. When the cop took the truck away, it was me he wanted to arrest, not Chris. And while Kevin, Jaq, and I worked our asses of to finish the house, Chris relaxed in rehab. Yes, from where I stood, God really loved him.

Chris reached up and rubbed my shoulders. "You just have to trust me that I'm going to make everything right, Jonna."

****

Three days after coming home Chris had a job working with a cabinetmaker. Three days. Fresh out of rehab. He made one phone call, went on one interview, and started the next day. Of course I was thrilled he landed a job. It's what I wanted and what we needed desperately. But still, three days? One phone call was all the effort he'd put into it and God instantly rewarded him.

When Chris received his first paycheck, I deposited it in the bank and immediately got on the computer to send all of it to Jodi and Jenn for the truck payment.

"Don't do that!" Chris demanded as I was logging onto the account.

"The truck payment is due. I have to pay it."

224

"Just call your sister and tell her part of it is gonna be late. We need to take care of ourselves first."

"I have an idea: why don't you call Jodi and tell her that," I snapped back.

"Fuck her. I ain't talkin to her," he said as he threw one hand in the air and left the room.

"Yeah, that's what I thought," I mumbled to myself as I hit Send.

The following Friday, when his next check came in, I did the same thing. Only this time I gave all the money to Jacqueline for rent.

"Stop giving all our money away!" Chris protested as he stood in the cramped kitchen. He snatched a pack of cigarettes off the counter and headed outside to the backyard.

I followed and sat on the concrete stairs leading to the back door. Chris was too angry to sit, choosing instead to pace in front of me.

"Can I have the lighter?" I asked.

Chris leaned down and lit my cigarette, then quickly put the lighter in his pocket. Perhaps he was afraid I would give that away too.

"Jaq and Kev could have waited for their money," he said. "I bust my ass all week and you just give it all away."

And then he began to imitate what I could only guess was supposed to be my voice, while simultaneously miming a prancing person handing out invisible things. The voice was high pitched and squeaky, and sounded nothing like me. "Oh, here you go, have some money. I don't care; just take it all. Take it. Take it."

The voice was really pissing me off. It made me sound like an airhead. I wasn't squeaky and girly like that. If anything, my voice was low for a woman, and for sure I wasn't prancy. I'd never pranced in my life. Never, not one time.

I shot him a dirty look; thankfully, he dropped the stupid voice. "I'm sick and tired of livin' like this," he said.

I could feel the anger rushing to my face. "Really? You're sick and tired? You realize right, that I was in that empty house for nearly six weeks? By myself. No television. No radio. Nothing. Me and Beaux in an empty house for six weeks. You get out of rehab and move straight here. Actually you didn't even have to move. I moved all your shit for you. You have food in the fridge, a television, a computer, a stereo, a ride back and forth to work every day, and you're sick and tired of living like this. You? You're sick and tired?" I stubbed out my cigarette and stood up, "You don't know the first thing about it."

I flung opened the door, then turned around to look back at Chris. Circling my face with an index finger, I added, "This is what someone looks like when they are really, truly, sick and fucking tired."

As I entered the house, I called back over my shoulder, "You're not even close."

The weeks slid into months. Although Chris was employed, it brought in just enough to scrap by. I was so happy when I finally landed an interview. Chris's boss at the cabinet shop knew a contractor that needed someone to help in the office. I spoke with him briefly on the phone. All I knew was that his name was Dean and I was supposed to meet him at his shop for an interview the following day.

I arrived a few minutes early. He arrived forty-five minutes late, roaring up to the front of the shop in a huge truck that was lifted to make it even bigger. His truck made mine look like a Tonka toy. I knew this must be Dean, because the guys in the shop—who moments before had been hanging out and talking—suddenly became really busy. I guessed him to be in his mid-thirties, a good-looking guy with dark hair and a large frame.

He jumped out of the truck, leaving it running, while speaking loudly into his cell phone. He paced up and down the cluttered driveway, stopping now and again to pick up random objects, pieces of wood, or tools, which he would then look at and toss to the side. I could hear his voice clearly, but I couldn't make out any words. I wondered if maybe he spoke another language. In this part of the county it was probably French.

He seemed really rushed. I didn't want to interrupt his call, so I just stood there watching him. When he got out of his truck he didn't close the driver's door; I could hear the music blasting from inside. He came around and opened the front passenger door while still on the phone. He reached inside and took out a couple of plastic shopping bags, then walked into the shop and tossed them on a workbench. He left the passenger door open as well.

I watched as he reached into one of the bags and pulled out a box of drill bits. I only knew this from watching Chris hang drywall. He continued to talk on the phone as he wandered around the shop looking for something. He shouted something at one of the other guys, and then that guy also started roaming around the shop looking for something. I assumed he finally found it when he came back to the table with a drill.

227

He must have gotten the wrong size bits because he kept trying to put one into the drill, then he'd toss it aside and grab another. Eventually, he gave up, taking his phone call back outside. As he passed by he gave no indication that he saw me standing in his driveway.

It was fascinating to watch this guy as he paced around the driveway, and then back into the shop, and then returned to his truck. He opened one of the back doors, and I wondered what he was going to bring out next. But apparently he changed his mind, and walked away. The door was left wide open too. By the time he hung up the phone, I had watched him find a hammer, use it to pull a few nails out of a random piece of wood that he ended up throwing in a big dumpster, pick up some paint cans, move them from one side of the shop to the other, and spend a moment sanding an unfinished table.

One thing I was absolutely certain of: he had no memory that we had an appointment, so I either needed to leave or introduce myself. If only he would stay in one place long enough. He went to the driver's side of his truck and I was worried he was going to hop in and drive away. When he grabbed a cigarette, I made my move. "Hi, Dean. I'm Jonna. We spoke yesterday about the office manager position."

There was barely a flicker of recognition in his eyes, so I shoved my resume at him, giving him no choice but to take it. "Oh yeah, Man," he replied, followed by something unintelligible

The day before, when we made the appointment, I thought we had a bad cell connection; earlier I had thought it was a language problem. Now I realized he just spoke exceptionally fast with a peculiar mix of mumbled gibberish. As he continued speaking I was lucky if I caught a third of what he was saying. Also, he kept calling me "man."

"Yeah, man, so (something something). What I need is (something). I had this other chick (something something something). You know what I'm sayin', man?"

I nodded without a clue as to what he was saying or what I was agreeing to, but it was a job and I needed it.

All of a sudden he turned and walked back into the shop heading up a flight of stairs. I didn't think we had finished our conversation, but I wasn't entirely sure, so I followed after him. Once upstairs, Dean entered an office where a dour-looking, heavy-set woman sat behind a desk.

"Debbie!" he barked, "(Something something!)"

"It's right there!" she drawled, pointing at a bookshelf.

He quickly snatched a book off the shelf and handed it to me. "You know QuickBooks?" he asked.

"I did have a job back in L.A. where I—"

"Yeah, man, this is (something something) QuickBooks. I need someone to (something) contractor."

"I worked on regular QuickBooks, so I'm sure I could—" I almost got my full sentence out.

"Yeah, yeah, man, that's (something something). Here, take this home." He shoved the guide QuickBooks for Contractors into my hand and walked out.

I glanced at Debbie for help. She clearly wasn't about to give me any indication of what to do so I quickly followed him as he raced out of the office, back down the stairs, and out to the driveway. He walked as fast as he spoke. Saying to me over his shoulder to me, "Read that book and call me (something) cell phone."

He abruptly stopped at his truck and turned around to face me. "I gotta go, man," he pleaded. He looked like an overgrown child begging his mother to leave him alone so he could go play.

I didn't know how to respond so I responded as any mother would, "Okay, go, go."

He turned away from me and yelled something incoherent to a young guy standing nearby. The guy seemed to understand Dean better than I did and quickly started loading stacks of wood into the back of his truck.

Dean turned his attention to me and handed back my résumé. "So yeah, fax this to Debbie."

I took it but was confused. "You want me to fax it to the lady in the office?"

"Yeah, man!" he said, implying I was the village idiot.

"Maybe I could just go upstairs and hand it to her since I'm already here?"

"Yeah, man, yeah. Do whatever you want. I gotta go," he begged."

It was by far the shortest and strangest interview I'd ever had. He didn't ask me a single question or even glance at my résumé. "Well, it was nice meeting you," I said. But his attention was already focused on the young guy stacking wood.

"No! No! (something something) What the fuck, man?" he shouted, pointing to a different stack of wood. Apparently I wasn't the only one who had trouble understanding him.

Over the next week and a half, I called and left Dean numerous messages that went unreturned. I couldn't understand why he had given me a brand new, thirty-dollar book if he didn't intend to call me again. I thought about just throwing it in the trash, but thought better of it; just because he was a jerk, didn't mean I had to be one too. The book didn't belong to me, so I needed to return it.

I left one last message, not even trying to hide my irritation. "Hey, (asshole was implied with my tone), this is Jonna. The one you gave the book to. Remember? You told me to call you and I left quite a few messages, but maybe you hired someone else. Anyway, I still have your book and I'm assuming you want it back, so I'll come to your office tomorrow and drop it off."

I knew I sounded like a pissed-off girlfriend making arrangements to return belongings after a breakup, but I didn't care. Within five minutes he called back and asked if I could start the next morning. What was it with these men who could only respond to a woman after she was pushed to the point of being pissed off? Of course, I said yes.

I tried to avoid it but it was only a matter of time before Chris and Dean met. It was like a hurricane being introduced to a tornado; I wanted no part of it. Dean wanted to start building his own cabinets in the shop and needed someone to run it. Chris told Dean that he had run a cabinet shop in Mississippi. I seriously doubted if this was even true, but Dean hired Chris at twice the pay I was getting. Once again Chris and I were joined at the hip.

As the lazy, humid months of summer rolled past life fell into a regular routine. It was too exhausting to stay actively angry at Chris. The resentment would never go away, but I was able to fake it enough to function on a day-to-day basis. We talked about work. We cooked dinner together. Eventually we were able to have fun and laugh again.

But still, I never forgot in the back of my mind that my plan was to leave him. I would never trust him. Some little stuff around the house had disappeared, and some tools at the shop were missing. I suspected it was Chris, but I could never prove it. If he was taking stuff, I couldn't for the life of me figure out where he was hiding it. I would look everywhere when he wasn't around and never found a thing. On top of it, Dean was so scattered, and there were so many different guys coming and going all day long, it could have been anyone. But I remembered all the things in the truck; I didn't put it past Chris to take things that didn't belong to him.

At least now with both of us working I was starting to save money. The more money I could save, the closer I was to getting away. One afternoon while I was at work, my sister Judy called from Arkansas. She told me that there was a mobile home right next to hers that was for sale. It was only $1,000; before she bought it she wanted to see if I wanted it. It was the perfect answer I had been looking for. Now when I left Chris I'd have a place to go.

I wanted to be near my family. Although we hadn't known each other long, I still needed that connection. Judy had told me a few months earlier that our father had been diagnosed with stomach cancer and his health was in rapid decline. I thought going to Arkansas and getting my head back on straight while reconnecting with my father was a good idea.

Chris still didn't have a bankcard, so he didn't have access to the account. I deposited our paychecks and gave him cash to spend for the week, but he still knew what we made and what we spent, so he had a rough idea of what was available. I couldn't hide taking $1,000 out of the account, plus there was also the monthly lot rental of $400. Ideally, it would have been nice to buy the trailer and not mention it, but I had to tell him.

I convinced Chris the trailer would be a good vacation place for us to have. The trailer was located in a town called Prairie Creek situated in the Ozark Mountains near Beaver Lake. I had been there on my first visit to see my father and I knew that the surrounding area was absolutely gorgeous. Chris loved anything to do with the outdoors—caving, fishing, hiking—so it wasn't a hard sell. He had no idea I never intended for him to see it. I quickly sent Judy the money and she paid for it.

The first step was taken. Now I just had to save a little more money so I had a cushion when I got there. The trailer, the deposit, and the first month's rent on the lot had depleted most of the savings, but I wasn't worried. In a couple of months we'd have it replenished and I would be gone. Or so I thought.

One evening Jaq came over to the house to pick up something. We were standing outside smoking when I confided in her how I was feeling.

"I'm so ready to grab my stuff, get in the truck, and take off."

Jacqueline looked me in the eyes and replied, "Don't you dare leave Chris here. You can stay as long as you want, but he can't stay here without you."

She was right. Of course she was right. I couldn't dump my problem on them. Sure, they liked Chris well enough to hang out with once in a while, but no one trusted him, especially now that things were missing. If I took off in the truck and left him there, what would they do with him? Why should this become their problem? I wasn't sure what to do, but it was okay, because I knew I still had time to come up with an alternative plan. Once again I was wrong.

It had not taken long working for Dean to figure out that this guy was flying high on some serious narcotics. I'd never seen anything like it in my life. The interview had been so quick, I figured he was just busy and full of himself, and had no regard for other people's time. I'd had bosses like that before. It was no big deal. But it became very clear very fast that this was a whole other level of chaos.

I told myself it was none of my business. All I needed to do was make money and stick to my plan. But when my job description started to include regular trips to the pharmacy and bailing Dean out of jail after arrests for possession, I knew things were rapidly disintegrating. I began to look into the finances of the business. Anyone with basic math skills could have figured out that way more money was going out than was coming in. The business, just like its owner, was about to implode.

What I miscalculated was how fast it would unravel. Soon after I bought the trailer, everything fell apart. Dean's checks were bouncing all over town and angry people were showing up wanting money. Dean would hire his random drug buddies to work for him. They would hang out in the shop after hours getting high and doing God-only-knows-what, then show up on Friday expecting to be paid. Dean became so drug crazed and paranoid that he began screwing the doors closed at night. It was complete and total chaos. When it ultimately went belly up, Chris and I were out of work.

It didn't take much to decide to pack up our things and move to the trailer that we were already paying for anyway. I had dreamed of taking this trip alone, but once again God had stepped in to look after his boy. I told myself things would be better in Arkansas. I told myself I'd be surrounded by family and that would help keep Chris in check. I guess I was getting as good at lying as he was.

Driving I-5 North

Somewhere in Oregon

I think about her. I can't help but think about her because I feel like I'm becoming like her: never able to stay in one place. As I maneuver the truck up the winding highway, through the beautiful lush mountains of Western Oregon, I can't help but see I am my mother's daughter.

I was eighteen—maybe nineteen—when Mom told me about the event that I think had the biggest impact in making her who she was. I believe it's the reason she was constantly piling us in the car and moving us to some new place, up and down the state of California. I believe it's the reason she married six times. And I believe it was why she was always restless and seeking change.

Mom and I were sitting in the living room in our little two-bedroom apartment in the Hollywood Hills. We were talking about Nana and Grandpa—just a casual, nothing-important conversation. They had moved to Lincoln, Oregon from Sacramento a number of years before; still, every time Nana called she would say "Hi, Honey. This is Nana from Oregon."

It cracked us up. We couldn't figure out if she thought we were going to confuse her with some other Nana or if we'd suddenly forgotten that she'd moved to Oregon. We'd laugh every time she said it.

Mom and I were sitting on the couch chatting one day, when she casually mentioned, "Well, you know Nana and Grandpa aren't your real grandparents."

"What?"

"Nana and Grandpa are not my biological parents. Grandpa was my real mother's brother and Nana was is his wife.

"What?"

"Grandpa was my uncle. Nana and Grandpa adopted your Uncle Mike, myself, and your Aunt Bobby after the accident," she threw this out there as if it had been common knowledge all along.

"What?"

Mom looked at me with the look she gave when she thought I was being overly dramatic. "Stop saying, what," she told me, indicating that if I wanted to hear the rest of the story I needed to be quiet and listen.

My mom rarely, if ever, expressed her feelings or private thoughts unless she was completely wasted, so I didn't want to blow this opportunity to learn something—anything—about her past. I nodded to encourage her to keep going.

"Nana and Grandpa adopted us kids after the accident. Your real grandfather, my father, drove our car off a cliff, killing my mother and your Uncle Patrick—"

"I had another uncle?" I interrupted.

"Yes. Well, at the time he was just a child, but had he lived he would have become your uncle. That's who your Uncle Mike named your cousin Patrick after. Anyway, there was also another man in the car, but I'm not sure who he was. Maybe a friend of the family, or just some guy they knew from the bar, but he died too.

I was only six or seven when it happened. You're Uncle Mike was just an infant. Mama was holding him in the front seat; since she was so obese her body protected him from the impact. Everyone sitting on the outside edges of the car died."

"So wait, what happened to your dad? Did he die too?" I asked, trying to wrap my head around this family saga.

"No, he jumped out. That's why the car went off the cliff: because no one was driving it."

"Are you saying your dad, my real grandfather, did that to all of you on purpose? He wanted the car to go off the cliff?"

She nodded. "We stayed in the orphanage for three months before Nana and Grandpa adopted us. I remember waking up every night screaming with nightmares. That's all I remember from that place: waking up screaming."

I searched her face for any sign of the pain this must have caused her, but there was no indication. My mother was not a heartless person and I knew that her lack of expression was not in any way a reflection on how she felt. It was simply the result of having spent a lifetime mastering the art of masking her feelings.

"So what happened to your dad?"

238

"Well, this was in the fifties, so at that time no one told us kids anything. Back then, children were meant to be seen and not heard, so we didn't know anything."

Mom lit a cigarette, and took a long drink from her Budweiser before continuing. "When I became an adult, Nana finally told me that there had been an investigation; the police had discovered footprints around the car and then leading away. Also, my mother's wedding ring had been taken off her hand. Before they could arrest him he was gone. Nana and grandpa thought he married another woman and went to Alaska. Back in those days people could disappear if they wanted to. Anyway, that's the whole story."

But there was more to the story Mom chose to leave out. My Aunt Kathy, Uncle Mike's wife, would fill in the missing piece for me after Mom passed away. It was this piece that would give me the greatest insight into understanding my mother. Unfortunately, I learned too late.

Aunt Kathy and I were sitting at the dining room table in the Pasadena house I shared with Adam. It was a few months after Mom passed away and Kathy was in Los Angeles visiting. We were looking at some of Mom's rings, when Kathy said, "You know your mother never got over your Uncle Patrick dying in that accident. She always blamed herself."

"But she was just a kid," I said, putting one of Mom's big garnet rings on my finger.

"She probably never told you."

"She told me about the crash and that he died."

Kathy sighed and began to explain, "Your Mom and Patrick were really close as children. They were only a year apart, and apparently they were inseparable. They did everything together. Mike was just a baby and your Aunt Bobby was older and doing her own thing, so Patrick and your Mom had each other. After the accident, your Mom woke up on the floorboards of the back seat, lying on top of Patrick; he was already dead. She grew up believing it was her fault—that she had killed him."

Kathy continued with her story, "Sometimes when your Mom and I and your Uncle Mike would all go out to the bars—and you know your Mom, she would get really drunk—there were times where she would go to this really dark place. She would start crying and tell me, 'You know, I killed my brother.' I would try to tell her it wasn't her fault, but when she got to that point there was no getting in." Aunt Kathy had tears in her eyes when she added, "It was heartbreaking."

Now, nine years after my mother's passing, as I continue driving north on I-5, I wonder if I have just picked up the path where she left off. Searching, always searching for something or someone to fill that empty space. I understand now the reasons why my mother ran. Why she ran from house to house, town to town. Why she ran from one marriage to the next, and from one drink to another. But no matter how fast or how far she ran, she could never get out of her own skin.

And neither can I.

Prairie Creek, Arkansas

My sister Judy had said the mobile needed work; she didn't lie. It was a broken down, ugly, piece of crap. And I loved it. I loved the minimalism of it. I loved the smallness of it. There was no excess space that needed to be filled. Everything needed was there and anything that wasn't needed wouldn't fit anyway.

I started to fantasize that maybe Chris would decide to leave me. Maybe he would meet another woman who lived in a big house and had money and lots of things. Chris liked things. He liked spending money; if he couldn't buy what he wanted, apparently he was willing to steal it. I began to hope that maybe—just maybe—he would grow bored of me. Bored of my desire to live only with what was needed. My need for simplicity and his need to be larger than life could not co-exist in this shabby little trailer.

Before unpacking the truck we walked down to see my dad. He lived with my stepmother in a mobile home three doors down. When he saw me he put a smile on his face and gave me a big hug, but I could see he was sick. Really sick. I didn't think he was long for this world.

For my entire childhood all I ever wanted was to be rescued by a big, strong man. I wanted a father, a protector. I wanted to feel safe and I wanted to be told what to do when I was confused and overwhelmed by this thing called life. I wanted him to know what was best for me when I didn't know for myself. Now I finally had him, but he wasn't strong and powerful. He was old and tired and dying.

The words echoed in my mind: Get a steak, you need a steak. How easy it had been for Chris. I was so ready and willing to hand my life over, just waiting for that hero to come along and make it all better. I might as well have worn a sign around my neck that read: "Will Love for Crumbs."

We settled in quickly and it didn't take long for Chris and me to find jobs. He found work as a tree-trimmer and I began work as a bartender at a local place called Tony C's. Even though I had never bartended in my life, I was hired. My sister Judy knew the owners Tony and Colleen; on her recommendation they were willing to take a chance on me. The idea of pouring drinks to regulars in a sleepy little bar appealed to me. I'd had enough excitement in the last year and welcomed the chance to hide away in the Ozark Mountains.

On my first day behind the bar, a tall, lanky guy in his mid-thirties slid onto a barstool. I could tell by his expression that I was a surprise. Things didn't change much around Prairie Creek and I wasn't who he'd expected to see. I immediately noticed his bright blue eyes.

"Well, hello," he said. "Who do we have here?" As he smiled, dimples appeared on both sides of his cheeks. I instantly liked him. There was an ease to his masculinity that was in total contrast to the intensity that Chris always exhibited.

I smiled in return. "Jonna," I answered as I set a bar napkin in front of him.

"I'm Greg. When did you start working here?"

"Today's my first day. Can I get you something?"

Like the rest of the regulars I helped that afternoon, Greg was obviously not used to having to say what he wanted, "Oh yeah, a Bud Light." I made a mental note that if I were going to win any friends I needed to start memorizing what people drank and have it ready before they sat down.

I set the beer in front of him and we held eye contact for a moment longer than necessary while we continued to smile at each other. There was an immediate physical attraction that was palpable, but underneath that, something else was happening. I was going to know him for a long time—or perhaps somehow, in that strange Universal way, I already did.

A man, whose name I couldn't remember but who was drinking Kessler and Coke, called out from the other side of the bar, "Hey Greg, don't bother. She has a boyfriend. I already asked."

"Ah, well, that's too bad," Greg answered, still looking at me. Then he broke into a wide grin and shrugged his shoulders. "Doesn't mean I can't still look." He stretched up to look over the bar to get a better view, "And from where I'm sittin' it looks pretty good."

It didn't take long to grow comfortable at the bar. Life slowed to a crawl and I was content to forget about my old life back in Los Angeles. I'd left behind the chaos of Louisiana and hoped that Chris would not drag it along with us.

It always made me smile when Greg came into the bar. I especially liked it when the bar was nearly empty and I could come around to the other side and sit on a stool beside him. Just being there, shooting the shit about nothing, I started to feel like a normal person again. I was able to forget about Chris and see again what it would be like to just be a regular girl talking to a regular guy. In those moments I felt free.

One day as we sat together Greg asked me, "So what's your old man like?"

I shrugged. "I don't know really. I mean we hadn't seen each other in like twenty-five years, so now—"

"No, not your dad, dumbass," Greg teased me. "Your boyfriend, what's he like? It's Chris right?"

"Yeah, Chris." I thought about what my answer should be. What was Chris like? Finally I settled on a generic answer, saying, "He's cool. You know, he likes fishing and outdoorsy stuff. You should get to know him. You'd probably have a lot in common."

"Nah," Greg said, shaking his head. "I don't want to get to know him."

"Why not? You guys could probably be good friends." The truth was I hoped Chris and I could make a circle of friends. The more people we were surrounded by, the more everyone would know us, and the harder it would be for Chris to tell lies. Safety in numbers.

Greg took a sip of his beer and looked at me, "Nah, I'm not gonna be Chris's friend."

"Why?" I asked again.

"Cause I plan on stealin' his woman, and I can't do that to a friend." He laughed loudly and slapped my knee a little harder than was necessary.

I got up and rolled my eyes in response before heading back behind the bar.

"Hey, at least I'm honest," he called out to me, still laughing.

He had no way of knowing the impact of his words.

Every day after work, I went to visit my Dad. We would sit, usually not talking, and watch television together. I didn't know if it was a normal father-daughter relationship, because I had nothing to compare it to, but it was pleasant. Just pleasant. Not warm. Not comforting. But pleasant.

I began to realize that "pleasant" was about as much as we would ever achieve. Dad's body began to shrink smaller and smaller and with it my hopes of having any kind of real connection. My own features were reflected back to me in his face. Physically there was no question that I had come into this would through him. But that's where it ended.

We didn't speak about the past or our lack of a shared past. Often he would talk about my siblings, Judy and Jake, telling me stories of their childhood and proudly describing their many accomplishments. He was a proud father, a loving father. I got the feeling that by telling me these stories he was letting me know that he had been a good father.

****

Early One January morning, before the sun came up, my cell phone awakened me. I knew by the hour of the call what the news would be.

Judy sounded drained as she spoke softly. "Dad died early this morning."

"Are you over there now?" I asked.

"Yeah, my mom came into the room about an hour ago and he was gone."

"I'll be right there."

Chris had heard me on the phone and rolled over in bed, "Is it your dad?"

"Yeah, he's gone," I answered, pulling on some slippers in the dark. "I'm gonna head over there now."

Chris sat up in bed, "I'll come with you."

"No it's fine. Just come over whenever you get up." I went to the closet and pulled out a heavy coat to wear over my pajamas.

"Okay," He said. "I won't be long."

"Okay."

Chris's voice stopped me before I reached the bedroom door. "I'm sorry, Babe, that your dad died. I really liked Jon; he was a good man."

I gave him a small smile that I'm sure he couldn't see in the dark. "Thanks. I'll see you in a little bit."

I stepped out of our trailer and was instantly hit by the cold, freezing air. The sun had just begun to peek out; the sky was still dark

246

but not quite dark enough to be considered night. It was the time of transition. A thin layer of snow covered the ground and everything was quiet. As I began to walk down to Dad's mobile home all I could hear were the faint crunches my footsteps made in the snow. I stopped for a moment to look around. The snow-dusted trailer park was pretty—as pretty as a trailer park can be.

I entered Dad's place without knocking and found Judy and her mom sitting in the back bedroom. Dad's body lay in the bed, his eyes open and staring up toward the ceiling. I wasn't expecting his eyes to be open; it was unnerving. Judy was sitting on the bed next to Dad, so I came around—trying not to look at him—to give her a hug. She looked how I felt after my mom had died.

I took a seat on the floor, which made it easier to not see his eyes. The three of us chatted quietly in the way people do when someone has died. We said all of the things people are supposed to say, reassuring each other that he was in a better place and expressing gratitude that he no longer suffered. Sometimes Judy would cry. Sometimes my stepmother would. I didn't. I felt like I was intruding on a private moment in someone else's family.

A little while later Chris came into the room. He sat comfortably on the bed next to Dad, looking at him.

"I wish his eyes were closed," Judy said. "But I can't bring myself to touch them."

Without any hesitation, Chris reached over and closed Dad's eyes, holding the lids in place until they would stay closed on their own. Judy and I both exhaled with relief. Now he just looked like he was sleeping.

"Thank you," I said to Chris.

"Yes, thank you, Chris," Judy reiterated.

Chris had been a big help with Dad ever since we'd arrived in Arkansas. He was the only one strong enough to lift Dad out of bed when we needed to move him or rearrange his bedding. He never hesitated for a moment to offer a helping hand, often stopping by on his own to check on Dad and say hello. It was in these moments that I genuinely missed the man I met in Texas.

When the funeral home arrived and they were taking Dad out, I took a moment for myself to go outside. I felt sad, with a longing in the pit of my stomach. But when I thought about Dad, he wasn't the cause. I took a little walk around the trailer park, unable to figure out what was really eating at me. As I walked I noticed a tall pine tree. My eyes followed it up toward the sky and then I knew: I missed my mother. Seeing the pain and deep lines of exhaustion in Judy's face had brought it all back. She loved our father as deeply as I loved my mother, and I understood exactly how she was feeling.

I had not spoken to Jodi in nearly a year, but I knew she and Judy had been in touch over the last couple of years. Jodi had made it clear she wanted nothing to do with my reunion with our dad, but I still felt she should know he was gone and allow her the chance to offer condolences to Judy.

Dad passed away this morning. I thought you might want to know so you could call Judy. It's been hard on her.

A minute or two passed before my phone vibrated with a response.

Thank you.

I interpreted the message as: I still think you're a stupid fucking bitch with stupid written all over your forehead, but I'll call Judy.

I returned the phone to my coat pocket and headed back to Dad's trailer. They were just bringing him out as I approached. Chris was helping the funeral director. I stood off to the side watching as Chris lifted the gurney into the back of the hearse. My father, zipped up in a black bag, was being hoisted into a hearse by a man I thought was going to be the love of my life, and I felt empty.

Dad's funeral was a couple of days later. On the way home I told Chris to stop at Tony C's because I wanted a drink. Apparently though, I wanted a lot more than one. Chris, who rarely ever drank, grew bored after my third shot and wanted to go home.

"Go ahead and go," I said. "I'll walk home."

Chris shrugged and left. I was happy to see him go. I wanted to sit at the bar with the regulars and drink. I wanted to hunch over the bar and spend a bit of time feeling sorry for myself. The more I drank, the surlier I got. By the time Chris returned a few hours later to pick me up, I was looking for a fight.

Once home, I went to the kitchen to get something to eat. Chris was behind me looking in one of the drawers when he accidently elbowed me in the side. Without a moment's hesitation I swung around and punched him right in the face. We both stood there for a moment in shock. I had never punched anyone in my life, and it felt amazing. It had been a long time coming and he deserved it.

Maybe I had wanted to punch someone my whole life. Maybe I had wanted to punch my father. Maybe I had wanted to punch God. But without a doubt I had wanted to punch Chris. I punched him for bringing to the surface all the qualities I hated in myself. I punched him for forcing me to confront my own weaknesses. I punched him because I had spent my entire life playing small. I punched him for my willingness to buy into his lies instead of listening to my own intuition. I punched him because I was tired of punching myself.

Chris stared at me with a frightening intensity; I could tell he was deciding what to do. For a moment I thought I was in serious danger. He had the strength to snap me in two and we both knew it. But then he did something I never would have expected. He turned and walked away. Maybe it was true what I had heard: when you face your fears they lose their power.

****

Over the next few months, people in Prairie Creek slowly got to know us as a couple. But just as I had in Louisiana, I kept everything about our past a closely guarded secret. On a regular basis I gave Chris little reminders that everyone knew everyone's business, in the hope that he would think twice before causing any trouble.

I'd causally drop into conversation things like, "Paul came into the bar today and was telling this story. And I swear, within hours five more people came in with the same story. It's amazing in these small towns how fast word travels. It's like there is no privacy. You say one thing to someone and before you know it everyone knows."

Whenever anyone asked why Chris and I had moved to Arkansas, I said it was because my father had been ill and I wanted to spend time with him. Everything else I kept private while I continued to play the part of one half of a happy couple. Everyone bought it. Except for Greg.

250

One afternoon Chris stopped by for one reason or another. He always found reasons to come into my work when he wasn't working. When he left, Greg looked at me as though he was trying to figure out a question.

"What?" I asked.

"You act different when Chris is around."

I poured another beer and set it in front of him. "That's so not true," I overemphasized, trying to play it off.

"Except that it is," he said seriously. I was used to Greg being jokey and flirty, so it was unsettling to see this side of him. I felt exposed. "It's not like you do anything different. You don't talk different or act different, but your face changes as soon as you see him walk through the door."

"I don't know what you're talking about."

"Yeah, you do. I can see it in your eyes right now." He tapped a cigarette on the bar and stood up to go smoke outside. "Look, it's no big deal, but if you ever feel like talking to someone, I'm here."

I didn't know how to respond so I stood there like a fool, staring at him.

Greg leaned over the bar and lowered his voice, "You know, you're not as tough as you pretend to be."

"I think you've had too much to drink."

He smiled a lopsided smile, showing those dimples that just killed me. "That may be true. It ain't the first time and it sure as hell ain't gonna be the last, but you still know I'm telling the truth." He laughed as he headed out to the back patio.

For the next week the idea of talking to Greg tugged on me. I knew him well enough by then to know he wouldn't judge me. It wasn't in his nature. But, taking the risk to trust, could I actually do it? If he repeated what I said to even one person, it would get back to Chris so fast.

I was standing behind the bar counting out my tips and preparing to get off my shift one evening. Greg was sitting at the bar facing me when I looked up to see Chris walk in the front door. My stomach sank just like it did every time Chris showed up, but I instantly hid it as I smiled and waved to him, "I'm almost ready."

"I'll be over here," Chris grumbled as he headed to a nearby table. He didn't usually like to sit at the bar, because he thought the people that came in the bar were losers; he made a point of letting me know this on a regular basis. Chris, of course, could spend all our money smoking crack for six days straight, but if someone stopped by the local bar for a couple of beers after work they were the loser.

I went back to counting my money, but I could still feel Greg's eyes on me. Finally I couldn't avoid it any longer; I looked up and made eye contact. His face said it all. I hadn't been quick enough to mask my face.

"Are you working tomorrow?" I asked.

Greg was in construction and often had gaps between jobs. He shook his head, "Nope."

"Do you want to meet me for coffee in the morning at the diner next door?"

"So you're finally going to tell me what the deal is, huh?"

"I don't know," I said still worried. "I haven't decided yet. Let's just get coffee and I'll see how I feel tomorrow."

"Okay."

I stuffed my tips in my pocket, "See ya," I said as I waved to Chris to let him know I was ready.

Chris stood up and met me as I came around the bar. I turned back for a brief moment and said to the bartender that was relieving me, "Oh yeah, I forgot to tell you, Joe is cut off."

Joe whipped his head around to look at me. His eyes caught up a moment later. "Hey you little shit, wha juis say that for?"

"Because you're drunk. Call your girlfriend to come pick you up."

"Imma not drunk you little shit," he said, trying to focus his eyes in my direction.

I laughed, "Okay, Joe, whatever you say."

Chris pulled on my arm. "Come on." He opened the front door for me and as I walked out he said, "You need to get another job."

"Why? I like my job. It's fun," I answered as I climbed into the truck and clicked my seatbelt.

"Yeah, I bet it is," he said backing up and tearing out of the parking lot too fast. "Guys like that dude, Greg, sittin' in there starin' at your ass all day is probably fun for you."

Chris quickly whipped a left turn past the little market and into the trailer park. Why he insisted on driving over to pick me up when the bar was across the street from where we lived was beyond me.

"Would you slow down? And no one is staring at my ass."

He shot me his, are you out of your mind, look—that I used to love and now despised—as he pulled into our driveway and shut off the engine. "Baby," he said as he got out of the truck and walked ahead to hold open the front door for me, "if you think for one second those guys down there aren't all staring—"

As I passed him, I cut him off. "Of course I know they are staring at my ass. I'm a woman and I'm the bartender. That's what they're supposed to do. But it's not personal. It's not like they're staring at me, Jonna, the real person. They're staring at whoever happens to be pouring the drinks, because I have breasts and a vagina."

Chris tossed the keys on the counter, then looked at me as if I were a used condom on the floor of a public restroom. "And you think that's all right?"

I was over this conversation. Actually, I was pretty much over all our conversations. I walked down the hall toward the bedroom as he called after me. "You think it's okay for guys to check out your ass?"

"Why not," I yelled back. "You did!" A moment later, I heard the front door slam and assumed he was over this conversation too.

The next morning after Chris left for work, I texted Greg, Did you still want to get coffee?

Sure. What time? He responded.

We set a time and then I got really nervous. It was only coffee, but it felt like cheating. Okay, on the outside it was only coffee, but there was more going on, and I knew it. Greg and I liked each other. There was a mutual attraction; just because we didn't act upon it didn't mean it wasn't there. Even Chris could see it.

Was I looking to be rescued again? Probably. Was Greg the man to do it? Probably not. He was just a guy hanging out at the local bar flirting with the bartender. And I certainly didn't need to add any drama to my situation, so I made the decision that Greg would be my friend.

I walked into the diner and immediately had butterflies in my stomach when I saw my "friend".

I was glad when he seemed kind of nervous too. This was the first time we were seeing each other outside of being customer and server. I got the feeling it was much easier for him to be the flirting, joking guy when there was the barrier of the bar between us. Now as we sat across from each other with nothing but our coffee, our conversation was patchy and quiet.

We both knew why we were there; I was either going to have to spill it or go home. So I started talking. I told him everything. He sat quietly, just listening. He never offered advice or told me his opinion. He just listened until I reached the part about the Special Forces and the tattoo.

Greg looked up from his cup of coffee. "Really? A tattoo?"

I nodded. "I know, right?"

"He better hope people around here don't find out about that. That will piss some people off."

"Do you see now, why you can't say anything to anyone?" I asked. "If word gets out about Chris, it's going to cause a ton of problems that I just can't deal with right now. That's why I just put a smile on my face and act like everything is normal."

Greg shook his head. "How long you plan on doing that for?"

"Until I can save up enough money, find a place to go, and leave him."

"Doesn't sound like much of a plan to me. Just tell him to get the fuck out."

"Oh gee, why didn't I think of that?"

Greg eyed me, letting me know my sarcasm wasn't appreciated.

"I know what you're saying, but I know Chris more; he's not just going to pack up his bags and say, 'Sorry Babe, I did you wrong. I'll go now.' He's not that kind of guy. If he knows where I live and he knows where I work, he'll make my life hell. I know he will."

Greg sat up straighter and leaned forward. "He doesn't hit you does he? Cause if he's hitting you—"

"No, no, he's never hit me—"

"Cause if he did—"

"No, I appreciate that, but no, he doesn't hit me. He's shadier than that, you know? He's the guy who will break into my place, and slash my tires, or throw a rock through my sister's salon window, and I won't be able to prove it's him. I don't trust him; he's unpredictable." I laughed. "He'd probably just kill me before he hit me."

256

"That's funny to you?" Greg asked.

"No, of course not. It's not funny at all. Please don't tell anyone what I told you, okay? I just need to keep the peace for a little while longer and then… I don't know. I'll figure something out."

Greg looked directly into my eyes, "I'm not going to say anything to anyone. I promise."

I took a chance and believed him.

A short time after my outpouring to Greg I found out that Chris had been stealing from a woman who lived in town. Her husband had died recently while trimming trees. He'd hit an electrical line and was killed instantly. The locals took the news hard. Chris took it as an opportunity to take advantage of a widow.

They met one night at the bar when Chris came in to pick me up. As he waited for me to finish my shift, he got to talking with this woman. She told him that she didn't know what to do with all her late husband's tools and equipment. Chris, being the big hero, offered to help.

She wanted to sell these things but had no idea what they were or what the value would be. Chris said he would sell them for her. My radar immediately went up. I didn't trust him, but what could I say? "Don't let my boyfriend help you. He's a liar and he'll rip you off." So I said nothing and hoped that all my seed planting of how small the town was would keep him from doing anything shady.

As the weeks passed, Chris continued to come home with various things that had belonged to this women's husband. He would list them on Craigslist and tell me that he was giving the widow the money.

I thought if he was selling these things and not giving her the money, I would have heard about it. She would have told someone or at least stopped giving him things to sell. I actually started to believe that maybe Chris was telling the truth and helping this woman out. This was all based on the assumption that she actually gave him things to sell. I would find out that my assumption was totally wrong.

One afternoon she came into the bar. She didn't come in very often so, when I saw her I took the opportunity to check in and make sure everything was still okay.

"So, Chris was able to help you sell some of your husband's things?" I asked as casually as I could.

She looked at me funny and my stomach dropped. I knew with that one look that he'd been lying to me and stealing from her.

"No," she said. "He's been coming up to the house and helping me sort though all the boxes in the garage, but we haven't sold anything yet."

"Oh, okay," I said. "I knew he was going to your place, but I must have misunderstood."

I turned to help another customer and thought *this has to end now.* I knew I had to just bite the bullet and tell Chris I wanted out of this relationship. If he flipped out and killed me, so be it. But I couldn't live like this anymore. Maybe he could lie and steal without a thought or care, but I felt like a scumbag lying with him. This woman, who had recently lost her husband, had no idea the amount of stuff Chris had stolen from her. I felt sick.

I didn't say anything to Chris that night when I came home from work. Instead I told him I wanted to find Beaux a new home. I said that the trailer was too small to have such a big dog, and I was tired of him crying and whining all the time to go out.

I didn't want to get rid of my dog. I loved Beaux. He'd been all I had in Louisiana. But I didn't know what was going to happen when I told Chris it was over. I had no doubt that I was going to have to move out, but I had no idea where I was going to go. Chris wasn't going anywhere, and I would rather see Beaux live with someone else than to leave him behind with Chris.

It took a lot of screening; I turned down numerous hillbillies before I eventually found the right family. The husband was a police officer and they already had one boxer that needed a friend. It broke my heart to watch him go, but I gained some relief when the next day the guy texted me a picture of Beaux curled up sleeping with his new friend.

After Beaux was gone it was time to end this. That night my stomach was in knots. I was scared but figured the best thing to do was just say it and get it over with. The faster the better, before I chickened out. And by faster I meant "a year and a half in the making" fast.

I made sure to keep the truck keys in my hand just in case I had to make a run for it, and then I asked Chris to join me outside for a cigarette. The way I saw it, telling him outside was a lot safer.

Chris followed me outside. I sat on the front steps, not knowing how to begin. As it turns out Chris began for me.

"Are you okay, Babe?" he asked, lighting a cigarette and handing it to me.

I took it and looked up at him. "No, I'm not okay. That woman you were supposed to be selling stuff for came into the bar the other day.

Big surprise: you never gave her any money and she never gave you any stuff to sell."

"What did you say to her?"

"I haven't said anything to anyone. I don't want some angry mob showing up here to run us out of town. Everyone will think I knew about it. But it doesn't matter. That's so not the point!" I placed my head in my hands for a moment then looked up at him, "I can't do this anymore. I can't be a part of this kind of shit. I mean, seriously—what the fuck is wrong with you? I don't get it. I don't get why you're like this and I can't be with you anymore."

I held my breath and waited for the explosion. It never came. Instead, Chris turned his back to me and looked up at the sky. After a moment he said, "I don't know why I'm like this either."

I had braced myself for a huge fight and it never came. Instead, his eyes welled up and he looked at me, "I know everything is my fault. I'm sorry I did this to you."

What was happening? I'd lived in fear, plotting and planning my great escape from this monster for the last year, and this was his response? Crying and saying he was sorry? I felt stupid. I could have had this conversation back in Louisiana. Had I really built this up in my mind? All the fear was for nothing? I'd built a prison of my own imagination, and for what? For nothing.

"I think I need professional help," Chris said to me, his eyes pleading with desperation.

"Um, yeah. You probably do," I answered, while thinking apparently I do too.

260

"If I can find a therapist, would you go with me?" he asked.

"Yeah, sure."

Was this really happening? Was he simply going to let me walk out of his life without a fight and go into therapy just like that? Something didn't feel right. This was too easy. I didn't trust it. Was this reluctance on my part to accept his response coming from my need for drama or was it my intuition telling me to sleep with one eye open? I guessed only time would tell.

One thing he made clear as we continued this bizarre, polite conversation was that he wasn't going anywhere.

"Have you already found a place?" Chris asked.

"No." I answered, irritated that in his new found clarity of what a douchebag he was, he didn't offer to move out.

"Well, Gal, you're welcome to stay here as long as you need." Chris smiled a mischievous grin. "You know I'm gonna win you back, right?"

"Oh really?" I said.

"Yes, Ma'am. You just wait. You'll see. I ain't sweatin' this cause I know my Baby will come back to me." He reached his hands out and I took them letting him pull me up. "Shoot Gal, you know I ain't no quitter."

Chris pulled me close. I could feel the tense muscles of his arms pulling tightly against my shoulders as he whispered in my ear, "I love you Jonna."

"I love you too," I murmured into his neck, and for a split second I almost let myself believe this was true.

A few days later I was at work when Greg bounded in with his lopsided grin and slapped his hand on the bar, "Well, Darlin', I'm outta here."

I laughed as I started to pour him a Budweiser. "You came in to tell me you're leaving? Wouldn't it be easier to just not come in at all?"

He slid onto the barstool. "No, I'm outta here. I'm moving to Kansas."

"What? When?" I looked at him, shocked.

"Next couple of days?"

"Why?"

"You're wasting good beer," he said, nodding toward the glass in my hands.

I quickly looked at the overflowing glass and shut off the tap. I wiped the glass with a napkin and set it in front of him. "I can't believe you're moving. This sucks."

"I have to. My dad's remodeling his house and there's no reason to pay someone else to do it when I'm sittin' down here doin' nothin'. I have to go where the work is."

I immediately felt sad. I didn't want Greg to go. He was the one person I felt I could talk to; now he was leaving. As we continued to talk I told him the whole story about finding out Chris had been stealing from the widow. I also told him that I had ended it and was looking for a place to live.

262

"How did he take it?" Greg asked.

"Really well, actually. I don't know if I trust it."

"Look the guy knows he fucked up. At some point you have to accept the fact that you blew it and move on. What's he gonna say?" Greg grinned showing his dimples, "Trust me. I fucked up nearly every relationship I ever had. Sometimes a guy just has to man up and take one on the chin."

"I hope you're right." I smiled sadly. "Kansas, huh?"

"Yep. I guess our timing sucks."

"Yeah."

A couple of hours later I was in the liquor closet, getting some bottles to restock the bar, when I heard the door open behind me. I turned around and Greg reached up behind my neck and pulled me toward him. Without a word he gave me a kiss that sent shivers down my spine. The butterflies in my stomach were still fluttering when he pulled back and said, "Kansas isn't that far away. You can always come and visit." Before I could answer, he opened the door and slipped back out.

Two days later, I met him again to say goodbye. It was early morning and we sat at the bar drinking coffee. There was nothing to say. He was leaving and I was staying behind. What might have been would have to be left unknown.

"So we won't say goodbye," he said. "We'll just say see ya down the road."

I wasn't as optimistic. "Unfortunately, see you down the road usually means I'll never see you again."

He started to reach out to touch my face but pulled back, "I know for sure I'll see you again someday."

I stared at my coffee cup and nodded. "Okay." I looked over and tried my best to smile. "If you say so."

****

After Greg left, life continued to mosey along in our little Ozark town. The same regulars came into the bar each day and I served them the same drinks. Life was quiet. I was still looking for a place to move. Although Chris and I tiptoed around each other—the way couples do when they are splitting up—there was very little excitement.

One night I was sitting in my favorite La-Z-Boy chair reading a book when Chris came home from work. I looked up and smiled hello as he tossed his keys on the counter. He had recently bought himself a truck. . Since I would be moving out, he needed his own vehicle. Of course he picked a jacked-up, bright-red truck with a loud engine that you could hear coming a mile away. It was definitely a Chris kind of truck.

"Hey, I was thinking," he said, "Would you have dinner with me on Friday night? I know things have been tough, but I'd like to spend some time with you. You know, as friends."

I was immediately struck with the thought that he must have been talking to the guys at work who, no doubt, assured him the best way to get a woman back was to woo her. I could hear them saying, "Take her out on a date. Wine and dine her. Chicks love that shit."

No, what chicks love is not telling them you were Army Special Forces when you were not. What chicks love is when you don't steal from widows. What chicks love is when you don't leave them stranded in the middle of the swamps of Louisiana while you are off smoking crack.

"Sure," I smiled. "That sounds nice." I didn't buy for a moment that Chris had any desire to be my buddy. But if having dinner meant that it would keep things peaceful until I moved out, then I could do that.

That Friday night we drove to Eureka Springs, about forty-five minutes away. It's an amazing historic town up in the Ozark Mountains and we had to drive beautiful winding mountain roads to get there. Dinner went well—not extremely comfortable—but we were polite and overly considerate, the way couples behave when they are trying to be nice while splitting up. Then Chris started telling a story about his ex-wife cheating on him.

"Was that because she found out you'd been arrested for stealing?" I asked.

To this day, I don't understand why I let those words come out of my mouth. Chris had told me when we first met the story of how he'd been arrested when he was younger. At the time, he said it was the reason he went into the Army because he was going down the wrong path. My bringing up the story was a dig, and we both knew it. I'd had such control, for so long, keeping every thought, every feeling, tightly packed away. And now that I was nearly free, I'd taken a stick and poked the bear.

Chris's face grew dark and he glared at me from across the table. It became so incredibly uncomfortable that finally I said, "Do you just want to go?" I wanted this night to be over. Chris pushed himself away from the table and walked out.

I walked half a block behind him all the way back to the truck. We both got in and I could tell by the way he started the truck and tore off down the tiny mountain road that this was a huge mistake. I tried to act nonchalant, and casually threw out, "There's cops all over; you may want to slow down." Once again it was the wrong thing to say.

Chris sped up and headed out of town. He turned to me with so much hatred in his eyes that I knew this was going someplace bad really fast. He started screaming, "Shut the fuck up! I don't want to hear you say anything!" He gunned the gas, whipping around other cars on the small mountain road.

I took a deep breath and tried to remain calm. My heart was pounding out of my chest, but I forced my voice to stay quiet and even, "Look, I'm sorry I made that comment. It was mean, I just—"

"Shut your fucking mouth! Why can't you ever let anything go?" Chris slammed on the brakes and the truck fishtailed across the road toward the ledge. At the last moment, he swerved the wheel, pulling back into the lane. I could barely breathe at this point, but muttered, "You need to calm down." I slowly tried to reach for the door handle, but he saw me and stomped on the gas so hard the tires screeched in protest.

266

Chris looked at me for a long time, not watching the road. "You think you're so fucking great! Just sit there and shut your fucking mouth! I'm sick of listening to you." To prove his point he slammed his fist repeatedly into the windshield shattering it in two places. As I watched the cracks in the windshield spread, Chris slammed on the brakes once again and sent us into another fishtail.

I turned to him. "Let me out of the truck." His response to this request was to punch the windshield a few more times and speed down the road. "Chris, just pull over and let me out." Again he slammed on the brakes while turning the wheel sharply. This time the truck skidded sideways rocking from side to side. I grabbed onto the door, fearing the truck was going to flip.

Chris turned to me and started screaming, "You want your truck? Huh? You want your fucking truck so bad?"

Before I completely realized what was happening, Chris had opened the driver's door and with his foot still flooring the gas, he hung out of the truck just barely holding the steering wheel with his one hand. "Then come get your fucking truck!" he shouted. Although I wasn't totally aware of what he was doing, one thing became crystal clear: I was buckled into the passenger seat of an F150 that was flying down a mountain road with no one in the driver's seat.

And in a flash it dawned on me. Chris knew the story of my mother's childhood, and how much suffering the accident had caused in her life. I'd told him the story just a few weeks before ending the relationship; now he was reenacting it for me. There was no doubt in my mind that this man was a sociopath. My brain knew I needed to do something, but my body was frozen. Chris's voice snapped me out of it, "Come on! Come get your truck, you stupid bitch!"

I quickly unhooked my seatbelt and crawled into the driver's seat. As soon as I put my hands on the wheel, I immediately felt relief. No longer at his mercy, I slammed down on the brakes and brought the truck to nearly a complete stop. I quickly glanced back over my shoulder to the open driver's door. Chris was gone. I didn't know if he had fallen, or if he had jumped, but I had no intention of finding out. I stepped on the gas and took off without looking back.

For all the years I had spent meditating, this was the first time in my life my mind actually went absolutely silent. The night road was black, and all I could see was the circle of my headlamps. I thought, "Drive. Just drive."

After about a mile my brain kicked back in and I was flooded with spinning thoughts. I wonder if he broke his legs when he jumped. No one will see him lying there. Could I get arrested for leaving him in the road? He might get run over by another car. Well yeah, that's what happens when you jump out of a moving car you stupid, redneck, lying, sociopath, motherfucking piece of shit! Fueled by my own rage now, I drove faster.

It was going on about two o'clock in the morning when I made it back to our little town. I didn't know where to go. I couldn't go to my sister Judy's. Her mobile home was right next door to the one I shared with Chris. If he managed to get a ride back I didn't want him seeing the truck parked at Judy's. I didn't know what he was capable of at this point; the last thing I wanted was to bring danger into my sister's home. As long as I wasn't at her house he certainly wouldn't go there. He sure as hell wasn't about to tell her what just happened.

I decided the best thing to do was stay hidden in the truck. I found an area off the main road where people parked cars and motor homes they were trying to sell. Someone had parked a big rig and I was able to hide my truck behind it. I wouldn't be seen by anyone driving by, but I would still be able to drive away quickly if he happened to pull up in front or behind me.

I was still shaking when I called Greg.

"Hey," he answered, sounding sleepy. "What's up, Darlin?"

The tears started flowing before I could get the first word out. Between gasps of air I related the story. I knew Greg was a little rough around the edges and didn't hold back his thoughts, so I wasn't completely surprised when, after hearing what I had to say, he replied, "You need to stop acting like an asshole. After everything you've told me, why would you go out to dinner with him? That's just stupid."

I sighed, "I wanted to keep things cool between us until I moved out." I looked up at my shattered windshield, and traced the cracks with a finger.

"Well, Baby, you need to stop trying to be so fucking nice all the time."

"I'm not trying to be nice. I was trying, in the only way I know how, to protect myself!" I protested, raising my voice.

"What are you going to do? Live in fear every day?" His voice became louder matching my own. "Is that your big plan, huh?"

"Do you have any idea how freakishly strong he is?"

"I don't fuckin' care how strong he is! You think I give a shit how strong Chris is?"

"No, of course you don't care. You're in Kansas! I care! He could break me in half."

"I can take Chris. He's not that tough."

I exhaled deeply, "Yes, I'm sure you could. You and Chris can beat each other to bloody pulps, but that doesn't help me. You're in Kansas and I'm in the woods hiding in my truck."

Greg's voice grew strict. "Quit feeling sorry for yourself. It's time to put your big-girl pants on and cut this guy out of your life."

I understood what he was saying, but my frustration caused my voice to rise again. "How do I do that? How do you get someone to go away? You can't. I'm the one who's going to have to go away. I've always known this and no one else seems to get it."

"So, come to Kansas. It's only a four-hour drive. You can stay here for a while."

"I appreciate the offer. I really do. But I can't show up at your dad's house, homeless, jobless, and broke with a truckload of my stuff. I doubt that would go over well."

Greg sighed, "It's not like you have anything keeping you there."

I told Greg I would think about it, but I knew it wasn't an option, at least not now. We both calmed down and he stayed on the phone with me until the sun started to come up. I will always love him for that. We didn't talk about anything in particular. Just talked. Just listened. He couldn't fix my problem. He couldn't save me. But for a little while, sitting in my truck hidden off the main road, I didn't feel alone.

When we finally hung up, I slept for about an hour, and then drove myself to my work. I was on the schedule for that morning, and had a few hours before my shift started. The place opened at 6 AM; I poured myself a cup of coffee, sat at the bar and thought, "Now what do I do?"

Since I had never found myself in a situation quite like this before, I thought I should call the police. I figured if anyone would know what to do, they would. Although from past experience I was reluctant to ask for their help. A woman answered the phone and I told her the situation. She told me that I needed to wait until Monday morning and then go to the courthouse to file an order of protection. I had my doubts about how a piece of paper was going to protect me. I reiterated to the woman that we lived out in Prairie Creek, which was a bit of a drive from the main town and, since it was Saturday, what did she suggest I do until Monday?

"Darlin', call the police if he shows up," she said in her twangy, hillbilly accent.

"But we're all the way out in Prairie Creek. It will take them a while to get here," I stressed, trying to get her to understand my situation.

"Don't you worry, sweetie, they like drivin' fast."

I have realized something about Southern accents and my tolerance for them. It varies greatly, depending on circumstance. When I first met Chris and he would call me "gal" or say things like "let me get that for you, darlin'," I used to melt. The accent had so much charm I just wanted to throw my panties at it. But when someone is telling me something I don't want to hear, it makes me want to scream obscenities and call them names. My mind immediately goes to every Southern stereotype and I become an uppity, big-city stereotype.

So there I sat with my uppity, big-city ways and my cup of coffee, not having a single clue what to do next. Eventually the hour came for me to start my shift and I went behind the bar. Every time a loud truck roared past I jumped out of my skin. I knew it was only a matter of time before he showed up. He would make it back to town, see my truck, and know I was working. Unless, of course, he was dead. That was always a possibility.

He wasn't dead. A few hours into my shift I saw his red truck roar into the parking lot. One of the regulars, Big Jay, met him outside and told him he couldn't come in. I don't think Chris wanted to see me any more than I wanted to see him. He just wanted his cell phone that had been left behind when he made his sudden departure. I gave it to Jay, who was running interference for us, and Chris roared off again.

That night when my shift ended, I was offered a couch to sleep on by a guy who was friends with the owners of the bar. I was just grateful for a place to sleep. As soon as we walked into his home, I lay down on the couch and was asleep within minutes. I slept for seventeen hours. Luckily, I had extra clothes in my truck to wear to work when I woke up.

I'd never lived in a small town before, but I experienced firsthand what if felt like to have a community reach out and give a helping hand. A woman named Nancy, after hearing what had happened, offered to let me move into the downstairs portion of her house.

I was honest with her when she made the offer, "I don't know what he's going to do, so if you don't want to get involved, I understand, because there could be drama. He could show up at your house—I don't know."

Nancy who was shorter than me and probably weighed ninety pounds soaking wet, replied, "I have a lot of guns. Let him show up."

I really wasn't sure about the whole gun thing, but I felt better that I'd given her a heads-up.

I began going by the trailer and picking things up while Chris was at work. It only took a couple of trips before my things were moved into Nancy's. The second morning I was at her house she came downstairs where I was unpacking a box. I wasn't in any hurry and was piddling about. She asked, "Do you need some speed?"

I laughed, answering, "I know I'm moving slow. I'm just kind of meandering."

I thought she was joking. Later, when I went upstairs to ask her a question, I walked into her room to find her inhaling smoke through a glass pipe off a folded piece of tinfoil. I went back downstairs and repacked my things.

Over the next few days Chris began texting me, full of apologies and promises to fix the shattered windshield. I accepted his apology, and I let him pay for the broken window. I wasn't being nice, as Greg had said; I was finally taking control of my own life. I set the date when I would leave and I kept it completely to myself. A few days before leaving I let my sister Judy know my plans. She offered to help me pack up my truck when the time came. I wasn't looking to be rescued. I didn't beg God to save me. I simply decided I'd had enough. It was time for this journey to come to an end.

A week later I would lie in bed listening for footsteps to leave the house. Footsteps that would tell me my cross-country journey was about to begin.

Vancouver, Washington

My friend Raquel recently sent me an email after reading a first draft of this story and she wrote, *Have you made peace with God?*

My answer to that is: God was never the problem. I was the problem all along. I don't need to make peace with God, because God was never at war with me. What I needed was to make peace with my life as it was and not as I wish it to be. God didn't put Chris into my life to torture me. I chose Chris, and when I look back on my history I see that it was not the first time I picked an unavailable man or the first time I was willing to love for crumbs. I have been falling in love with unavailable men for as long as I can remember. Either they were alcoholics, or they lived a thousand miles away, or at my worst, involved in other relationships. I'd never picked a man quite as extreme as Chris, in that he was so unattainable that he didn't actually exist, but the pattern was there long before the man came along. Sometimes, I guess, we have to go to the furthest end before we can hear the wakeup call and make our way back.

In writing this memoir, I have come to realize that I am a "piner." I seem to be happiest when I am sadly pining away for someone or something I can't have. Actually, I won't say I'm happiest; it's more that the feeling of longing for things to be different is more familiar than anything I know. I've lived with it for so long, it's become a part of me. I think I have spent most of my life stuck in a state of wishful thinking. Pining for my father. Pining for a sober mother. Pining for the unavailable man. Always wanting life to be different than what it is.

The biggest eye-opener in writing this book was that I could finally see that all along the way, I'd had choices. If I had have only paused long enough to accept life as it was, and stopped trying to plot and plan my next moves, I may have realized this sooner. But I'm okay with that, because living through this experience is what brought me to where I am today. Living my life, day-to-day and accepting life on life's terms.

Jonna Ivin is the author of the crime thriller 8th Amendment and Will Love For Crumbs - A Memoir

She is the editor of Loving For Crumbs - An Anthology of Moving On

Visit Jonna on her website at www.wix.com/jonnaivin/jonnaivin or on Facebook www.facebook.com/jonna.ivin

Excerpt from 8th Amendment

Prologue

A bell rang inside the small brick schoolhouse. The empty halls soon filled with the laughter and chatter of children. One little girl, eight-year-old Sarah LaPonte walked down the crowded hall with her best friend Maggie. Sarah, with her curly blond hair and big brown eyes, was half the size of Maggie. She was delicate and small boned, often mistaken by strangers to be younger than she was. Sarah hated it when adults spoke to her with baby voices asking her how old she was as if they expected her to hold up fingers to count her age. Just because she was small that didn't make her a baby.

The two girls talked excitedly about their plans for a sleepover at Sarah's house for the coming weekend. "My mom said we can make cupcakes when you come over," Sarah said.

Maggie's eyes grew wide as she answered, "Can they be chocolate?" Both girls knew making cupcakes was a special treat because when they were finished the kitchen usually looked like a bomb had gone off. After the last time, Sarah's mom was found swearing under her breath, "never again," as she tried to mop frosting off the ceiling.

The girls had been best friends since kindergarten. On the first day of school another girl had taken a doll away from Sarah leaving her in tears. It was Maggie who yanked the doll out of the girl's hands and gave it back to Sarah. Since then they'd been inseparable with weekend sleepovers growing into a regular occurrence. They often alternated between houses, which gave their parents some much needed alone time.

As the girls approached the front doors one of Sarah's schoolbooks fell from her tiny grasp and landed with a thud on the concrete floor. She turned back to get the book and saw a man bending down to pick it up. As he stood up he slowly held it out to her.

"Thank you," Sarah said as she took hold of the book but he didn't let go. The man was smiling at her like he had a secret. A secret that Sarah didn't think she wanted to know. She gave the book another slight tug hoping he would loosen his grip. He didn't. She'd always been taught to treat adults with respect and didn't want to get in trouble for being rude but she needed her book to complete her homework.

It was Maggie's voice that finally broke the moment. Turning with her hands on her hips she shouted, "Hurry up Sarah, my mom is waiting." This was one time Sarah was glad Maggie could get bossy.

He let go of the book but his eyes never left Sarah as she ran to catch up to her friend.

* * * * * * * * *

From inside the beat up station wagon he could see Sarah playing in her front yard with her dolls. She was the most beautiful girl he'd ever seen and he knew he must have her. He'd been watching her for weeks since the first day he was hired as a janitor at the elementary school. The family's routine was fairly predictable. The father would return from work between five-thirty and six. The mother stayed home. She picked Sarah up from school Mondays, Wednesdays and Fridays. The bigger, bossy girl's mother dropped Sarah off on the alternating days. Once or twice a week, Sarah was allowed to play alone in the front yard, but her mother would often poke her head out the front door every fifteen minutes or so to make sure her little girl was okay. He would have to be quick.

Taking a final drag off his cigarette he stubbed it out in the over flowing ashtray before reaching into the backseat and opening a cardboard box. Inside was a little orange and white striped kitten he'd pick up off an ad in the local Penny Saver. As soon as he didn't need it anymore he would dump it on the side of the road. Placing the kitten on his lap, he started up the engine and slowly drove toward the house.

****

Nancy LaPonte had just finished putting another load of laundry into the dryer when she smelled the smoke. "Oh crap! The biscuits!" she said, wiping a mass of blonde curls away from her face. The ear piercing beeps of the smoke detector soon followed.

Nancy ran down the hall into the kitchen and flung open the oven door. Black smoke poured out as she used a potholder to yank the charred biscuits out of the oven before tossing the baking sheet on top of the stove. She shut off the oven while wildly waving the potholders to clear the air. The incessant beeping wouldn't stop. She threw the useless potholders down and grabbed a larger dishtowel to wave in front of the smoke alarm. Nothing was working. The damn thing wouldn't shut off. Climbing on a kitchen chair Nancy reached up to remove the batteries from the offensive device.

When silence had resumed, and she could gather her thoughts, Nancy began the task of clearing the house of smoke. All the while muttering, "Why do I try to bake?" With the windows in the kitchen open, Nancy could see again and she moved to the living room to open the front door.

Laying in the front yard were Sarah's dolls, but there was no sign of her daughter anywhere. The small white gate on the fence around their yard swung slowly back and forth. Sarah knew to never leave the yard.

Nancy exited the house calling out, "Sarah? Sarah?" When no answer came she walked to the sidewalk and looked up and down the street. Everything looked perfectly normal. It was then the panic set in.

Chapter One

Lauren Atkinson was led down the corridor of the prison by two armed guards. It was a routine she'd become use to over the years but still it rattled her nerves. Each time they approached a set of iron bars a buzzer sounded sliding the gate open. It was the clanging of the bars behind her that chilled her spine.

She always made a point to look as plain as possible when visiting a client in prison. No makeup, her black hair pulled back in a tight ponytail, loose dark slacks, sensible shoes and a jacket to hide her breasts. It was impossible to completely hide her natural beauty. Her eyes always gave her away. Even without all the feminine frills, the high cheekbones and wide blue eyes grabbed the attention of most men who looked upon her as a sexual object they wanted to possess. But it was those same unflinching eyes that let her clients know she was someone they could trust, someone who wouldn't lie, and who stood by her word. These were the most important qualities a person could posses when dealing with inmates on death row.

It had been an irritating morning and Lauren was anxious to get this meeting over with but she didn't let it show. Having practiced law for over fifteen years she'd become a master at masking her emotions. Compartmentalizing her feelings was her greatest strength. Her stoic exterior made it impossible for others to guess what she was thinking until she was ready to let them know.

As another set of bars slammed shut, Lauren turned to the older guard to her right. Jerry, a portly man in his mid-fifties had known Lauren for over five years. Their relationship had grown friendly in that time and they often spent the long walk to death row catching up on each other's lives.

"So Jerry how's your daughter?" Lauren asked while ignoring the younger guard who was walking slightly behind her. She could feel that he was trying to check out her ass. She'd learned over the years that when dealing with new guards it was best to keep her head held high and pretend not to notice the looks. The guards weren't much different than the prisoners in that respect.

"She left for Harvard Law School Monday morning," Jerry answered as a grin warmed his face.

"You must be very proud."

"I sure am."

"Well," Lauren added, "when she graduates have her give me a call. We can always use some help at the office."

Jerry chuckled as he said, "No offense Lauren, but I'm pretty sure she plans on fighting for the other side. She is her father's daughter."

Lauren smiled warmly. She respected Jerry. He was a good family man, and worked hard to support his family. "Then I look forward to the challenge."

Another buzzer sounded and they stepped through the opening of the gates. "How's your family doing?" Jerry asked.

"Good. City championships are today. Gillian is pitching."

With the sound of the last gate slamming behind them, they had arrived in the section of the prison that housed the death row inmates. Not many people ever saw this part of the prison, but Lauren had seen it far too often.

"Female on grounds!" The younger guard shouted to announce Lauren's arrival.

Lauren rolled her eyes, "Is that really necessary?"

"No," he smiled then added, "I just like the way it sounds."

Lauren leaned close to Jerry's ear whispering, "I hate rookies."

"Me too," he agreed.

Within a few minutes, Lauren was seated in a small bare room separated into two parts by a shatter proof Plexiglas partition. Her foot tapping in agitation for having to wait even though she knew there was nothing to be done to speed up the process. There were rules and regulations for visitation, but still she had a little league game to get to. If she was late to one more game, she feared her daughter's reaction more than any inmate on death row. A convicted murderer paled in comparison to the wrath of a pre-teen girl.

Just as Lauren was glancing at the clock on the wall for the third time the door on the other side of the partition opened and Eddie James was led in shackled and cuffed. With his hardened face, menacing eyes and linebacker size, Eddie would intimidate most people on the street, but when he saw Lauren, his mouth broke into a wide smile showing underneath it all there was still a human being.

Lauren didn't return his smile. Instead she reached into her briefcase pulling out the morning newspaper which had been the source of her irritation. While Eddie situated himself into the hard plastic chair opposite Lauren, she held the paper up against the glass for him to see. The headline read: I'm The Victim Here in bold caps with a picture of Eddie in his prison uniform.

"What the hell were you thinking?" Lauren demanded.

"You don't like it?" Eddie asked playfully trying get a smile out of her.

"No, I don't like it. I told you specifically not to talk to anyone about your case except me."

Eddie lowered his head, looking almost childlike in his defense. "This guy come around from the paper asking me a bunch of questions."

"I am trying to save your life here and it doesn't make it any easier when you say stupid things like," Lauren lowered the paper and read the text out loud, "If George Davis had stayed in his own neighborhood he wouldn't have been shot."

"I didn't know they were going to print it all messed up like that. That's not how I meant it. I was just talking about how bad the neighborhood was."

Disgusted, Lauren shoved the paper back into her briefcase and continued, "Are you trying to get yourself executed? Is that what you want? You know, I have a lot of other clients who actually want my help."

Eddie shifted uncomfortably in his chair as he answered, "It's just that this guy wanted to hear my side. No one ever wants to hear my side."

"Eddie, look at me," Lauren narrowed her gaze on him, "George Davis was a Pediatrician who was in *your* neighborhood because in his spare time he made house calls to underprivileged children. You were robbing a liquor store so you could buy more crack. Understand when I say this, you don't have a side."

Eddie pleaded with Lauren, "That's not what I meant. I swear!" Out of frustration he punched the Plexiglas with his fist.

The two guards in the corner of the room stepped forward as Lauren lowered her voice speaking calmly. "Well, that's what the

Appeals Board is going to think when they read what's in this paper and it's going to make it that much easier for them to kill you."

The news began to sink in with Eddie and Lauren watched his tough demeanor soften. She looked to the guards, waving them off that everything was okay.

Eddie slumped deeper into his chair. "I never meant to hurt those people. I was high and I was trippin'.

"I know and I believe you but please trust me on this. Do not talk to any more reporters. I can promise they are not interested in helping you. They want to sell papers by painting you as an unapologetic monster. Okay?"

Eddie nodded, "Yeah, okay."

"Now tomorrow at the hearing the prosecutors will be saying some pretty awful stuff about you. I need to know that you're going to keep your cool."

"People been sayin' shit about me all my life. After a while you get used to it." Eddie raised his eyes, and was met with Lauren's reassuring gaze.

After forty-five minutes of going over every detail for the hearing the next morning, Lauren finally stepped outside the prison into the warm sunshine. Walking across the parking lot toward her car she saw Tom Branson, the Prison Warden. Like Jerry, Lauren and Tom had an easy-going relationship built on mutual respect.

Tom stood near the fence smoking a cigarette while watching the prisoners in the yard. Lauren approached him saying, "Hey Tom."

He turned around and smiled when he saw her but that wasn't unusual, most men smiled when they saw Lauren. She was use to it. "Oh hey Lauren. You here to see Eddie?" he asked. "Yeah. Can I get a cigarette?"

Tom reached into his pack and pulled one out to give to her. "I thought you quit," he said handing it over.

Lauren reached into her bag, taking out a lighter and lit her cigarette. She drew the strong smoke into her lungs and exhaled with satisfaction. "I did."

It had already been a long day for Lauren. Standing there looking out over the men in the yard, she began to wonder if she was fighting a losing battle. It seemed the system grew in numbers every year. More crime. More violence. More pain.

"Do you like your job, Tom?" Lauren asked almost more to herself than to him.

"Sure," he answered then after thinking about it added, "Of course, some days more than others."

Lauren glanced to Tom out of the corner of her eye, "Do you think they deserve to die?"

He knew what she was asking. Everyone knew Lauren Atkinson only represented men and women on death row. "Doesn't matter what I think," Tom answered. And then squaring his shoulders and standing straighter he continued in the tone of a rehearsed sound bite, "I was hired by the state to carry out the law of the people. This is what they want."

Lauren tossed her half smoked cigarette onto the ground and stepped on it. Smiling she turned to Tom, "With bullshit answers like that, you should have gone into politics."

Tom laughed knowing this was probably true. "Maybe so. Why the question?"

Lauren sighed deeply as she looked to the multitude of men in matching uniforms wandering around the yard while armed guards watched their every move "Oh, just another long day I suppose."

"You ever think about quitting?" Tom asked while taking a last drag before flicking his own cigarette to the ground.

"All the time. But, then I think, what if just one is innocent and I didn't do anything to stop it."

This made Tom laugh. He waved his arm out in front of him indicating the yard full of criminals, "Well, you should know by now Lauren, they're *all* innocent."

"So I've been told. Thanks for the cigarette Tom. I'll see ya soon."

"See ya."

Lauren gave Tom a tired smile then headed back toward her car. The day wasn't even half way over. She still needed go to the office and meet with her partner Gary Brudeoux, and then in no way shape or form could she be late for Gillian's big game.

Thirty minutes later, Lauren arrived at her office. Walking into the shabby run down building, she could feel herself relax. It was her home away from home. With phones constantly ringing and unpaid interns pouring through the wall of library books, there was always a buzz of excitement and urgency swirling in the air. Lauren needed the buzz. It helped her relax to know that things were happening. Problems were being solved. Well maybe not solved, but at least the energy in the room made it feel as such.

Lauren always felt proud of what she and Gary had built when she looked around at the volunteers, law students, and lawyers sitting at cramped desks pouring over stacks of files. The dingy paneled walls were covered in various signs and posters repeating the same sentiment: End the Death Penalty. Yes, it was a shit-hole. But it was her shit-hole and she loved it. She loved every dusty shelf, broken filing cabinet and uncomfortable chair. They were fighting the good fight and they were doing it with a minimal budget.

She'd barely entered the door and crossed the room when Gary was at her side followed closely by an eager female intern. The girl, Lisa, was a law student who'd recently joined their office. She was a straight "A" student at the top of her class, an overachiever, who in Lauren's opinion was a little too eager to please. But, they needed all the help they could get so Lauren agreed when Gary suggested hiring her. Who was Lauren to argue when it came to free help?

Lauren wasn't above admitting to herself that she was probably a little jealous of Lisa. The girl had grown up in a wealthy family, excelled in equestrian events and attended all the best private schools. She could afford to intern in the summer with her father paying all her bills.

It had been different for Lauren. She'd worked her way through college on a shoestring budget. Living in cramped apartments with other poor students eating Top Ramon every night. Her grades always fell somewhere in the middle, not bad, not good, while she juggled two part time jobs. What her professors at school always remembered about Lauren was not her excellent grades, it was her balls. She never backed down from a fight and she never quit.

"How did it go?" Gary asked Lauren as they headed to her tiny private office.

"Pretty well. You know, considering we're screwed." Lauren answered.

"Well," shrugged Gary, "It's not the first time."

"Um Lauren," Lisa timidly interrupted, "Here's the motion for appeal on the Johnson case."

Lauren took the file and asked, "Did you site Woodson versus North Carolina?"

Lisa stopped walking and stared at Lauren with a blank expression. Gary reached over taking the file from Lauren and handed it back to Lisa, "Look it up."

As Lisa's shoulders slumped at thinking she's disappointed them she gave one final puppy dog glance to Gary then took the file and slunk off. It was in that moment that Lauren knew yet another intern had fallen for Gary. It happened all the time. She was used to it.

"I just love students," Gary said with a wide grin. "So damn eager to please. You know, save the world and all that shit."

"You are not…?" Lauren asked, indicating the rest of her sentence with a sideways nod, "…with her?"

"No!" Gary protested. "What kind of man do you take me for?"

She knew exactly the kind of man he was. He was the best kind. Loyal, intelligent, strong, but Lauren was also aware that he closely resembled a young Denzel Washington and that women threw themselves at him often. She'd like to believe he turned them all away, but wasn't that naïve. He was a man after all.

Gary never spoke of his love life to her. It was as if they had an unspoken rule, she kept her relationship with her husband Michael private and Gary did the same with whomever he might be seeing at the moment.

They reached Lauren's office and she opened the door. A wave of exhaustion fell over her as she stepped in and sat behind her desk. Gary noticed immediately, "You want some coffee?" he asked.

Lauren raised her eyes and nodded slowly. "Did I ever mention that you are the very best person in the whole wide world?"

Gary laughed, "You need to raise your standards." He left Lauren alone shutting the door behind him.

Much like the outer office, Lauren's private office had few frills. Plain and simple was the way she liked it. And since most of the funding for the firm was acquired through private donations and fund raising there was barely a penny to spare. The luxurious mahogany desk Lauren sat behind seemed out of place among the simple file cabinets and bare furnishings, but it had been a gift from her husband Michael on their fifth wedding anniversary and she loved it.

Lauren's parents once had high hopes that Lauren would be the head of her own high powered law firm, bringing in millions and living a life of prestige. Perhaps even going into politics one day. Lauren could still see the disappointment on their faces when she told them that she would be starting her career at the Public Defenders Office, and even more disappointment came when she left the Public Defender's Office to open her own law office specializing in Death Row cases. Translation: ridiculously long hours with very little pay.

But her parents could take heart in the fact that Lauren's husband Michael had gone on to build a very successful architectural firm. It was his financial success that kept their family living in a more than comfortable lifestyle. Her mother had told her on more than one occasion that marrying Michael was the smartest decision of her life. Lauren agreed, not for her mother's materialistic reasons but because she loved her husband dearly.

She hoped that love would be strong enough to get them through their current rough patch. They'd weathered tough times before. It seemed whenever Lauren was working on a particularly difficult case her attention was diverted away from her family and tensions grew. Lauren knew she had trouble leaving work behind and she was trying to work on it, but still time after time, Michael would wake up in the middle of the night to find her sitting at the kitchen table obsessing over a case.

After the hearing for Eddie James the following day, Lauren vowed to herself to spend more time with her husband and daughter. If she could just get through tomorrow, all would be well.

Lauren's thoughts were interrupted by a light tapping on the door followed by Lisa poking her head in. "Sorry to bother you but I need the Tyson file," she said timidly.

"It's up there," Lauren answered pointing to a stack of files on top of a cabinet to the right of her desk.

Lisa sifted through the large stack of files trying to find what she was looking for. "If you wanted, I could organize your office for you."

"Don't bother it just gets messed up again."

Lisa found the file. As she turned to leave, her eyes fell to a cluster of photos taped to the wall behind Lauren. She had seen the photos every time she entered the room, various snap shots of different men and a few women. The photos had always intrigued her. They were taped to the wall in a haphazard way as if they'd been slapped there in a hurry or out of frustration.

"Are those all the people you have helped?" Lisa asked.

She took a chance by asking the question hoping she wasn't disturbing Lauren. The woman intimidated the hell out of her and she didn't want to get on her bad side. It was the way Lauren seemed to study people while seemingly being able to see right through them. Lauren Atkinson often reminded Lisa of a stray dog who was deciding if she could trust the stranger who held out food. Lisa found it unsettling and difficult to know if the stray lurking with her boss was going to accept what was being offered, run away or attack.

Lauren turned in her chair and scanned the photos before answering, "No I didn't help any of them. I tried but I failed."

"You mean they've all been executed?" Lisa asked as she absentmindedly sat down in a chair across from Lauren's desk. She studied the faces in the photos. They were mostly men but also a couple of women. Some were smiling, arms wrapped around loved ones and family members. Some were hardened mug shots, and others were candid moments when the subject of the photo wasn't aware their picture was being taken.

As Lisa studied the photos, Lauren studied Lisa. The young woman was out of place. Too sweet. Too wholesome. There was a lack of grit that most interns coming into this office had. Lisa seemed better suited for corporate law. A place where everything was organized and neat, where the copy machine wasn't constantly breaking and where a latte could be whipped up in a matter of moments on the company espresso machine.

"Why are you here?" Lauren finally broke the silence.

Lisa stood nervously. "Sorry. I didn't mean to take up your time."

"No, sit. It's okay. I don't mean why you are here, I mean why are you *here?*" Lauren emphasized her point by making a larger circle with her index finger.

Lisa returned to her chair, straightened her back and lifted her chin. She leaned forward with her elbows on the desk, the fingers of both hands intertwined. Lauren figured this was a move the girl spent hours perfecting in order to show she was serious and a force to be reckoned with. It probably served her quite well on the high school debate team but it would be useless here. She'd be branded a newbie before her elbows brushed the table.

Lauren thought about calling her out on the move and saving her the embarrassment when somewhere down the road another attorney would mock her for it. She quickly dismissed the idea figuring it was a right of passage for a young hot shot to get knocked down at least once.

"We're dealing with human beings, not animals and I believe executions are wrong," Lisa stated with certainty and conviction.

Lauren put on her best poker face to keep from laughing. "Why is it wrong?" she asked with feigned seriousness. She was actually curious about what this determined but naïve girl had to say.

Lisa fidgeted in her seat having a bad feeling the dog was about to bite. "I believe in the goodness of people. I think with the right rehabilitation everyone deserves a chance to redeem themselves," she answered nervously, her confidence having been shattered by Lauren's gaze.

Amused by Lisa, Lauren pointed to a mug shot of a man with stringy, dirty hair and a dangerous sneer. "You see this guy? His name is Louis Clemons. He shot an eighty-nine year old grandmother in the head and stole her purse, which had all of four dollars and sixty-three cents. When they asked him why he did it, he replied that he wanted a cheeseburger and that shooting her was easier than 'pushing the old bitch over'. You think a man like that could ever be redeemed?"

Lisa was confused. She didn't understand why Lauren was seemingly arguing for the other side. She stammered, not knowing the right thing to say, "I don't know. I guess not."

"Maybe you should think about that before you decide if this is the place for you."

Lisa stiffened her back once again preparing her argument. "I just know that I finally feel like I'm a part of something important. It feels good knowing that I'm helping to get someone paroled."

Lauren leaned forward making direct eye contact with Lisa. She wanted to make sure the young girl really understood where she was coming from. "That's not what we do. When I lose a case, my client is put to death and when I win, he or she spends the rest of their life in prison. Whatever the outcome, when it's over I walk away. I don't send cards and well wishes and I don't put flowers on their graves. Every person on this wall was guilty of the crime they were charged with, rape, murder, child molestation. The list goes on. Don't kid yourself. They are animals. I fight against the death penalty because the system is flawed not because I'm in the business of freeing convicted criminals. There's a difference."

The door to the office opened and Gary entered with a cup of coffee that he handed to Lauren. He sat down in the chair next to Lisa and fixed his gaze on her as she once again shifted in her seat. "Don't you have something to do? Let's go! Lives are at stake. Times a ticking."

As Lisa rushed out of the room, Gary let out a laugh.

"Why do you do that?" Lauren asked joining in his laughter.

"Just helping to build a little character."

"Have you checked out the elbows on the desk, fingers crossed, maneuver?"

"Oh yeah," he laughed. "She pulled it on me when she came in for the interview and I questioned her decision to list four years as head cheerleader on her resume under special skills."

"And you still hired her?" Lauren asked raising an eyebrow.

"She gave a very compelling argument. Did you know that despite popular opinion the primary goal of a cheerleader is not to jump around in a short skirt but to motivate and sway the common goal of a crowd... much like a jury?"

"You're an ass."

Gary shrugged, "Oh come on. You know you had a signature move too. We all did."

She grinned. "What was yours?"

"You first."

"Oh hell no."

"Guess we'll never know then."

Gary noticed that Lauren had begun to rub the back of her neck. He knew whenever the stress became too much it always built up in her neck. Standing and coming around the desk, he said, "Here let me do that."

His hands felt good working out the kinks and Lauren allowed herself to relax under his touch. She didn't know what she would do without Gary. He was a brilliant lawyer and her best friend. He understood her commitment to her work more than anyone, even more than her own husband and at times she allowed herself to imagine what their life would be like if she wasn't married to someone else. It was a dangerous line to allow her mind to cross. She loved Michael. But sometimes, just sometimes, in times like this, when she felt Gary's strong hands touching her, she wondered what could be.

Gary too had thought about it often. Probably more often than Lauren had, but he kept his feelings to himself. He respected Lauren and Michael and would never cross that line, but if only she knew the hold she had on his heart.

Lauren let out a deep sigh when Gary hit the right spot. He could feel her relax under his touch, and he longed to stay like this with her forever. The tension in the room was thick and they both felt it. Almost simultaneously they were also aware of the power of the line they should not cross. Lauren sat up straight just as Gary released his grip and stepped back.

"Thank you. That feels much better."

"Glad I could help." Gary quickly came back around the desk and headed for the door.

Lauren's voice stopped him as he reached for the doorknob. "I don't know what to do about Eddie. That article really messed things up."

Gary turned to her and smiled. "Don't worry, we'll think of something. We always do."

"I wish I had your confidence."

Hours later, having gone over Eddie's file for the hundredth time, Lauren found herself speeding through traffic on her way to the baseball field. She had once again lost track of time and was late for the one game she promised her daughter Gillian she wouldn't miss. Lauren pulled into the parking lot and quickly found a spot. Getting out of the car her heart sank as she jogged toward the field. On the other side of the chain link fence the players of both teams lined up to slap each other's hands signaling the end of the game. She'd missed it.

Lauren waited by the bleachers along with the other parents. She felt like an outsider. They all knew each other and knew her husband well since he coached the team but Lauren was practically a stranger in this circle. Most of the other parents recognized her from the television.

The various news conferences and interviews she gave regarding high profile death penalty cases kept her in the spotlight. Lauren could feel the disdain for her and her work pulsating all around.

She turned her focus to her husband and child. Michael had the team in a circle on bended knee listening as he gave the last pep talk of the season. Gillian's team had lost by two points and she could hear snippets of Michael's speech saying how proud he was of their effort throughout the season and that they would come back even stronger the next year. With a final throwing of mitts into the air, the game was over.

Walking back to her car, Lauren kept her arm slung over Gillian's shoulder. At eleven years old, Gillian was already showing signs of her mother's beauty, the same black hair and wide eyes. Only hers were a deep chocolate brown like her fathers. The eyes came from the Spanish side of his roots. The wide smile and full lips came from Lauren but the straight nose and high cheeks were definitely all Michael. Both of her parents were tall so there was no doubt she too would grow into her gangly frame one day and become a beautiful woman.

"Don't worry, you'll get them next year," Lauren comforted her daughter.

In response Gillian shrugged her mother's arm off her shoulder while grumbling, "How would you know? You weren't even there." With that she veered away from her parents to go and talk with one of the other players on her team. Gillian apparently was also developing her mother's fiery temper.

Michael and Lauren reached her car and stopped. Lauren dropped her head into Michael's shoulder as he wrapped his arms around her. She loved his smell, fresh cut grass mixed with his own masculine scent always made her feel safe.

Michael knew Lauren felt bad about the game and he tried to lift her spirits by murmuring in her ear, "Don't worry she'll get over it."

Lauren pulled back looking into his warm brown eyes. "The last game of the season and I missed it. I'm so sorry."

"It's not that big of a deal. Gillian is fine."

"You say that now, but just wait. One day this will end up costing thousands of dollars in therapy to find out why she hates her mother."

Michael shrugged. "At least she likes me. One out of two isn't so bad."

Lauren playfully shoved Michael away. "Jerk."

He pulled her close and nuzzled into her neck. "Don't worry, Babe. I still like you. And when the time comes, I'll tell her therapist you really weren't that bad."

Lauren's attention was pulled away by a familiar woman passing by. She was one of the other mom's whose son was on the same team as Gillian. More importantly Lauren knew her as the woman who nearly came between herself and Michael.

"I thought you said she was moving to Arizona or something?" Lauren questioned Michael.

Seeing that Lauren was looking directly at her, the woman lowered her head, picking up the pace while pulling her son along. It was at times like this that Lauren wished she could behave more like her clients. Of course she had no desire to harm the woman, but she wouldn't mind shouting across the parking lot, "That's right bitch, keep walking. Keep your ass away from my man!"

Reaching up Michael brought Lauren out of her ghetto fantasy by softly pulling her chin so that her focus was back on him. "There is nothing going on. And yes, she is moving. To New Mexico."

"Well, what is she doing here?"

"Come on Lauren," Michael assured his wife, "I can't stop a mother from watching her son's little league game."

But Lauren had heard enough. She was ready to go home. She'd disappointed her daughter by getting caught up in her work once again and to top it off she still had no idea what she was going to say to the Appeals Board the next morning regarding Eddie's case. Lauren was in no mood to have a fight with her husband. Her fingers reached back finding the handle of her car and opened the door. "I'll see you at home," she said feeling defeated.

Michael held Lauren tightly not letting her get away that easily. The more she tried to avoid eye contact the closer he pulled her to him. Determined to make her look him in the eyes he followed hers with his own until eventually she had no choice but to match his gaze. "I love you," he said and he meant it.

She tried to fight it, but eventually couldn't help but smile. Their marriage may not have been perfect but it was strong and in Michael she knew she was loved and supported. "I love you too," she grumbled half heartedly.

"Oh come on. You can do better than that. If I were on a jury I wouldn't believe you."

Lauren tried to wiggle out of his firm grip, but it was no use. Despite her best intentions to remain tough she giggled. "Okay. Okay."

"Okay, what?" he asked.

Lauren stopped wiggling and looked directly in his eyes. "I love you too."

"That's much better." He gave her a kiss and finally released his grip allowing her to get in the car. "I'll see you at home, Babe."

Lauren started the car and pulled away. As she was leaving the parking lot she saw Gillian speaking to a boy on her team. Danny, was a year older than Gillian but not much taller. He had blond hair that often poked out in odd places, giving him the disheveled look of a real boy's boy. He was a rough and tumble kid and Lauren hoped her daughter would not grow up with a fascination for bad-boys.

Lauren slowed to stop the car in order to say good-bye to Gillian, but thought better of it. She was seeing the first awkward stages of young love. Not wanting to embarrass her, Lauren drove on. Gillian was already upset; she didn't need to make it worse.

Gillian watched her mom's car slow down but was relieved when it didn't stop. Most of the time her mom was pretty cool, she just wished she didn't work so much. The other mom's made it to the games. Why couldn't hers? She knew her mother worked as a lawyer and was often on television, but Gillian wasn't allowed to watch any of the press conferences or interviews and Lauren's office at home was strictly off-limits.

She'd once opened the door without knocking and before Lauren could shove the pictures she was looking at into the drawer Gillian was pretty sure she saw what looked like a dead person. Her mom had been pissed. She'd yelled at her to never open her door without permission.

One time when she was in the third grade a kid in another class, told the whole school that Gillian's mom loved murderers. She didn't understand at the time why he did that, but she didn't like it and she let the kid know by socking him in the nose. It must have been a lucky punch because blood poured from his nose and no one ever said anything bad about Gillian's mom again. At least not to her face.

Danny's voice broke into Gillian's thoughts; "You pitched a pretty good game today."

"Thanks," she muttered. Danny made her nervous and she never knew what to say when he was around. With her other friends she chatted away easily but when he was around her stomach twitched and her mind went blank.

"If you wanted, maybe we could play catch some time," Danny said before quickly clarifying. "You know, so you can practice. Your curve ball is pretty weak."

Gillian swung her glove hitting him in the arm. "No it's not!"

Danny laughed, "I just wanted to get a smile out of you. Guess that didn't work."

Gillian did smile then. She always wanted to smile when Danny was around, even if he made her mad most of the time. "I guess we could practice if you want."

"Cool." Danny looked down at his shoes for a moment not knowing what else to say. "Well, I better go. My dad is waiting for me. I'll call you, okay?"

"Okay."

With a knot in his stomach and sweaty palms, Danny quickly looked around to see that no one was watching. He quickly leaned in and kissed her on the lips before running off. It was Gillian's first kiss and happened so fast she nearly missed it. Not knowing what else to do, she did what came naturally. She threw her mitt into the air. It was how they celebrated the end of a game, and she felt this moment deserved some kind of celebration. In her enthusiasm Gillian threw the mitt too high. It sailed high over her head landing with a thud behind her.

Gillian spun around to reach for the mitt that lay on the pavement behind her. As she turned she saw that a man already held it in his hands. Gillian reached out and took hold of the mitt but he didn't let go.

"Did I just see Danny kiss you?" her father asked as he let go of the mitt.

Gillian turned thirteen shades of red before nodding her head.

"Oh God, I am not ready for this," Michael sighed. "Come on, let's go."

As they walked back to the car, Michael threw an arm over Gillian's shoulder pulling her close for a noogie until she squealed with laughter. "Give your mom a break okay. She's doing the best she can."

Later that night Lauren tapped lightly on Gillian's bedroom door. Dinner had been quiet. Gillian was still upset about losing the game and Lauren was lost in her own thoughts about the hearing the next morning. Not wanting her daughter to go to bed angry, Lauren decided to make one last attempt at making amends.

"Come in," Gillian answered in reply to the tapping.

Lauren opened the door and stepped inside to find Gillian lying on her bed tossing her baseball glove into the air. "Can I talk to you for a second," she asked not waiting for an answer before sitting on the bed. Lauren was the parent after all. It was one thing to give her daughter space, but she wasn't about to walk around on eggshells and allow a child to rule her house. She was fair but she was firm.

In response Gillian pulled herself up to a sitting position, tucking her knees up under her chin. At the age of eleven she already felt she knew everything her mother could possible say, and so she decided to patiently and silently suffer through whatever "talk" her mom had in mind. The sooner it was over the sooner she could go back to daydreaming about Danny and her first kiss.

Lauren reached into her pocket and pulled out a small white box that she presented to Gillian. It wasn't wrapped. She'd barely had time to pick the gift up from the jeweler let alone wrap it. It would have to do as it was.

"I wanted you to have this." Lauren said as Gillian opened the box. "I ordered it a few weeks ago, but it just came in today."

It pleased Lauren to see a small smile form at the corners of Gillian's mouth as she removed the silver charm bracelet. Attached to the bracelet were several small charms each with a baseball theme; a home plate, glove, a little bat and ball, and Lauren's favorite, the number 15, Gillian's number. Although Gillian was still playing it cool Lauren knew she liked it. This feeling was confirmed when Gillian stretched out her arm and allowed Lauren to clasp the delicate piece of jewelry around Gillian's more delicate wrist.

"I wanted to tell you…"

"This isn't going to be one of those, 'it doesn't matter if you win or lose' speeches, is it?" Gillian asked.

"No." Lauren smiled then added, "Losing sucks but it happens so you have to get used to it and deal with it. But what I wanted to say was I am so very proud of you all the time. I love that you are not a quitter and that you always give your best no matter what you're doing. And I am really very sorry that I missed a few of your games."

"Most of them," Gillian corrected.

"Some of them," Lauren countered.

"Half."

Lauren realized that perhaps her daughter would follow in her footsteps and there would be two lawyers in the family. "Okay. I'm very, very, very, sorry I missed *half* your games."

"It's okay, Mom."

"Are you just saying that so I'll get out of your room?"

"No. It's really okay. Thanks for the bracelet. It's cool."

Lauren stood to leave, bending down to kiss Gillian good night. At least she felt better that things were okay between them. "Good night. I love you."

"I love you too, Mom."

Just as Lauren reached the door, Gillian said, "Mom?"

"Yes?"

"Can I get my nose pierced?"

"No."

Gillian flopped back on the bed with a dramatic exhale. Her parents would never understand what it felt like to be a kid! And with that, Lauren closed the door putting an end to another day while Gillian continued to admire her bracelet by twirling it around her wrist.

15089745R00177

Made in the USA
Charleston, SC
16 October 2012